The Great American Political Quiz

From the Constitution to Capitol Hill - Your Ultimate Test of U.S Politics.

Parker Monroe

Contents

Thank you for your purchase. If you enjoyed this book, please consider dropping us a review. Scan the QR Code below:

Introduction

"The Great American Political Quiz" is a comprehensive exploration of the rich and complex history of American politics, spanning from the birth of the nation to the modern era. This quiz book is designed to challenge and educate readers on the key events, figures, and ideologies that have shaped the United States' political landscape over the past two and a half centuries.

The American political system is a unique and ever-evolving amalgamation of ideas, values, and practices that have been influenced by a diverse array of factors, including the nation's founding principles, its geographic and demographic makeup, and its interactions with the rest of the world. From the early debates over federalism and states' rights to the contemporary discussions surrounding issues like healthcare, immigration, and climate change, American politics has always been characterized by a lively and often contentious exchange of ideas.

This quiz book is divided into several chapters, each focusing on a specific period or aspect of American political history. The first chapters cover the early years of the republic, from the signing of the Declaration of Independence in 1776 to the end of the Antebellum era in 1860. During this time, the nation's founders grappled with the challenges of establishing a new form of government based on the principles of liberty, equality, and self-governance. Readers will be tested on their knowledge of key events like the drafting of the Constitution, the formation of the first political parties, and the presidency of George Washington.

Then book deals with the tumultuous period of the Civil War and Reconstruction, which saw the nation torn apart by the issue of slavery and the struggle to reunite and rebuild in the war's aftermath. Readers will encounter questions about the major battles and leaders of the Civil War, the Emancipation Proclamation, and the efforts to extend civil rights to formerly enslaved African Americans during Reconstruction.

Moving into the 20th century, the quiz book then covers the Progressive Era, World War I, and the Roaring Twenties. This period saw significant changes in American society and politics, including the rise of the labor movement, the expansion of women's suffrage, and the emergence of the United States as a global power. Readers will be tested on their knowledge of figures like Theodore Roosevelt and Woodrow Wilson, as well as important events like the passage of the 19th Amendment and the nation's involvement in World War I.

Then the books moves Great Depression, World War II, and the early Cold War era. During this time, the United States faced unprecedented economic challenges and emerged as a superpower in the aftermath of World War II. Readers will encounter questions about Franklin D. Roosevelt's New Deal policies, the nation's role in the Allied victory in World War II, and the onset of the Cold War with the Soviet Union.

The final chapters the quiz book covers the latter half of the 20th century and the early 21st century, a period marked by significant social and political upheaval, as well as rapid technological change. Readers will be tested on their knowledge of the Civil Rights Movement, the Vietnam War, the Watergate scandal, and the presidencies of figures like John F. Kennedy, Ronald Reagan, and Barack Obama. The book also includes questions about more recent events, such as the 9/11 terrorist attacks, the wars in Afghanistan and Iraq, and the rise of social media as a political tool.

The book includes chapters that cover various political institutions. The Supreme Court chapter discusses landmark cases and the significant impact of judicial decisions on American law. In the Congress chapter, you will explore the legislative process, uncovering the complexities of lawmaking and the influential roles of the Senate and House of Representatives. The Constitution chapter provides an in-depth examination of the document that forms the foundation of American democracy, from its creation to its contemporary interpretations. State Politics highlights the diverse political climates and issues unique to each state, emphasizing the importance of local governance. Our Electoral System chapter offers insights into the mechanisms of American elections, from voting processes to the intricacies of the Electoral College. Finally, the chapters on the FBI and CIA reveal the inner workings of the nation's intelligence and security agencies, exploring their histories, missions, and the controversies that surround them.

In addition to testing readers' knowledge, "The Great American Political Quiz" also aims to provide a broader understanding of the themes and trends that have shaped American politics over time. By exploring the nation's political history in a comprehensive and engaging way, this book encourages readers to think critically about the ways in which the past continues to influence the present, and to consider the role that they themselves can play in shaping the future of American democracy.

Whether you are a history buff, a political junkie, a student of politics or simply someone who wants to learn more about the fascinating story of American politics, "The Great American Political Quiz" is the perfect way to test your knowledge and deepen your understanding of this complex and endlessly fascinating subject. So sharpen your pencil, put on your thinking cap, and get ready for a journey through the rich and storied history of American politics – from the halls of Congress to the campaign trail, and everything in between.

The American Revolution (1775-1783)

The American Revolution was a colonial revolt that began in 1765 and culminated in the independence of the United States from Great Britain. The revolution was driven by growing tensions between the 13 American colonies and the British government, fueled by issues such as taxation without representation, British attempts to control colonial trade and economy, and increasing desires for self-governance among the colonists. The conflict began with the battles of Lexington and Concord in 1775 and ended with the signing of the Treaty of Paris in 1783, which recognized American independence. The American Revolution had far-reaching consequences, inspiring other colonial independence movements and shaping the political and social landscape of the newly formed United States.

1. What was the primary political reason colonists protested British taxes?

A) The taxes were too high
B) The colonists lacked representation in Parliament
C) They believed in total economic independence
D) The taxes were solely used to benefit Britain

Answer: **B)**

2. The Tea Act of 1773 resulted in:

A) A widespread boycott of tea
B) The Boston Tea Party
C) The creation of the First Continental Congress
D) An increase in tea prices

Answer: **B)**

3. What was the purpose of the Coercive Acts (Intolerable Acts)?

A) To help strengthen the colonial economies
B) To improve relations between Britain and the colonies
C) To encourage loyalty to the British crown
D) To punish the colonies for acts of defiance

Answer: **D)**

4. Which body served as the primary government of the colonies during the Revolutionary War?

A) The House of Burgesses
B) The First Continental Congress
C) The Second Continental Congress
D) The Sons of Liberty

Answer: **C)**

5. The Declaration of Independence primarily asserts:

A) The right of the colonies to form a new government
B) The need to increase exports to Britain
C) The importance of maintaining a strong monarchy
D) The right to impose taxes on British citizens

Answer: **A)**

6. The first constitution of the United States was called:

A) The Bill of Rights
B) The Articles of Confederation
C) The Declaration of Independence
D) The U.S. Constitution

Answer: **B)**

7. One major weakness of the Articles of Confederation was:

A) Too much power given to the states
B) A strong central government
C) Lack of power to collect taxes
D) Overly strict trade regulations

Answer: **C)**

8. The Committees of Correspondence were created to:

A) Improve communication and collaboration between the colonies
B) Raise money to support the Continental Army
C) Draft a new constitution
D) Facilitate trade between colonists and Native Americans

Answer: **A)**

9. Which Enlightenment thinker heavily influenced the ideas expressed in the Declaration of Independence?

A) John Locke
B) Thomas Hobbes
C) Voltaire
D) Jean-Jacques Rousseau

Answer: **A)**

10. The concept of "popular sovereignty" means that:

A) The king's rule is absolute
B) Government power comes from the people
C) Only the wealthy should participate in government
D) State governments should have more power than the federal government

Answer: **B)**

11. Benjamin Franklin played a critical diplomatic role in securing support from which nation?

A) Spain
B) France
C) Prussia
D) The Netherlands

Answer: **B)**

12. What were colonists who supported the Revolution called?

A) Loyalists
B) Tories
C) Federalists
D) Patriots

Answer: **D)**

13. The practice of boycotting British goods was also known as:

A) The Townshend Acts
B) The Embargo
C) Non-importation agreements
D) Quartering

Answer: **C)**

14. Excessive printing of paper money by the Continental Congress led to which economic problem?

A) Deflation
B) Increased trade
C) Economic prosperity
D) Inflation

Answer: **D)**

15. Those opposed to ratifying the Constitution were known as:

A) Loyalists
B) Tories
C) Federalists
D) Anti-Federalists

Answer: **D)**

16. Which Founding Father was the primary author of the Federalist Papers?

A) Thomas Jefferson
B) George Washington
C) Alexander Hamilton
D) James Madison

Answer: **C)**

17. Shays' Rebellion demonstrated the weakness of the Articles of Confederation and highlighted the need for:

A) A weaker military
B) A stronger central government
C) Returning to a monarchy
D) Increased power for the states

Answer: **B)**

18. The primary goal of the Constitutional Convention of 1787 was to:

A) Declare war on Britain
B) Revise the Articles of Confederation
C) Write the Bill of Rights
D) Elect the first president

Answer: **B)**

19. The Great Compromise (or Connecticut Compromise) resolved a dispute about:

A) Slavery
B) Taxation
C) Representation in Congress
D) Presidential powers

Answer: **C)**

20. The system designed to prevent any one branch of government from becoming too powerful is called:

A) Popular sovereignty
B) Republicanism
C) Federalism
D) Checks and balances

Answer: **D)**

21. Which influential document served as a precursor to the U.S. Bill of Rights?

A) The Virginia Declaration of Rights
B) The Articles of Confederation
C) The Mayflower Compact
D) The Declaration of Independence

Answer: **A)**

22. The Quartering Act required colonists to:

A) Pay taxes on imported goods
B) House British soldiers
C) Serve in the British army
D) Abolish colonial assemblies

Answer: **B)**

23. The pamphlet "Common Sense" by Thomas Paine argued in favor of:

A) Reconciliation with Britain
B) Increased taxes to support the war effort
C) Complete independence from Britain
D) Forming an alliance with Spain

Answer: **C)**

24. Which figure was a key advocate for a strong federal government and the creation of a national bank?

A) Thomas Jefferson
B) Alexander Hamilton
C) Samuel Adams
D) Patrick Henry

Answer: **B)**

25. Protests against the Stamp Act marked an important turning point because they:

A) Demonstrated widespread colonial unity against the British
B) Were completely ignored by the British government
C) Resulted in the death of many British soldiers
D) Caused King George III to abdicate the throne

Answer: **A)**

26. Which Virginian famously declared, "Give me liberty, or give me death!"?

A) Thomas Jefferson
B) George Washington
C) Patrick Henry
D) George Mason

Answer: **C)**

27. The British strategy to isolate New England from the rest of the colonies led to which major battle?

A) Battle of Yorktown
B) Battle of Saratoga
C) Battle of Trenton
D) Battle of Bunker Hill

Answer: **B)**

28. Which figure was instrumental in training and professionalizing the Continental Army?

A) Benedict Arnold
B) Marquis de Lafayette
C) Baron von Steuben
D) Horatio Gates

Answer: **C)**

29. What influential protest involved colonists disguised as Mohawk Native Americans?

A) The Boston Massacre
B) The Boston Tea Party
C) Burning of the Gaspee
D) Shays' Rebellion

Answer: **B)**

30. Which term describes colonists who remained loyal to the British Crown?

A) Patriots
B) Loyalists
C) Federalists
D) Tories

Answer: **B)**

31. The first major victory for the Continental Army, significantly boosting morale, was the:

A) Battle of Trenton
B) Battle of Saratoga
C) Battle of Bunker Hill
D) Battle of Long Island

Answer: **A)**

32. Which international treaty formally recognized American independence?

A) Treaty of Versailles (1783)
B) Treaty of Paris (1783)
C) Treaty of Ghent (1814)
D) Treaty of Alliance (1778)

Answer: **B)**

33. The "shot heard 'round the world" refers to the first battles of the Revolutionary War, which took place in:

A) Yorktown and Philadelphia
B) Boston and New York City
C) Lexington and Concord
D) Charleston and Savannah

Answer: **C)**

34. Which early figure in the Revolution organized the Sons of Liberty?

A) John Adams
B) Samuel Adams
C) Alexander Hamilton
D) Paul Revere

Answer: **B)**

35. Which 1770 event heightened tensions between colonists and British soldiers?

A) The Stamp Act
B) The Boston Massacre
C) The Battle of Saratoga
D) The Tea Act

Answer: **B)**

36. Colonial women played a significant role in the Revolution through:

A) Spinning their own cloth to support boycotts
B) Serving as nurses and aiding the troops
C) Taking up arms in battle
D) All of the above

Answer: **D)**

37. Which figure famously became a traitor after defecting to the British side?

A) Benedict Arnold
B) Nathan Hale
C) Paul Revere
D) George Washington

Answer: **A)**

38. The final major battle of the Revolutionary War was the:

A) Battle of Trenton
B) Battle of Saratoga
C) Battle of Yorktown
D) Battle of Bunker Hill

Answer: **C)**

39. Life, liberty, and the pursuit of happiness" are considered unalienable rights outlined in the:

A) Articles of Confederation
B) U.S. Constitution
C) Declaration of Independence
D) Mayflower Compact

Answer: **C)**

40. Which state was the last of the original 13 colonies to ratify the Constitution?

A) Virginia
B) Massachusetts
C) Rhode Island
D) New York

Answer: **C)**

Declaration of Independence

The Declaration of Independence, adopted on July 4, 1776, was a formal statement by the Continental Congress announcing the thirteen American colonies' independence from Great Britain. The document, primarily written by Thomas Jefferson, outlined the colonies' grievances against King George III and the British government, and asserted the colonies' right to self-governance and freedom. The Declaration of Independence became a cornerstone of American political philosophy, enshrining the ideas of individual liberty, equality, and the right to resist oppressive government, and has since served as an inspiration for democratic movements around the world.

1. The Declaration of Independence was primarily written by:

A) Benjamin Franklin
B) John Adams
C) Thomas Jefferson
D) George Washington

Answer: **C)**

2. The Declaration of Independence declared the colonies' separation from:

A) France
B) Spain
C) Great Britain
D) The Netherlands

Answer: **C)**

3. The Declaration of Independence was adopted on:

A) July 4th, 1776
B) December 25th, 1776
C) March 1st, 1776
D) August 2nd, 1776

Answer: **A)**

4. The Declaration of Independence was signed in which city?

A) New York City
B) Boston
C) Philadelphia
D) Jamestown

Answer: **C)**

5. How many colonies adopted the Declaration of Independence?

A) 9
B) 13
C) 10
D) 12

Answer: **B)**

Key Concepts

6. Which of the following is an "unalienable right" listed in the Declaration?

    A) The right to own property
    B) The right to bear arms
    C) The right to free speech
    D) The right to life

Answer: **D)**

7. According to the Declaration, a government's power comes from:

    A) The will of God
    B) The strength of the military
    C) The consent of the governed
    D) The power of the King

Answer: **C)**

8. The Declaration refers to an unjust ruler as a:

    A) Despot
    B) Dictator
    C) Tyrant
    D) Monarch

Answer: **C)**

9. The Declaration of Independence argued that the British government had violated the colonists':

    A) Natural rights
    B) Right to privacy
    C) Religious freedom
    D) Right to a fair trial

Answer: **A)**

10. The Declaration of Independence was meant to justify:

A) A peaceful resolution with England
B) Starting a war for independence
C) Surrendering to British forces
D) Requesting aid from France

Answer: **B)**

The Signers and Beyond

11. Which signer of the Declaration is known for his large signature?

A) Samuel Adams
B) Benjamin Franklin
C) John Hancock
D) Thomas Jefferson

Answer: **C)**

12. Which future president did NOT sign the Declaration of Independence?

A) James Madison
B) Thomas Jefferson
C) John Adams
D) George Washington

Answer: **D)**

13. How many delegates signed the Declaration of Independence?

A) 13
B) 39
C) 56
D) 100

Answer: **C)**

14. One signer of the Declaration later became a Loyalist. Who was he?

A) John Hancock
B) Richard Stockton
C) Samuel Adams
D) Benjamin Rush

Answer: **B)**

15. Which delegate also served as the supreme commander of the Continental Army?

A) George Washington
B) Benjamin Franklin
C) John Adams
D) Thomas Jefferson

Answer: **A)**

16. The Enlightenment philosopher John Locke influenced the Declaration of Independence. His ideas are reflected in which part of the document?

A) The list of grievances against the King of England
B) The statement about unalienable rights
C) The call for a new form of government
D) The signatures of the delegates

Answer: **B)**

17. Which of these was a major grievance the colonists accused King George III of committing?

A) Imposing taxes without their consent
B) Providing free land to all colonists
C) Outlawing religious practices that didn't align with the Church of England
D) Forcing colonists to join the British army

Answer: **A)**

18. What is the purpose of the long list of accusations against King George III within the Declaration of Independence?

A) To persuade other nations to declare war on England
B) To record the complaints of the colonists for history
C) To justify the colonists' decision to break away from England
D) To embarrass the King publicly

Answer: **C)**

19. Which of the following best describes the Preamble of the Declaration of Independence?

A) A list of new laws to govern the colonies
B) A statement of the reasons for the colonies' separation from Britain
C) A call for other countries to come to the aid of the colonies
D) A detailed battle plan for the Revolutionary War

Answer: **B)**

20. An early draft of the Declaration of Independence included a section condemning the slave trade. Why was this section removed?

A) To gain support from Southern colonies
B) To show respect to the British, who had just abolished slavery
C) Because it was seen as unrelated to the fight for independence
D) Due to a printing error

Answer: **A)**

21. Which other revolutionary document was heavily influenced by the Declaration of Independence?

A) The U.S. Constitution
B) The Magna Carta
C) The Declaration of the Rights of Man and Citizen (France)
D) The Communist Manifesto

Answer: **C)**

22. Martin Luther King Jr. made a famous reference to the Declaration of Independence in which speech?

    A) "I Have a Dream"
    B) "Letter from a Birmingham Jail"
    C) "The Ballot or the Bullet"
    D) "I've Been to the Mountaintop

Answer: **A)**

23. The original Declaration of Independence is currently on display at:

    A) The White House
    B) The Smithsonian Museum of American History
    C) The National Archives
    D) The Liberty Bell Center

Answer: **C)**

24. Independence Day in the United States is celebrated on:

    A) July 2nd
    B) July 4th
    C) December 25th
    D) November 11th

Answer: **B)**

25. The Declaration of Independence has inspired movements for liberation around the world. Which of these is an example?

    A) The Indian Independence Movement
    B) The Chinese Revolution
    C) The French Revolution
    D) All of the above

Answer: **D)**

Constitutional Convention

The Constitutional Convention, also known as the Philadelphia Convention, took place from May 25 to September 17, 1787, in Philadelphia, Pennsylvania. Delegates from 12 of the 13 states (Rhode Island did not attend) gathered to address the weaknesses of the Articles of Confederation and create a new system of government. The Convention, presided over by George Washington, resulted in the drafting of the United States Constitution, which established a federal system with a stronger central government. The Constitution was signed by 39 of the 55 delegates on September 17, 1787, and was later ratified by the states, becoming the supreme law of the land.

The Basics

1. The Constitutional Convention was held in which city?

A) Boston, Massachusetts
B) New York City, New York
C) Philadelphia, Pennsylvania
D) Jamestown, Virginia

Answer: **C)**

2. The main purpose of the Constitutional Convention was to:

A) Revise the Articles of Confederation
B) Declare war on Great Britain
C) Elect the first President of the United States
D) Settle a trade dispute with France

Answer: **A)**

3. Which Founding Father is known as the "Father of the Constitution"?

A) George Washington
B) Benjamin Franklin
C) Thomas Jefferson
D) James Madison

Answer: **D)**

4. Which state did NOT send delegates to the Constitutional Convention?

A) Delaware
B) New York
C) Rhode Island
D) Virginia

Answer: **C)**

5. The Constitutional Convention took place in which year?

A) 1776
B) 1783
C) 1787
D) 1791

Answer: **C)**

Key Debates

6. The Virginia Plan proposed a system of representation in Congress based on: The New Jersey Plan proposed a system of representation in Congress based on:

A) Equal representation for each state
B) Representation based on a state's population
C) Representation based on a state's wealth
D) Representation based on military strength

Answer: **A)**

7. The Great Compromise (also known as the Connecticut Compromise) resolved the debate about representation by creating:

A) A single legislative body with equal representation
B) A two-house legislature with one chamber based on population and the other with equal representation
C) A system where the president would select representatives to Congress
D) A rotation system where states would alternate between different representation systems

Answer: **B)**

8. The Three-Fifths Compromise dealt with the issue of:

A) Counting slaves for the purposes of representation and taxation.
B) Setting the term limit for the presidency.
C) Dividing power between the federal and state governments.
D) International trade regulations.

Answer: **A)**

9. Which of these issues was NOT a major point of debate at the Constitutional Convention?

A) Representation in Congress
B) The power of the presidency
C) Slavery
D) Women's right to vote

Answer: **D)**

Key Figures & Concept

10. Who served as the President of the Constitutional Convention?

A) Alexander Hamilton
B) John Adams
C) Thomas Jefferson
D) George Washington

Answer: **D)**

11. Which delegate to the Convention was a strong proponent of a powerful central government?

A) Alexander Hamilton
B) James Madison
C) Roger Sherman
D) George Mason

Answer: **A)**

12. Delegates who opposed a strong central government and supported states' rights were known as:

A) Federalists
B) Whigs
C) Anti-Federalists
D) Loyalists

Answer: **C)**

13. The series of essays written in support of the ratification of the Constitution is called:

A) The Federalist Papers
B) Common Sense
C) The Anti-Federalist Papers
D) The Declaration of Independence

Answer: **A)**

14. Which of these was a key argument made by the Federalists in support of the Constitution?

    A) It would create a strong and efficient national government
    B) It would concentrate too much power in the hands of a few
    C) It did not adequately protect individual liberties
    D) It would weaken the ability of states to govern themselves

Answer: **A)**

Ratification & Legacy

15. How many states were needed to ratify the Constitution for it to go into effect?

    A) 7
    B) 9
    C) 11
    D) All 13

Answer: **B)**

16. The first state to ratify the Constitution was:

    A) Virginia
    B) Delaware
    C) New York
    D) Pennsylvania

Answer: **B)**

17. Which two important states initially generated strong opposition to the Constitution?

    A) Rhode Island and Connecticut
    B) Virginia and New York
    C) Pennsylvania and Georgia
    D) Massachusetts and South Carolina

Answer: **B)**

18. The addition of this document was crucial to securing the ratification of the Constitution:

    A) The Magna Carta
    B) The Articles of Confederation
    C) The Bill of Rights
    D) The Emancipation Proclamation

Answer: **C)**

19. The U.S. Constitution created three branches of government, a concept known as:

    A) Checks and Balances
    B) Federalism
    C) Popular Sovereignty
    D) Separation of Powers

Answer: **D)**

Broader Context

20. Which earlier document heavily influenced the ideas of government outlined in the U.S. Constitution?

    A) The English Bill of Rights
    B) The Declaration of Independence
    C) The Communist Manifesto
    D) The Bible

Answer: **A)**

21. Which earlier document heavily influenced the ideas of government outlined in the U.S. Constitution?

    A) The English Bill of Rights
    B) The Declaration of Independence
    C) The Communist Manifesto
    D) The Bible

Answer: **A)**

22. The concept of dividing power between the national government and state governments is known as:

A) Judicial Review
B) Federalism
C) Republicanism
D) Impeachment

Answer: **B)**

23. The legislative branch of the U.S. government is made up of what two bodies?

A) The President and the Vice President
B) The Senate and the House of Representatives
C) The Supreme Court and the Cabinet
D) Governors and State Legislators

Answer: **B)**

24. The executive branch of the U.S. government is headed by the:

A) President
B) Speaker of the House
C) Chief Justice of the Supreme Court
D) Senate Majority Leader

Answer: **A)**

25. The judicial branch of the U.S. government has the power to:

A) Declare laws unconstitutional
B) Impeach the president
C) Raise taxes
D) Declare war

Answer: **A)**

Bill of Rights (1791)

The United States Bill of Rights, ratified on December 15, 1791, consists of the first ten amendments to the U.S. Constitution. These amendments were designed to protect individual liberties and limit the power of the federal government. The Bill of Rights guarantees various rights, including freedom of speech, religion, and the press, the right to bear arms, protection against unreasonable searches and seizures, and the right to a fair and speedy trial. The adoption of the Bill of Rights was crucial in addressing the concerns of Anti-Federalists and securing the necessary support for the ratification of the Constitution.

The Basics

1. The Bill of Rights refers to the first ten amendments to:

  A) The Declaration of Independence
  B) The Articles of Confederation
  C) The U.S. Constitution
  D) The Federalist Papers

Answer: **C)**

2. The Bill of Rights was ratified in:

A) 1776
B) 1783
C) 1787
D) 1791

Answer: **D)**

3. The Bill of Rights was added to the Constitution in response to concerns about:

A) The power of the individual states
B) The strength of the national government
C) The lack of protection for individual liberties
D) The role of the military

Answer: **C)**

4. How many amendments are included in the Bill of Rights?

A) 5
B) 8
C) 10
D) 13

Answer: **C)**

5. Which amendment guarantees freedom of religion, speech, press, assembly, and the right to petition the government?

A) First Amendment
B) Second Amendment
C) Third Amendment
D) Fourth Amendment

Answer: **A)**

Specific Rights

6. The Second Amendment protects the right to:

A) A fair trial
B) Bear arms
C) Freedom of religion
D) Vote in elections

Answer: **B)**

7. The Third Amendment prohibits the government from:

A) Quartering soldiers in private homes during peacetime without consent
B) Denying a person the right to an attorney
C) Imposing cruel and unusual punishment
D) Conducting unreasonable searches and seizures

Answer: **A)**

8. The Fourth Amendment protects against unreasonable searches and seizures and requires a warrant for:

A) Arrests
B) Interviews with suspects
C) Public speeches
D) All of the above

Answer: **A)**

9. The Fifth Amendment protects against:

A) Cruel and unusual punishment
B) Self-incrimination during a criminal trial
C) Denial of a speedy trial
D) All of the above

Answer: **D)**

10. The Sixth Amendment guarantees the right to a speedy and public trial by an impartial jury. It also ensures the right to:

    A) Face one's accuser
    B) An attorney (if cannot afford one)
    C) Both A and B
    D) Neither A nor B

Answer: **C)**

Understanding the Bill of Rights

11. The Bill of Rights can be amended through a specific process outlined in the Constitution.

    A) Yes, with a 2/3 majority vote by both houses of Congress and ratification by 3/4 of state legislatures.
    B) The President can amend it unilaterally in times of crisis.
    C) Each state has the power to amend it as they see fit.
    D) No, the Bill of Rights is permanent and cannot be altered.

Answer: **A)**

12. The Bill of Rights applies only to the federal government and does not limit the power of state governments.

    A) That's how it was originally designed.
    B) The 14th Amendment changed that, now it applies to states too.
    C) Only the first five amendments restrict state powers.
    D) States can opt out of specific parts of the Bill of Rights.

Answer: **B)**

13. The Supreme Court plays a crucial role in interpreting the meaning and application of the Bill of Rights through landmark court cases.

A) Yes, they are the final authority on what the Bill of Rights means in practice.
B) Only Congress can interpret it, as they wrote it.
C) It's up to each individual to decide how the Bill of Rights applies to them.
D) Supreme Court rulings on the Bill of Rights are just suggestions, not binding.

Answer: **A)**

Louisiana Purchase

The Louisiana Purchase was a landmark transaction between the United States and France, finalized on April 30, 1803. The U.S., under President Thomas Jefferson, acquired approximately 828,000 square miles of land west of the Mississippi River for $15 million, effectively doubling the size of the nation. The purchase included land that would later form 15 states and two Canadian provinces, stretching from the Mississippi River to the Rocky Mountains. The Louisiana Purchase was a pivotal moment in U.S. history, setting the stage for westward expansion and shaping the country's future.

The Basics

1. The Louisiana Purchase was:

A) The acquisition of a massive territory from France.
B) A trade treaty allowing free navigation of the Mississippi River for U.S. trade vessels
C) The military defeat of Napoleon Bonaparte in North America
D) The settlement of a territory dispute with Spain

Answer: **A)**

2. Which country sold the Louisiana Territory to the United States in 1803?

    A) Spain
    B) France
    C) Great Britain
    D) Russia

Answer: **B)**

3. Who was the President of the United States at the time of the Louisiana Purchase?

    A) George Washington
    B) John Adams
    C) Thomas Jefferson
    D) James Madison

Answer: **C)**

4. In what year was the Louisiana Purchase made?

    A) 1776
    B) 1803
    C) 1812
    D) 1845

Answer: **B)**

5. Approximately how much did the United States pay for the Louisiana Territory?

    A) $1 million
    B) $15 million
    C) $100 million
    D) $1 billion

Answer: **B)**

6. The Louisiana Purchase roughly doubled the size of the United States.

    A) True
    B) False

Answer: **A)**

Reasons & Context

7. Why was Napoleon Bonaparte willing to sell the Louisiana Territory?

    A) He needed money to fund his wars in Europe
    B) He wanted to strengthen the new United States
    C) He feared losing the territory to Great Britain
    D) All of the above

Answer: **D)**

8. Thomas Jefferson originally sent negotiators to France to purchase:

    A) The entire Louisiana Territory
    B) Just the city of New Orleans
    C) Rights to trade in the Caribbean
    D) Territory in Florida

Answer: **B)**

9. The Lewis and Clark Expedition was sent to:

    A) Explore the newly acquired Louisiana Territory
    B) Negotiate trade deals with Native American tribes
    C) Find a route to the Pacific Ocean
    D) All of the above

Answer: **D)**

Impact

10. Which present-day state was NOT part of the original Louisiana Purchase?

    A) Texas
    B) Missouri
    C) Iowa
    D) Arkansas

Answer: **A)**

11. The Louisiana Purchase led to increased conflict with:

    A) Great Britain
    B) Native Americans
    C) Spain
    D) Russia

Answer: **B)**

12. One major consequence of the Louisiana Purchase was:

    A) Westward expansion by the United States
    B) Increased tensions that led to the War of 1812
    C) Resolution of all border disputes with France
    D) The end of slavery in the Southern states

Answer: **A)**

13. The Louisiana Purchase is considered one of the greatest real estate deals in history. Why?

    A) The United States paid very little per acre
    B) Gold was discovered in the territory shortly after the purchase
    C) It led to the discovery of oil in the region
    D) The land was immediately resold to Spain for a profit

Answer: **A)**

Deeper Understanding

14. The Louisiana Purchase raised questions about:

A) The constitutionality of acquiring new territory
B) The rights of Native Americans living in the territory
C) The issue of slavery in newly acquired lands
D) All of the above

Answer: **D)**

15. Which legal principle did the Supreme Court establish in response to legal challenges regarding the Louisiana Purchase?

A) That the federal government has implied powers
B) That states can nullify federal laws they disagree with
C) That the president cannot make treaties without Senate approval
D) That the Constitution does not apply to newly acquired territories

Answer: **A)**

16. Which famous Native American woman aided Lewis and Clark in their exploration?

A) Pocahontas
B) Sacajawea
C) Sitting Bull
D) Tecumseh

Answer: **B)**

Legacy

17. The Louisiana Purchase contributed to the idea of Manifest Destiny, which was:

A) The belief the U.S. was destined to expand across North America
B) The right of states to secede from the Union
C) The doctrine that the U.S. should remain isolated from Europe
D) The belief in abolishing slavery throughout the United States

Answer: **A)**

18. Which later territorial acquisition by the United States was partially inspired by the success of the Louisiana Purchase?

A) The Alaska Purchase
B) The annexation of Texas
C) The Oregon Territory
D) The Gadsden Purchase

Answer: **B)**

19. The Gateway Arch in St. Louis, Missouri, commemorates:

A) The starting point of the Lewis and Clark Expedition
B) The centennial of the Louisiana Purchase
C) The victory over the French in the Battle of New Orleans
D) The birthplace of Thomas Jefferson

Answer: **A)**

20. The Louisiana Purchase was a major turning point in American history because it:

A) Set the stage for westward expansion
B) Increased tensions over slavery
C) Sparked the creation of new states
D) All of the above

Answer: **D)**

21. Today, the legacy of the Louisiana Purchase is still debated, particularly in regard to:

A) Its impact on Native American populations
B) The constitutionality of federal land acquisition
C) Environmental concerns about land development
D) All of the above

Answer: **D)**

War of 1812 (1812–1815)

The War of 1812 was a conflict between the United States and Great Britain that lasted from 1812 to 1815. The main causes of the war included trade restrictions, the impressment of American sailors by the British, and the U.S. desire to expand its territory. Key events included the burning of Washington D.C., the Battle of Baltimore (which inspired the U.S. national anthem), and the Battle of New Orleans. The war ended with the Treaty of Ghent in 1815, which restored the pre-war borders and left many of the underlying issues unresolved, but it also boosted American nationalism and established the U.S. as a significant military power.

Causes of the War

1. What was NOT a major cause of the War of 1812?

A) British impressment of American sailors
B) French encouragement of Native American resistance on the American frontier
C) American desire to expand westward
D) Ongoing trade restrictions imposed by both Britain and France

Answer: **D)** (While trade restrictions played a role, it wasn't a primary cause)

2. What is impressment?

  A) The act of forcing foreign sailors to serve in the British Navy
  B) The taxation of goods imported into the United States
  C) The practice of kidnapping enslaved people from Africa
  D) A military tactic involving surprise attacks

Answer: **A)**

3. Which famous American political figure argued for a strong military response to British actions?

  A) John Adams
  B) Alexander Hamilton
  C) James Madison
  D) Thomas Jefferson

Answer: **B)**

The War

4. In what year did the War of 1812 begin?

  A) 1807
  B) 1810
  C) 1812
  D) 1814

Answer: **C)**

5. Which U.S. city successfully defended itself against a major British attack during the War of 1812?

  A) New York City
  B) Philadelphia
  C) Boston
  D) Baltimore

Answer: **D)**

6. The Battle of New Orleans, a major American victory, actually took place:

A) Before the official peace treaty was signed
B) As part of a larger invasion of the eastern United States
C) In response to a direct attack on the American capital
D) Entirely at sea, with no land battles involved

Answer: **A)**

7. What was the role of First Nations (Native American) allies in the War of 1812?

A) They remained neutral in the conflict.
B) They primarily fought alongside the British.
C) They fought alongside both the British and Americans depending on the tribe.
D) They sided entirely with the United States.

Answer: **C)**

8. Which famous American naval hero emerged during the War of 1812?

A) George Washington
B) Andrew Jackson
C) John Paul Jones
D) Oliver Hazard Perry

Answer: **D)**

The War's End and Legacy

9. The War of 1812 officially ended with the signing of what treaty?

A) Treaty of Paris (1783)
B) Treaty of Ghent
C) Louisiana Purchase Treaty
D) Constitution of the United States

Answer: **B)**

10. What were the major outcomes of the War of 1812?

A) Britain gained control of the Mississippi River.
B) The war resolved none of the pre-war issues and ended in a stalemate.
C) The United States gained significant territory from Canada.
D) Both Britain and the United States emerged as clear victors.

Answer: **B)**

11. How did the War of 1812 contribute to a rise in American nationalism?

A) By highlighting the failures of the national government
B) By showcasing American military weakness compared to European powers
C) By creating a sense of national pride and unity through shared victories
D) By leading to increased political divisions between Federalists and Democratic-Republicans

Answer: **C)**

12. The War of 1812 is sometimes referred to as the "Second War for Independence." Why?

A) Because it secured American independence from British economic domination.
B) Because it involved similar battles and tactics to the American Revolution.
C) Because it finally drove out all remaining British forces from North America.
D) Because many of the same Founding Fathers were still alive and involved in the war effort.

Answer: **A)**

Deeper Understanding

13. The British burned the White House and other public buildings during which event in the War of 1812?

    A) The Battle of New Orleans
    B) The Invasion of Canada
    C) The Siege of Baltimore
    D) The Burning of Washington D.C.

Answer: **D)**

14. Which American national anthem was inspired by the events of the War of 1812?

    A) America the Beautiful
    B) The Star-Spangled Banner
    C) Yankee Doodle
    D) My Country, 'Tis of Thee

Answer: **B)**

15. The Hartford Convention, involving Federalist politicians opposed to the war, ultimately:

    A) Successfully blocked further U.S. involvement in the war.
    B) Led to the breakup of the Federalist Party
    C) Resulted in concessions made by the British to end the war.
    D) Caused President Madison to resign in mid-term.

Answer: **B)**

16. Which prominent American general, later a president, gained fame in the War of 1812 due to his victory at the Battle of New Orleans?

    A) William Henry Harrison
    B) Zachary Taylor
    C) George Washington
    D) Andrew Jackson

Answer: **D)**

Broader Context

17. The War of 1812 hampered the growth of American manufacturing due to restricted trade during the war.

    A) True
    B) False

Answer: **B)** (It actually spurred American manufacturing growth)

18. Which major European event was happening concurrently with the War of 1812?

    A) The French Revolution
    B) The Napoleonic Wars
    C) The Spanish Inquisition
    D) The Crimean War

Answer: **B)**

19. Despite ending in a stalemate, the War of 1812 is seen as significant in U.S. history because it:

    A) Led directly to the abolition of slavery.
    B) Affirmed American independence and fostered a sense of national identity.
    C) Resulted in the acquisition of Florida from Spain.
    D) Ended the threat of Native American resistance on the frontier.

Answer: **B)**

20. The War of 1812 and its legacy have been depicted in various art forms. Which of the following is an example?

    A) The novel "Gone with the Wind"
    B) The painting "Washington Crossing the Delaware"
    C) The folk song "The Battle of New Orleans" by Johnny Horton
    D) The musical "Hamilton"

Answer: **C)**

21. Which future U.S. president served as an army officer in the War of 1812?

A) Abraham Lincoln
B) James K. Polk
C) Theodore Roosevelt
D) Zachary Taylor

Answer: **D)**

22. American expansionism, fueled by the perceived success of the War of 1812, contributed to which later event?

A) The Mexican-American War
B) The annexation of Hawaii
C) The Louisiana Purchase
D) The Spanish-American War

Answer: **A)**

23. Which American poet wrote "The Star-Spangled Banner"?

A) Walt Whitman
B) Francis Scott Key
C) Edgar Allan Poe
D) Emily Dickinson

Answer: **B)**

24. Which major figure of the War of 1812 died in a duel several years later?

A) Alexander Hamilton
B) Tecumseh
C) Commodore Oliver Hazard Perry
D) General Andrew Jackson

Answer: **A)** (though his duel was in 1804, a decade before the war)

25. The War of 1812 contributed to the decline of which political party?

A) The Federalists
B) The Democratic-Republicans
C) The Whigs
D) The Republicans

Answer: **A)**

26. The rise of U.S. manufacturing in the aftermath of the War of 1812 is considered a key part of:

A) The Industrial Revolution
B) The Second Great Awakening
C) The Era of Good Feelings
D) The Civil War

Answer: **A)**

27. Which Native American leader was allied with the British and died during the War of 1812?

A) Sitting Bull
B) Crazy Horse
C) Geronimo
D) Tecumseh

Answer: **D)**

28. Which U.S. Naval hero is famous for the words "We have met the enemy and they are ours"?

A) Stephen Decatur
B) John Paul Jones
C) Oliver Hazard Perry
D) William Bainbridge

Answer: **C)**

29. Dolley Madison, the First Lady, is famous for saving what important item before the British burned the White House?

A) A portrait of George Washington
B) The original Declaration of Independence
C) Treasury funds and important documents
D) Her personal jewelry collection

Answer: **A)**

30. Although the U.S. did not gain territory from the War of 1812, it did secure better relations with Britain and established its status as a rising power.

A) True
B) False

Answer: **A)**

Challenge Questions

31. The War of 1812 is often seen as a war the U.S. was ill-prepared to fight. Which of these is evidence of this unpreparedness?

A) The small size of the U.S. Army and Navy
B) The lack of popular support in certain regions of the country
C) Insufficient supplies and funding for the military
D) All of the above

Answer: **D)**

32. While the War of 1812 is usually portrayed as a conflict between the U.S. and Britain, in what ways could it be considered a three-way war?

A) Due to the involvement of France as a background player influencing events.
B) Because of the divided participation of First Nations (Native American) tribes, some siding with the British, others with the U.S.
C) Because it involved battles on land, in coastal waters, and on the Great Lakes.
D) Due to the internal political division between Federalists and Democratic-Republicans.

Answer: **B)**

33. In the immediate aftermath of the War of 1812, there was a surge of American nationalism. BUT this was NOT universally positive. Why is this the case?

A) It led to increased aggression towards Native American groups.
B) It deepened divisions between the North and South over future expansion.
C) It made compromise with Britain on remaining issues more difficult.
D) All of the above

Answer: **D)**

34. Despite being a "stalemate", why didn't the War of 1812 just lead to everything returning to the way it was before?

A) Britain became less interested in meddling in North America afterwards.
B) The U.S. proved its military capabilities, gaining respect.
C) Native American resistance on the frontier was significantly weakened.
D) All of the above.

Answer: **D)**

35. Select the statement that is FALSE about the War of 1812's legacy:

A) It propelled Andrew Jackson to national prominence.
B) It contributed to a sense of American "Manifest Destiny".
C) It resolved the issue of British impressment of American sailors.
D) It contributed to growing sectionalism (North vs. South) within the United States.

Answer: **C)**

Monroe Doctrine

The Monroe Doctrine was a foreign policy statement delivered by President James Monroe in his annual message to Congress on December 2, 1823. The doctrine asserted that the United States would view further European colonization or interference in the Americas as an act of aggression, requiring U.S. intervention. It also stated that the U.S. would remain neutral in European affairs and wars. The Monroe Doctrine became a cornerstone of U.S. foreign policy, shaping the nation's role in the Western Hemisphere for many years to come.

The Basics

1. Which U.S. president is the Monroe Doctrine named after?

A) George Washington
B) Thomas Jefferson
C) John Adams
D) James Monroe

Answer: **D)**

2. In what year was the Monroe Doctrine issued?

   A) 1776
   B) 1789
   C) 1812
   D) 1823

Answer: **D)**

3. The Monroe Doctrine was primarily a statement of:

   A) Economic policy
   B) Military strategy
   C) Social reform
   D) Foreign policy

Answer: **D)**

4. Which document was the primary inspiration for the Monroe Doctrine?

   A) The Declaration of Independence
   B) George Washington's Farewell Address
   C) The U.S. Constitution
   D) The Federalist Papers

Answer: **B)**

5. The Monroe Doctrine was issued in response to fears that European powers might:

   A) Interfere in the newly independent nations of Latin America
   B) Attack the United States directly
   C) Cut off U.S. trade with Asia
   D) Ally with Native American tribes on the frontier

Answer: **A)**

Key Components

6. Which of these is a key principle of the Monroe Doctrine?

A) America should avoid intervention in European wars and conflicts.
B) Europe should not interfere in the Western Hemisphere.
C) The United States would actively promote democracy abroad.
D) All of the above

Answer: **D)**

7. The Monroe Doctrine asserted the separation of spheres of influence between:

A) The Northern and Southern parts of the United States
B) The federal and state governments
C) The Americas and Europe
D) Britain and France

Answer: **C)**

8. The Monroe Doctrine was largely drafted by:

A) James Monroe
B) John Quincy Adams
C) Andrew Jackson
D) Thomas Jefferson

Answer: **B)**

Impact and Interpretation

9. Which European power supported the Monroe Doctrine, helping to enforce it?

A) France
B) Spain
C) Great Britain
D) Russia

Answer: **C)**

10. In the immediate aftermath of its announcement, the Monroe Doctrine had:

A) Very little impact on European policies.
B) A dramatic effect, causing European nations to abandon their ambitions in the Americas.
C) Mixed results, with some nations respecting it and others disregarding it.
D) Resulted in a declaration of war by Spain

Answer: **A)**

11. One early consequence of the Monroe Doctrine was the:

A) U.S. acquisition of Florida
B) Mexican-American War
C) War of 1812
D) Louisiana Purchase

Answer: **A)**

12. The Monroe Doctrine became a cornerstone of U.S. foreign policy and was invoked by later presidents like:

A) Abraham Lincoln
B) Theodore Roosevelt
C) Woodrow Wilson
D) Franklin D. Roosevelt

Answer: **B)**

Jacksonian Era (1829-1837)

The Jacksonian Era, spanning from 1829 to 1837, was a period in U.S. history marked by the presidency of Andrew Jackson and the rise of the Democratic Party. This era was characterized by a shift towards greater democracy, increased suffrage for white males, and a focus on the common man. Jackson's policies, such as the Indian Removal Act and the destruction of the Second Bank of the United States, were controversial and had lasting impacts on the nation. The Jacksonian Era also saw the emergence of the Second Party System, with the Democratic Party and the Whig Party competing for power.

Andrew Jackson

1. Andrew Jackson was the _____ President of the United States.

A) 5th
B) 7th
C) 9th
D) 11th

Answer: **B)**

2. Which nickname reflected Andrew Jackson's popularity and reputation as a military leader?

A) "Old Hickory"
B) "The Great Compromiser"
C) "Silent Sam"
D) "The Rail Splitter"

Answer: **A)**

3. Which famous battle of the War of 1812 made him a national hero?

A) Battle of Bunker Hill
B) Battle of Yorktown
C) Battle of New Orleans
D) Battle of the Alamo

Answer: **C)**

4. Before becoming President, Andrew Jackson had a successful career as a:

A) Lawyer, senator, and military general
B) Banker, businessman, and plantation owner
C) Teacher, inventor, and newspaper editor
D) Doctor, minister, and college professor

Answer: **A)**

5. Andrew Jackson came from humble beginnings and was seen as a symbol of:

A) Eastern elites and the wealthy
B) Experienced statesmen and politicians
C) Native American resistance and cooperation
D) The common man and Western expansion

Answer: **D)**

Jacksonian Democracy

6. The expansion of voting rights to include white men without property ownership is a hallmark of:

 A) Jacksonian Democracy
 B) Manifest Destiny
 C) The Second Great Awakening
 D) The Industrial Revolution

Answer: **A)**

7. Jackson's use of the "spoils system" involved:

 A) Rewarding political supporters with government jobs
 B) Using government funds to purchase large tracts of land
 C) Bribing officials to gain political advantage
 D) Appointing Native Americans to key government positions

Answer: **A)**

8. The belief that ordinary citizens should play a more prominent role in government is a key aspect of:

 A) Jacksonian Democracy
 B) The Federalist Papers
 C) The Whig philosophy
 D) The Articles of Confederation

Answer: **A)**

Policies and Controversies

9. Andrew Jackson strongly opposed which institution?

 A) The National Bank
 B) The Supreme Court
 C) The Presidency
 D) The Electoral College

Answer: **A)**

10. The Nullification Crisis involved a dispute over:

A) Whether states could refuse to enforce federal laws
B) The expansion of slavery into new territories
C) Whether to increase tariffs on foreign goods
D) Foreign policy disputes with France

Answer: **A)**

11. The Indian Removal Act of 1830 resulted in:

A) The creation of reservations for Native American tribes
B) The peaceful relocation and fair compensation for displaced tribes
C) The Trail of Tears and the forced displacement of thousands of Native Americans
D) Increased cooperation and peaceful coexistence between settlers and tribes

Answer: **C)**

12. Which Native American tribes were primarily affected by the Indian Removal Act?

A) The Cherokee, Creek, Choctaw, Chickasaw, and Seminole
B) The Iroquois, Sioux, and Apache
C) The Pueblo, Navajo, and Hopi
D) The tribes of the Pacific Northwest

Answer: **A)**

13. Andrew Jackson's conflict with the Second Bank of the United States ultimately led to:

A) The stabilization of the U.S. economy
B) An economic crisis known as the Panic of 1837
C) Strengthening the power of the national bank
D) The founding of a new national bank

Answer: **B)**

14. Andrew Jackson's policies are seen by some historians as strengthening the presidency, while others see them as:

A) Overly cautious and ineffective
B) An abuse of power and expansion of executive authority
C) Leading to increased cooperation between the branches of government
D) Mostly focused on foreign policy and international relations

Answer: **B)**

Social and Economic Change

15. Which religious movement swept the United States during the Jacksonian Era and emphasized personal salvation?

A) The First Great Awakening
B) The Second Great Awakening
C) The Enlightenment
D) The Protestant Reformation

Answer: **B)**

16. The expansion of the market economy, along with developments in transportation like canals and railroads, occurred during the:

A) American Civil War
B) Transcendentalist movement
C) Gilded Age
D) Market Revolution

Answer: **D)**

17. The growth of cotton production in the South during the Jacksonian Era fueled the expansion of:

A) Industry and manufacturing
B) Western migration
C) Slavery
D) Urbanization in the Northeast

Answer: **C)**

18. One outcome of the market revolution and the rise of industry was:

A) Increased equality between men and women
B) More people becoming self-employed farmers
C) The growth of a working class dependent on wages
D) A decline in immigration to the United States

Answer: **C)**

Opposition and Legacy

19. Which political party formed in opposition to Andrew Jackson and his policies?

A) The Democrats
B) The Whigs
C) The Federalists
D) The Know-Nothings

Answer: **B)**

20. Which issue was NOT a major point of contention between the Whigs and Jacksonian Democrats?

A) The role of the federal government
B) The future of slavery
C) Economic policy and the national bank
D) The right of women to vote

Answer: D)

21. Which state fiercely opposed the Tariff of 1828 (Tariff of Abominations), leading to the Nullification Crisis?

A) Virginia
B) Kentucky
C) Georgia
D) South Carolina

Answer: **D)**

22. Andrew Jackson's presidency is associated with a rise in:

A) Sectionalism (North vs. South)
B) Economic inequality
C) Political participation among ordinary citizens
D) All of the above

Answer: **D)**

The Indian Removal Act

Between 1838 and 1839 there was a series of forced relocations of approximately 60,000 Native Americans from their ancestral homelands in the Southeastern United States to designated Indian Territory west of the Mississippi River. The affected tribes, including the Cherokee, Muscogee (Creek), Seminole, Chickasaw, and Choctaw nations, were compelled to leave their lands due to the Indian Removal Act of 1830, which was signed into law by President Andrew Jackson. The journey, which covered around 1,000 miles, was marked by severe hardship, disease, and starvation, resulting in the deaths of an estimated 4,000 to 8,000 Native Americans.

Background

1. Which U.S. President spearheaded the Indian Removal Act, ultimately leading to the Trail of Tears?

    A) John Quincy Adams
    B) Thomas Jefferson
    C) Andrew Jackson
    D) James Monroe

Answer: **C)**

2. The Trail of Tears refers to the forced relocation of primarily which Native American tribes?

A) Sioux, Cheyenne, and Arapaho
B) Iroquois, Mohawk, and Seneca
C) Cherokee, Creek, Choctaw, Chickasaw, and Seminole
D) Navajo, Apache, and Hopi

Answer: **C)**

3. What was the main motivation behind the Indian Removal Act of 1830?

A) To protect Native American tribes from warfare with other tribes
B) To allow white settlers access to valuable land in the Southeast
C) To establish reservations for Native Americans in the West
D) To spread Christianity among Native American populations

Answer: **B)**

4. Which state was the original homeland of the Cherokee Nation prior to the Trail of Tears?

A) Mississippi
B) Oklahoma
C) Georgia
D) Florida

Answer: **C)**

The Journey

5. The Trail of Tears primarily ended in what is now the state of:

A) Texas
B) Kansas
C) New Mexico
D) Oklahoma

Answer: **D)**

6. Approximately how many miles did those forced to travel on the Trail of Tears cover?

    A) 200-500 miles
    B) 500-1000 miles
    C) 1000-2000 miles
    D) Over 2000 miles

Answer: **C)**

7. What was the primary mode of travel for many forced onto the Trail of Tears?

    A) Horse-drawn wagons
    B) Steamboats
    C) On foot
    D) Trains

Answer: **C)**

8. The Trail of Tears was particularly devastating due to taking place during:

    A) Summer heat waves
    B) Brutal winter conditions
    C) A time of ongoing warfare with other tribes
    D) A smallpox epidemic

Answer: **B)**

Consequences

9. Roughly how many Native Americans died as a direct result of the Trail of Tears?

    A) 500
    B) 2,000
    C) 4,000
    D) 10,000

Answer: **C)**

10. The Trail of Tears led to a major loss of life among the affected tribes due to:

A) Starvation
B) Disease
C) Exposure to harsh elements
D) All of the above

Answer: **D)**

11. The Cherokee Nation filed numerous lawsuits against the U.S. government, but the Supreme Court, though ruling in their favor, was unable to stop their removal. Why?

A) Andrew Jackson ignored the rulings
B) The state of Georgia passed its own laws defying the Supreme Court
C) There was no mechanism to enforce Supreme Court decisions at the time
D) All of the above

Answer: **A)**

Manifest Destiny (1840s)

Manifest Destiny was a popular belief in the United States during the 19th century, particularly in the 1840s. The concept held that American settlers were destined by God to expand across the North American continent, spreading democracy and civilization. This belief was used to justify westward expansion, including the annexation of Texas, the Oregon Territory, and the Mexican-American War. While Manifest Destiny promoted American exceptionalism and nationalism, it also led to the displacement and mistreatment of Native Americans and other indigenous peoples.

The Concept

1. Manifest Destiny was the belief that the United States was:

A) Destined to expand across North America from coast to coast.
B) Superior to European nations and should dominate the world.
C) Destined to abolish slavery and spread democracy.
D) A nation chosen by God with a special mission.

Answer: **A)** (though elements of B, C and D were often intertwined with the idea)

2. The term "Manifest Destiny" was first coined by:

A) Andrew Jackson
B) John O'Sullivan
C) James K. Polk
D) Thomas Jefferson

Answer: **B)**

3. Which of the following ideas does NOT represent the philosophy of Manifest Destiny?

A) The United States has a right to expand its territory.
B) Expansion will help spread American values and institutions.
C) Native Americans have equal rights to the land.
D) Expansion is inevitable and divinely ordained.

Answer: **C)**

Motivations for Expansion

4. Which economic factor drove the ideology of Manifest Destiny?

A) Access to fertile farmland and natural resources
B) The desire to find gold and other precious metals
C) The need for new markets for American goods
D) All of the above

Answer: **D)**

5. Many proponents of Manifest Destiny believed that expansion would help:

A) Reduce tensions between the North and South over slavery.
B) Resolve political disputes with European powers.
C) Provide a "safety valve" for social unrest by offering new opportunities.
D) Improve relations with Native American tribes.

Answer: **C)**

6. Missionaries who traveled westward often played a role in Manifest Destiny by:

A) Promoting the idea of American cultural superiority.
B) Establishing schools and settlements.
C) Advocating for the rights of Native Americans.
D) Both A and B.

Answer: **D)**

Manifest Destiny in Action

7. Which territorial acquisition is considered a major success of Manifest Destiny?

A) The annexation of Texas
B) The Louisiana Purchase
C) The War of 1812
D) The Gadsden Purchase

Answer: **A)**

8. The Mexican-American War (1846-1848) resulted in the United States gaining:

A) California, Nevada, Utah, and parts of other Southwestern states.
B) Florida and parts of the Gulf Coast.
C) The Oregon Territory.
D) Control of the Great Lakes.

Answer: **A)**

9. The belief in Manifest Destiny led to conflict with:

A.) Native American tribes
B) Mexico
C) Great Britain (over Oregon)
D) All of the above

Answer: **D)**

10. Which famous trail played a critical role in westward migration under the influence of Manifest Destiny?

    A) The Santa Fe Trail
    B) The Oregon Trail
    C) The Erie Canal
    D) The Appalachian Trail

Answer: **B)**

Mexican-American War

The Mexican-American War, lasting from 1846 to 1848, was a conflict between the United States and Mexico, primarily driven by the U.S. annexation of Texas and the desire to expand westward. The war began with the U.S. invasion of Mexico and included major battles such as the Battle of Palo Alto, the Battle of Monterrey, and the Battle of Buena Vista. The conflict ended with the signing of the Treaty of Guadalupe Hidalgo in 1848, which resulted in Mexico ceding a significant portion of its northern territory (present-day California, Nevada, Utah, and parts of Arizona, New Mexico, Colorado, and Wyoming) to the United States in exchange for $15 million. The Mexican-American War had far-reaching consequences, including the expansion of U.S. territory to the Pacific Ocean and the intensification of the debate over the expansion of slavery in the newly acquired lands.

Causes of the War

1. Which event is considered an immediate trigger for the outbreak of the Mexican-American War?

A) The annexation of Texas by the United States
B) Mexican attacks on American settlers in Texas
C) Disputes over the Texas-Mexico border
D) American interest in California

Answer: **C)**

2. The annexation of Texas by the United States in 1845 was:

A) Welcomed by the Mexican government.
B) A major point of contention between the U.S. and Mexico.
C) Primarily motivated by a desire to spread slavery.
D) Both B and C

Answer: **D)**

3. Manifest Destiny, the belief in U.S. territorial expansion, played a role in:

A) Justifying the war with Mexico.
B) Increasing tensions over the Oregon Territory.
C) Encouraging trade relations with Mexico.
D) Supporting Mexican claims to Texas.

Answer: **A)**

Key Events and Battles

4. U.S. General Zachary Taylor achieved a key victory over Mexican forces at the Battle of:

A) The Alamo
B) San Jacinto
C) Buena Vista
D) Chapultepec

Answer: **C)**

5. The Mexican surrender at the Battle of _____ led to the U.S. capture of Mexico City.

A) Buena Vista
B) Monterey
C) Palo Alto
D) Chapultepec

Answer: **D)**

6. Which American military leader emerged as a national hero during the Mexican-American War?

A) Zachary Taylor
B) Winfield Scott
C) Ulysses S. Grant
D) Robert E. Lee

Answer: **A)**

Outcomes and Impact

7. The Treaty of Guadalupe Hidalgo (1848) formally ended the Mexican-American War and resulted in:

A) The U.S. gaining California, Nevada, Utah, and parts of other Southwestern territories.
B) The establishment of a neutral border zone between the U.S. and Mexico.
C) The annexation of Texas by Mexico.
D) The creation of a protectorate over Mexico by the U.S.

Answer: **A)**

8. The Mexican Cession, land gained by the U.S. in the war, significantly increased the size of the:

A) Eastern seaboard states.
B) Southern plantation states.
C) Western territories.
D) Great Plains region.

Answer: **C)**

9. The Mexican-American War contributed to increased tensions over slavery in the United States because:

A) The newly acquired territories would become slave or free states.
B) Many northerners opposed the war and its expansionist aims.
C) Southern planters sought to expand slavery into new territories.
D) All of the above

Answer: **D)**

Legacy

10. The Mexican-American War is considered by some historians as a:

A) Just war fought to defend American interests.
B) Unnecessary war fueled by expansionist ambitions.
C) War that ultimately benefited both nations.
D) Minor conflict with little lasting impact.

Answer: **B)**

11. The war had a lasting impact on relations between the U.S. and Mexico, including:

A) Increased animosity and suspicion.
B) Close economic and political cooperation.
C) A mass migration of Mexicans to the U.S.
D) A period of cultural exchange and understanding.

Answer: **A)**

The Civil War and Reconstruction

The American Civil War (1861-1865) was a conflict between the Union (Northern states) and the Confederacy (Southern states) primarily over the issues of slavery and states' rights. The war began with the Confederate attack on Fort Sumter in April 1861 and ended with the surrender of Confederate General Robert E. Lee at Appomattox Court House in April 1865. The Union victory resulted in the abolition of slavery, the reunification of the nation, and the beginning of the Reconstruction era (1865-1877). Reconstruction aimed to rebuild the South, establish civil rights for freed slaves, and reintegrate the Southern states into the Union, but it faced numerous challenges, including political opposition, economic struggles, and the rise of white supremacist groups like the Ku Klux Klan.

Compromise of 1850

1. The Compromise of 1850 attempted to maintain a balance between:

A) Slave states and free states
B) Northern and Southern economic interests
C) Federal and state powers
D) All of the above

Answer: **D)**

2. Which key provision of the Compromise of 1850 was highly controversial among abolitionists?

A) California admitted as a free state
B) New Mexico and Utah territories organized under popular sovereignty
C) Stronger Fugitive Slave Act
D) Slave trade abolished in Washington D.C.

Answer: **C)**

3. One prominent politician who played a key role in crafting the Compromise of 1850 was:

A) Abraham Lincoln
B) Henry Clay
C) Jefferson Davis
D) John C. Calhoun

Answer: **B)**

4. The Compromise of 1850 provided a:

A) Permanent resolution to the issue of slavery's expansion
B) Increase in pro-slavery sentiment in the North
C) Temporary fix that ultimately heightened tensions
D) Decisive victory for abolitionist forces

Answer: **C)**

Kansas-Nebraska Act (1854)

5. The Kansas-Nebraska Act of 1854 effectively repealed which earlier legislation?

A) The Compromise of 1850
B) The Three-Fifths Compromise
C) The Missouri Compromise
D) The Northwest Ordinance

Answer: **C)**

6. The concept of "popular sovereignty" meant that the issue of slavery in Kansas and Nebraska would be decided by:

A) A vote of the residents in those territories
B) A specially appointed federal commission
C) The Supreme Court
D) The President of the United States

Answer: **A)**

7. The Kansas-Nebraska Act was a major political victory for:

A) Northern Abolitionists
B) Southern slaveholders
C) Anti-immigrant factions
D) Native American tribes

Answer: **B)**

8. "Bleeding Kansas" refers to:

A) The violent clashes between pro-slavery and anti-slavery forces in Kansas Territory
B) A military battle between the U.S. Army and Native American tribes in Kansas
C) An epidemic that spread through Kansas during this period
D) An economic depression triggered by the Kansas-Nebraska Act

Answer: **A)**

Dred Scott Decision (1857)

9. Dred Scott sued for his freedom on the grounds that:

A) His owner had physically abused him, violating the law.
B) He had lived in free states and territories, making him free.
C) The Constitution guaranteed freedom to all U.S. citizens
D) He had been illegally purchased in a state where slavery was banned.

Answer: **B)**

10. Chief Justice Roger Taney's ruling in the Dred Scott case declared that:

A) Enslaved people were property, not citizens, and had no rights
B) States had the sole right to determine the legality of slavery
C) Free black Americans were entitled to full citizenship rights
D) Popular sovereignty should decide the issue of slavery in territories.

Answer: **A)**

11. What was NOT a direct consequence of the Dred Scott decision?

A) Heightened tensions between the North and South over slavery
B) Increased support for the abolitionist movement
C) Damage to the Supreme Court's reputation
D) The legality of slavery decided once and for all

Answer: **D)**

12. The Republican Party, formed in the 1850s, took a stance:

A) In strong support of slavery's expansion
B) Against the further spread of slavery into new territories
C) In favor of complete and immediate abolition of slavery
D) Promoting compromise with the South on slavery

Answer: **B)**

13. What event in 1859 further inflamed tensions and convinced many Southerners that secession was necessary?

A) The election of Abraham Lincoln as President
B) John Brown's raid on Harpers Ferry
C) The passage of the Fugitive Slave Act
D) The Supreme Court's ruling on the Dred Scott case

Answer: **B)**

14. Which political figure argued that a "house divided against itself cannot stand", believing the nation could not remain permanently half-slave and half-free?

A) Stephen Douglas
B) Jefferson Davis
C) John C. Calhoun
D) Abraham Lincoln

Answer: **D)**

15. Which Southern state was the first to secede from the Union after Lincoln's election in 1860?

A) Virginia
B) Georgia
C) Texas
D) South Carolina

Answer: **D)**

16. The concept of nullification, the idea that states could ignore federal laws, was a recurring theme in debates over:

A) Immigration policy
B) Expansion of voting rights
C) Slavery and states' rights
D) Foreign trade agreements

Answer: **C)**

17. The Crittenden Compromise in 1860 was a last-ditch effort to:

A) Organize a peace conference between Northern and Southern leaders
B) Guarantee the right to own slaves in both existing and future territories
C) Provide compensation to slaveholders who voluntarily emancipated their slaves
D) Prevent the Civil War by offering concessions to the South

Answer: **D)**

18. The Fugitive Slave Act of 1850 caused controversy and deepened divisions because it:

A) Required Northerners to assist in the capture and return of escaped slaves.
B) Banned the slave trade in all new U.S. territories.
C) Granted citizenship rights to free black Americans.
D) Established funding for education in former slave states.

Answer: **A)**

19. Which of these figures was a prominent abolitionist and published the anti-slavery newspaper "The Liberator"?

A) Frederick Douglass
B) William Lloyd Garrison
C) Harriet Tubman
D) Harriet Beecher Stowe

Answer: **B)**

The Outbreak and Early Battles

1. The Civil War began after the Confederate attack on:

A) Fort Sumter
B) Antietam Creek
C) Gettysburg
D) Appomattox Court House

Answer: **A)**

2. Which state seceded from the Union first?

A) Virginia
B) South Carolina
C) Georgia
D) Alabama

Answer: **B)**

3. Abraham Lincoln, the President during the Civil War, belonged to which political party?

    A) Democrat
    B) Whig
    C) Republican
    D) Independent

Answer: **C)**

4. The early years of the war saw more victories for which side?

    A) The Union (North)
    B) The Confederacy (South)
    C) Victories were evenly split.
    D) There were no major battles in the early years.

Answer: **B)**

5. General Ulysses S. Grant emerged as a key Union leader after victories at:

    A) Shiloh and Antietam
    B) Bull Run (Manassas) and Fredericksburg
    C) Gettysburg and Chancellorsville
    D) Vicksburg and Atlanta

Answer: **A)**

Strategies and Turning Points

6. The Union's strategy of Anaconda Plan aimed to:

    A) Quickly capture the Confederate capital, Richmond.
    B) Encircle and strangle the Confederacy through blockades and river control.
    C) Focus on major battles to deplete Confederate manpower.
    D) Incite slave rebellions throughout the South.

Answer: **B)**

7. The Confederacy's strategy often relied on:

A) Superior industrial and technological resources
B) Strong leadership and well-trained military tactics
C) Numerical advantage in troop size
D) Support from European powers

Answer: **B)**

8. The Emancipation Proclamation, issued by Lincoln in 1863, aimed to:

A) Grant immediate freedom to all enslaved people in the United States.
B) Free enslaved people in Confederate states only.
C) Encourage slave rebellions and weaken the Confederacy.
D) Compensate slaveholders who voluntarily freed their slaves.

Answer: **B)**

9. The Battle of Antietam, although a tactical draw, is considered a turning point because:

A) It ended General Lee's Maryland campaign.
B) It convinced Britain to recognize the Confederacy.
C) It led to the first major use of ironclad warships.
D) It resulted in the heaviest casualties of the war.

Answer: **A)**

10. The Battle of Gettysburg, the deadliest battle of the war, resulted in a victory for the:

A) Confederacy, halting their Northern invasion.
B) Union, marking a major turning point.
C) Neither side achieved a decisive victory.
D) War ended in a stalemate.

Answer: **B)**

The War's End and Legacy

11. General William T. Sherman's strategy in the South included the capture of Atlanta and the use of:

A) Total war tactics, devastating infrastructure and resources.
B) Guerilla warfare tactics to disrupt Confederate supply lines.
C) Focus on major battles to destroy Confederate armies.
D) Naval blockades to cut off Confederate trade.

Answer: **A)**

12. The surrender of General Lee at Appomattox Court House in 1865 marked the:

A) Official end of the Civil War
B) Beginning of Reconstruction
C) Abolition of slavery throughout the United States
D) Impeachment of President Lincoln

Answer: **A)**

13. The Thirteenth Amendment to the Constitution formally abolished slavery in the United States.

A) True
B) False

Answer: **A)**

14. Which of the following was NOT a direct consequence of the Civil War?

A) The preservation of the Union
B) The abolition of slavery
C) Devastation of the South's infrastructure
D) The immediate granting of full citizenship rights to freed slaves

Answer: **D)**

15. Lincoln was assassinated shortly after the war's end by:

A) A disgruntled Union soldier
B) A Confederate sympathizer, John Wilkes Booth
C) An enraged former slave
D) Vice President Andrew Johnson

Answer: **B)**

Social and Political Change

16. The Civil War had a profound impact on the role of women, with many serving as:

A) Spies and saboteurs behind enemy lines
B) Nurses, aiding the wounded and managing hospitals
C) Soldiers disguised as men on the battlefront
D) All of the above

Answer: **D)**

17. The period immediately after the Civil War, focused on reintegrating the South and rebuilding the nation, is known as:

A) The Progressive Era
B) The Great Depression
C) The Industrial Revolution
D) Reconstruction

Answer: **D)**

18. One legacy of the Civil War was the passage of amendments to the U.S. Constitution that:

A) Expanded federal power and guaranteed rights for freed slaves.
B) Repealed the income tax and banned the formation of labor unions.
C) Granted women the right to vote and limited presidential terms.
D) Prohibited alcohol and established the gold standard for currency.

Answer: **A)**

19. The Civil War left a devastating toll, with approximately how many casualties?

A) 100,000
B) 300,000
C) 600,000-850,000
D) Over 1 million

Answer: **C)**

20. The Civil War is often seen as a watershed moment in US history because it:

A) Led directly to America becoming a major world power.
B) Settled the issue of states' rights and the supremacy of the federal government.
C) Ended political disputes and led to lasting unity.
D) Marked the beginning of a struggle for racial equality that continues today.

Answer: **D)**

Broader Perspectives

21. Which military conflict served as a precursor to the Civil War, showcasing the use of new technologies and trench warfare tactics?

A) The Spanish-American War
B) World War I
C) The Mexican-American War
D) The War of 1812

Answer: **B)**

22. The Civil War is considered the first "modern war" due to:

A) Its focus on naval power and international alliances.
B) Its large-scale destruction and disregard for civilian casualties.
C) The widespread use of railroads, telegraphs, and industrialized weaponry.
D) Its reliance on guerrilla warfare tactics and avoiding major battles.

Answer: **C)**

23. Which prominent African American leader advocated for full citizenship rights and economic opportunities for freed slaves during the Civil War and Reconstruction?

A) Martin Luther King Jr.
B) Booker T. Washington
C) Frederick Douglass
D) Malcolm X

Answer: **C)**

24. The Battle of Gettysburg is often commemorated, but which battle was arguably more consequential in securing Union victory?

A) The Battle of Fredericksburg
B) The Capture of Atlanta
C) The Siege of Vicksburg
D) The Battle of New Orleans

Answer: **C)**

25. What medical innovation emerged during the Civil War that revolutionized field treatment of wounded soldiers?

A) Amputation procedures
B) The use of anesthesia
C) Early techniques in plastic surgery
D) Hygienic practices to prevent infection

Answer: **A)**

26. The Union's victory in the Civil War had an impact on international affairs, specifically by:

A) Discouraging European powers from meddling in the Americas.
B) Sparking a wave of revolutions in Europe for greater democracy.
C) Weakening the U.S. military, making it vulnerable to invasion.
D) Creating lasting alliances between the U.S. and Britain.

Answer: **A)**

27. Which Civil War General is known for harsh tactics like his "March to the Sea," yet later advocated for reconciliation and lenient treatment of former Confederates?

A) Ulysses S. Grant
B) Robert E. Lee
C) George McClellan
D) William T. Sherman

Answer: **D)**

28. While Abraham Lincoln is celebrated as the president who oversaw the end of slavery, his initial wartime goal was focused on:

A) Punishing the South for seceding
B) Preserving the Union, even if slavery continued
C) Granting full equality to freed slaves throughout the country.
D) Expansion of U.S. territory into Mexico and the Caribbean.

Answer: **B)**

29. The Civil War continues to be debated amongst historians. Which of these is a major area of disagreement?

A) Whether the primary cause was slavery or states' rights.
B) Which side had superior military tactics and leadership.
C) Which battle had the greatest impact on the war's outcome.
D) Whether the Confederacy could have won with more outside support.

Answer: **A)**

30. Which piece of Civil War-era literature provides a fictionalized but visceral account of a Southern woman's experience during and after the war?

A) Uncle Tom's Cabin
B) Little Women
C) Gone with the Wind
D) The Adventures of Huckleberry Finn

Answer: **C)**

Emancipation Proclamation

The Emancipation Proclamation was an executive order issued by U.S. President Abraham Lincoln on January 1, 1863, during the American Civil War. The proclamation declared that all enslaved people in the Confederate states in rebellion against the Union were henceforth free. While the Emancipation Proclamation did not immediately free all slaves in the United States, it was a crucial turning point in the war and a significant step towards the abolition of slavery. The proclamation also allowed for the enlistment of African Americans in the Union Army, which provided a much-needed boost to the Union's military efforts.

The Basics

1. The Emancipation Proclamation was issued by:

A) The U.S. Congress
B) President Abraham Lincoln
C) The Supreme Court
D) General Ulysses S. Grant

Answer: **B)**

2. In what year was the Emancipation Proclamation issued?

    A) 1861
    B) 1863
    C) 1865
    D) 1868

Answer: **B)**

3. The Emancipation Proclamation declared free:

    A) Only slaves in the Union states
    B) Only slaves who escaped to the North
    C) All slaves in the United States
    D) Enslaved people in Confederate states and territories in rebellion

Answer: **D)**

4. Which of these is a reason why the Emancipation Proclamation is considered a limited document?

    A) It didn't apply to slaves in border states that remained loyal to the Union.
    B) It lacked immediate, practical mechanisms for enforcement.
    C) It caused a wave of slave rebellions in the South.
    D) It was later overturned by the Supreme Court.

Answer: **A) and B)**

Motivations

5. One of Abraham Lincoln's primary reasons for issuing the Emancipation Proclamation was to:

    A) Weaken the Confederacy's war effort by disrupting their labor source.
    B) Fulfill a campaign promise to abolitionists.
    C) Inspire enslaved people to rise up in rebellion.
    D) Secure British support for the Union cause.

Answer: **A)**

6. The Emancipation Proclamation shifted the focus of the Civil War to include:

    A) The issue of slavery and freedom
    B) Expansion of the war into Mexico and the Caribbean
    C) Trade agreements with European powers
    D) Native American land rights in the West

Answer: **A)**

Responses & Impact

7. How did many enslaved people in the Confederacy react to the news of the Emancipation Proclamation?

    A) It sparked widespread uprisings and revolts.
    B) Many escaped to Union lines, seeking freedom.
    C) Most ignored it, believing it was propaganda.
    D) They continued working but demanded higher wages.

Answer: **B)**

8. How did the South react to the Emancipation Proclamation?

    A) They accepted it as the law and moved to abolish slavery.
    B) They offered to negotiate a peace treaty.
    C) They largely dismissed it as irrelevant and illegal.
    D) They increased efforts to recapture escaped slaves.

Answer: **C)**

9. The Emancipation Proclamation helped pave the way for the recruitment of:

    A) Native Americans into the Union Army
    B) Women as nurses and battlefield aids
    C) African American soldiers into the Union Army
    D) Immigrants as factory workers in the North

Answer: **C)**

10. The Emancipation Proclamation had a diplomatic impact in that it:

A) Secured an alliance with France and Spain against the Confederacy.
B) Led to the immediate end of the Civil War through British mediation.
C) Deterred Britain from recognizing or supporting the Confederacy.
D) Caused widespread protests and riots in Europe.

Answer: **C)**

Legacy

11. While symbolically important, the Emancipation Proclamation did not immediately end slavery. This was achieved through:

A) The work of abolitionists after the war
B) A Supreme Court decision in 1868
C) The Thirteenth Amendment to the Constitution
D) Compensation to former slaveholders

Answer: **C)**

Reconstruction Era

The Reconstruction Era was the period following the American Civil War from 1865 to 1877, during which the United States government worked to rebuild the Southern states and address the issues caused by the war, particularly the status of newly freed slaves. The era saw the passage of the 13th, 14th, and 15th Amendments, which abolished slavery, granted citizenship to African Americans, and prohibited racial discrimination in voting, respectively. However, the Reconstruction Era faced numerous challenges, including Southern resistance, the rise of white supremacist groups like the Ku Klux Klan, and the struggle to integrate African Americans into post-war society. The period ended with the Compromise of 1877, which led to the withdrawal of federal troops from the South and the end of many Reconstruction-era policies, setting the stage for the Jim Crow era of segregation and discrimination.

The Basics

1. Reconstruction refers to the period immediately after the Civil War focused on:

A) Expanding U.S. territory westward
B) Rebuilding the South and reintegrating the former Confederate states
C) Punishing the South for causing the war
D) Establishing trade agreements with Europe

Answer: **B)**

2. The assassination of Abraham Lincoln in 1865 resulted in his Vice President assuming the presidency:

A) Ulysses S. Grant
B) Andrew Johnson
C) Thaddeus Stevens
D) William Seward

Answer: **B)**

3. The main goals of Reconstruction included:

A) Guaranteeing rights to former slaves
B) Rebuilding the Southern economy
C) Reconciling the North and South
D) All of the above

Answer: **D)**

Federal Agencies & Amendments

4. The government agency tasked with assisting freed slaves, providing aid, and establishing schools in the South was the:

A) Department of Education
B) Southern Claims Commission
C) Freedmen's Bureau
D) Bureau of Indian Affairs

Answer: **C)**

5. The 13th Amendment abolished:

A) Slavery
B) Segregation
C) Poll taxes
D) The Ku Klux Klan

Answer: **A)**

6. The 14th Amendment granted:

A) Former slaves the right to vote
B) Women the right to vote
C) Citizenship to those born or naturalized in the U.S.
D) Land ownership to former slaves

Answer: **C)**

7. The 15th Amendment prohibited denying voting rights based on:

A) Race, color, or previous condition of servitude
B) Gender
C) Property ownership
D) Age

Answer: **A)**

Presidential vs. Radical Reconstruction

8. President Andrew Johnson's Reconstruction plan was seen as:

A) Very harsh towards former Confederate leaders
B) Lenient towards the South and offered few protections for freed slaves
C) Highly successful in bringing about lasting change
D) focused on punishing plantation owners economically

Answer: **B)**

9. Radical Republicans in Congress advocated for:

A) A quick return of the South to the Union
B) Punishing the South and forced social change
C) Stronger protections for freed slaves and more federal power
D) Limiting the federal government's role in the South

Answer: **C)**

10. Congressional Reconstruction, dominated by Radical Republicans, involved:

A) Temporarily dividing the South into military districts
B) Requiring Southern states to ratify amendments for readmission
C) A focus on addressing the rights of former slaves
D) All of the above

Answer: **D)**

Achievements & Failures

11. A positive outcome of Reconstruction for African Americans was:

A) Widespread land ownership and economic prosperity
B) The end of segregation and discrimination
C) Increased political participation and elected offices
D) Complete social equality with whites

Answer: **C)**

12. Successful programs established during Reconstruction included:

A) Public schools in the South
B) 40 acres and a mule land distribution
C) Immediate granting of full voting rights to women
D) Desegregation of public transportation and spaces

Answer: **A)**

13. The "40 acres and a mule" promise to former slaves was:

A) Successfully implemented across the South
B) Largely unfulfilled
C) Part of Andrew Johnson's Reconstruction plan
D) Established by the 14th Amendment

Answer: **B)**

14. Reconstruction governments in the South were a mix of:

A) Former Confederates and white supremacists
B) Northern "carpetbaggers", Scalawags (Southern white Republicans), and African Americans.
C) Native Americans and newly arrived immigrants
D) Abolitionists and industrialists from the North

Answer: **B)**

15. Which of these figures was a prominent African American senator from Mississippi during Reconstruction?

A) Frederick Douglass
B) Booker T. Washington
C) Hiram Revels
D) W.E.B. Du Bois

Answer: **C)**

Opposition to Reconstruction

16. The Ku Klux Klan and other white supremacist groups emerged in the South to:

A) Support Reconstruction efforts and protect the rights of freed slaves
B) Promote economic development and cooperation in the South
C) Intimidate and terrorize African Americans to prevent them from exercising their rights.
D) Lobby for stricter voting regulations for all citizens

Answer: **C)**

17. White Southerners who cooperated with Reconstruction efforts and Republicans were often labeled as:

A) Carpetbaggers
B) Scalawags
C) Redeemers
D) Radicals

Answer: **B)**

18. "Redeemers" were:

A) Northern Abolitionists who moved to the South during Reconstruction
B) Southern Democrats who regained control of state governments from Republicans
C) Former enslaved people who became wealthy landowners
D) Members of the Freedmen's Bureau assisting with education efforts

Answer: **B)**

19. Enforcement of Reconstruction policies weakened over time due to:

A) Diminished Northern support and political will
B) Economic recession and shift of focus to industrialization
C) Violent resistance from white Southerners
D) All of the above

Answer: **D)**

The End of Reconstruction

20. The Compromise of 1877 effectively ended Reconstruction by:

A) Removing federal troops from the South in exchange for Hayes becoming president.
B) Granting land and economic opportunity to former slaves.
C) Outlawing the Ku Klux Klan and securing voting rights for African Americans.
D) Guaranteeing equal access to education and public facilities for all races.

Answer: **A)**

21. Jim Crow laws in the South were designed to:

A) Provide land and economic opportunity to freed slaves.
B) Enforce racial segregation and restrict African American rights.
C) Guarantee equal access to education and voting.
D) Protect the rights of Northern "carpetbaggers" in the South.

Answer: **B)**

22. The "Lost Cause" mythology that developed after Reconstruction:

A) Reflected the Union victory and celebrated emancipation.
B) Romanticized the Confederacy and downplayed the role of slavery in the war.
C) Accurately portrayed the corruption and failures of Reconstruction.
D) Emphasized the suffering and hardship experienced by white Southerners.

Answer: **B)**

23. Which Supreme Court case in 1896 upheld racial segregation under the doctrine of "separate but equal"?

A) Dred Scott v. Sandford
B) Brown v. Board of Education
C) Marbury v. Madison
D) Plessy v. Ferguson

Answer: **D)**

Legacy of Reconstruction

24. Reconstruction is seen by historians as:

A) A period of complete success in achieving its goals
B) A tragically missed opportunity with lasting consequences.
C) A necessary period of punishment for the South.
D) An unnecessary overreach of federal power.

Answer: **B)**

25. Despite its failures, which of these was a lasting impact of Reconstruction?

A) Passage of the 13th, 14th, and 15th Amendments
B) Immediate equality and integration in Southern society
C) Widespread land ownership for former slaves
D) The end of racism and white supremacy in the South

Answer: **A)**

Gilded Age (late 1800s)

The Gilded Age, spanning from the 1870s to the 1890s, was a period of rapid economic growth, industrialization, and technological advancement in the United States. The term "Gilded Age" suggests that beneath the glittering surface of prosperity lay serious social problems, such as income inequality, political corruption, and poor working conditions. This era saw the rise of powerful industrialists and financiers, often referred to as "robber barons," who amassed enormous wealth and influence. The Gilded Age also witnessed significant immigration, urbanization, and the emergence of labor unions as workers sought to improve their conditions and rights.

The Rise of Industry

1. The Gilded Age was a period of rapid _____ in the United States.

    A) Industrialization
    B) Social reform
    C) Environmental protection
    D) Westward expansion

Answer: **A)**

2. Which invention revolutionized communication and helped expand businesses during the Gilded Age?

A) The automobile
B) The light bulb
C) The telephone
D) The airplane

Answer: **C)**

3. Which industry was central to the growth of industrialization in this era?

A) Textile manufacturing
B) Railroad construction
C) Shipbuilding
D) Agriculture

Answer: **B)**

4. The Bessemer process was a breakthrough in the efficient production of:

A) Textiles
B) Glass
C) Steel
D) Oil

Answer: **C)**

5. Prominent industrialists, sometimes called "robber barons", like Andrew Carnegie and John D. Rockefeller, accumulated vast wealth through:

A) Business innovation and at times ruthless practices.
B) Inheritance from wealthy families
C) Political patronage and government contracts
D) Land speculation in newly acquired territories

Answer: **A)**

Labor and Social Change

6. The rise of factories and mass production led to:

A) The decline of skilled craftsmanship.
B) Dangerous working conditions and long hours for laborers.
C) A growing gap between wealthy capitalists and the working class.
D) All of the above

Answer: **D)**

7. To address poor working conditions and low wages, workers formed:

A) Political parties
B) Militias
C) Labor unions
D) Religious organizations

Answer: **C)**

8. A major labor organization of this time was the:

A) Knights of Labor
B) International Workers of the World
C) United Farm Workers
D) National Labor Relations Board

Answer: **A)**

9. Which event in Chicago in 1886 marked a turning point in public perception of the labor movement?

A) The Great Railroad Strike
B) The Pullman Strike
C) The Haymarket Affair
D) The Homestead Strike

Answer: **C)**

10. A major demographic shift of the Gilded Age was rapid:

A) Urbanization as people flocked to cities for factory jobs.
B) Westward migration of those seeking farmland
C) A sharp decline in population due to epidemics.
D) Increased emigration from Asia leading to ethnic diversity.

Answer: **A)**

Immigration and Cultural Shifts

11. The Gilded Age saw a large influx of immigrants from:

A) Southern and Eastern Europe
B) Mexico and Central America
C) Canada and Western Europe
D) Africa and East Asia

Answer: **A)**

12. Where were many new immigrants initially processed upon arrival in the United States?

A) San Francisco
B) New Orleans
C) Boston
D) Ellis Island

Answer: **D)**

13. Nativism during the Gilded Age was:

A) An embrace of multiculturalism and immigrant contributions.
B) A movement promoting the interests of native-born Americans.
C) Legislation offering citizenship pathways for new arrivals.
D) The belief in the superiority of traditional American culture.

Answer: **B (often combined with elements of D)**

14. Immigrants often settled in ethnic enclaves in cities, which:

A) Helped them preserve their culture and community ties.
B) Led to the decline of traditional American values.
C) Made it difficult for them to integrate into American society.
D) Provided them with political power and economic advantages.

Answer: **A)**

15. The Chinese Exclusion Act of 1882 was a response to:

A) Nativist sentiment and anti-Chinese discrimination.
B) Chinese businesses unfairly competing with American companies.
C) Religious differences and rising anti-Buddhist sentiment.
D) China's refusal to trade with the United States.

Answer: **A)**

Politics and Corruption

16. Political machines, such as Tammany Hall, exerted power in cities by:

A) Promoting honest government and efficient public services.
B) Trading favors and services for votes, often engaging in corruption.
C) Advocating for labor rights and worker protections.
D) Supporting immigration restrictions and nativist policies.

Answer: **B)**

17. The term "Gilded Age" suggests that:

A) The era was a time of true equality and prosperity for all.
B) Beneath the surface of economic progress lay corruption and inequality.
C) The U.S. was focused on expanding its empire overseas.
D) American society was dominated by traditional values and social stability.

Answer: **B)**

18. The spoils system, also known as patronage, involved:

A) Politicians rewarding supporters with government jobs.
B) Strict campaign finance regulations to limit corruption.
C) A focus on merit-based appointments in civil service.
D) Regulations controlling the influence of big businesses on elections.

Answer: **A)**

19. Which President was assassinated by a disgruntled office seeker, leading to civil service reforms?

A) Ulysses S. Grant
B) Grover Cleveland
C) James Garfield
D) Abraham Lincoln

Answer: **C)**

20. The Pendleton Civil Service Act of 1883 aimed to:

A) Reduce political corruption by creating a merit-based system for some government jobs.
B) Expand voting rights to women and African Americans.
C) Break up monopolies and promote fair competition in business.
D) Establish national parks and protect wilderness areas.

Answer: **A)**

Society and Culture

21. The gap between the wealthy and the working class was starkly visible in:

A) The opulent lifestyles of the rich contrasted with urban slums.
B) Equal access to education and opportunity regardless of class.
C) The political dominance of labor unions and working-class parties.
D) The widespread rejection of materialism and industrial capitalism.

Answer: **A)**

22. Conspicuous consumption refers to:

A) The lavish spending of the wealthy on mansions and luxury goods.
B) Efforts to recycle and conserve resources in response to pollution.
C) Middle-class consumerism and the rise of department stores.
D) Charitable donations by wealthy philanthropists.

Answer: **A)**

23. The Social Gospel movement was an effort by:

A) Social reformers to address poverty and inequality based on Christian principles.
B) Secular philosophers promoting reason over religious faith.
C) Wealthy industrialists to justify their fortunes as divinely ordained.
D) Nativists to restrict immigration and preserve traditional values.

Answer: **A)**

24. Which novel by Upton Sinclair exposed the unsanitary conditions of the meatpacking industry?

A) The Jungle
B) The Grapes of Wrath
C) The Great Gatsby
D) Uncle Tom's Cabin

Answer: **A)**

25. "Yellow journalism" refers to:

A) Newspapers using sensationalism and exaggeration to sell copies.
B) Objective and fact-based reporting.
C) News publications focused on economic and business news.
D) The rise of investigative journalism exposing corruption.

Answer: **A)**

26. Which woman was a prominent leader in the settlement house movement, establishing Hull House in Chicago to serve the poor and immigrant communities?

A) Susan B. Anthony
B) Ida Tarbell
C) Jane Addams
D) Carrie Nation

Answer: **C)**

27. The Populist movement, which gained support among farmers and laborers, advocated for reforms such as:

A) Higher tariffs and protection for American industries.
B) The gold standard and reduced government spending.
C) Government regulation of railroads and greater control of the money supply.
D) Restrictions on immigration and labor unions.

Answer: **C)**

28. The Gilded Age saw a rise in popular forms of entertainment like:

A) Vaudeville shows
B) Amusement parks
C) Professional sports like baseball
D) All of the above

Answer: **D)**

Broader Context

29. The Gilded Age coincided with a period of U.S. expansionism and imperialism, reflected in events like:

A) The Spanish-American War and the acquisition of overseas territories.
B) Increased trade and diplomatic ties with European powers.
C) The Louisiana Purchase and expansion into Native American lands.
D) The annexation of Texas and the Mexican-American War.

Answer: **A)**

30. Which doctrine did Theodore Roosevelt add to the Monroe Doctrine, asserting U.S. dominance and interventionist policies in Latin America?

A) Manifest Destiny
B) Roosevelt Corollary
C) Good Neighbor Policy
D) Containment Strategy

Answer: **B)**

31. The debate over trusts involved:

A) Government regulation of large monopolies and corporate power.
B) Labor unions' rights to organize and collectively bargain.
C) Tariffs on imported goods and protectionist policies.
D) Environmental conservation and protection of natural resources.

Answer: **A)**

32. Which piece of legislation was passed in 1890 to break up monopolies and promote competition in business?

A) Interstate Commerce Act
B) Clayton Antitrust Act
C) Pure Food and Drug Act
D) Sherman Antitrust Act

Answer: **D)**

33. Muckrakers were:

A) Investigative journalists who exposed social problems and corruption.
B) Wealthy industrialists who used their fortunes for philanthropy.
C) Politicians who supported the spoils system and machine politics.
D) Activists who fought for environmental protection laws.

Answer: **A)**

34. The Progressive Era, which followed the Gilded Age, sought to address many of the era's problems through:

A) Government regulation, social reforms, and fighting corruption.
B) Overseas expansion and increased military power.
C) Reduced government intervention and promotion of big business.
D) Isolationism and avoiding involvement in foreign affairs.

Answer: **A)**

35. Which constitutional amendment granted women the right to vote?

A) 13th Amendment
B) 15th Amendment
C) 18th Amendment
D) 19th Amendment

Answer: **D)**

36. The Gilded Age is notable because it was a time of:

A) Dramatic transformation, progress, but also social and economic inequality.
B) Cultural decline and widespread rejection of materialism.
C) Unprecedented equality and opportunity for all Americans.
D) Global isolationism and lack of industrial innovation.

Answer: **A)**

Progressive Era (1890s-1920s)

The Progressive Era was a period of widespread social activism and political reform in the United States that spanned from the 1890s to the 1920s. Progressives sought to address the economic, political, and social issues that arose from rapid industrialization, urbanization, and corruption. They advocated for reforms such as women's suffrage, child labor laws, antitrust legislation, and the direct election of U.S. Senators. The era also saw the emergence of investigative journalism, known as "muckraking," which exposed social and economic injustices, as well as the implementation of initiatives like Prohibition and the income tax.

The Roots of Progressive Reform

1. The Progressive Era was a period primarily focused on:

A) Expanding U.S. territory through overseas imperialism
B) Promoting social justice and addressing problems caused by industrialization
C) Reducing the size and influence of the federal government
D) Strengthening ties with European powers through alliances

Answer: **B)**

2. Problems associated with the Gilded Age, which motivated Progressive reformers, included:

A) Political corruption and the influence of big business
B) Urban poverty, unsafe working conditions, and child labor
C) Environmental pollution and depletion of natural resources
D) All of the above

Answer: **D)**

3. Muckrakers contributed to Progressive reforms by:

A) Leading labor strikes and organizing unions.
B) Running for political office on reform platforms.
C) Using investigative journalism to expose social problems.
D) Establishing settlement houses to aid the poor.

Answer: **C)**

4. Jane Addams was a prominent figure in which Progressive movement?

A) The suffrage movement
B) The Settlement House movement
C) The Anti-Saloon League and Temperance movement
D) The conservation movement

Answer: **B)**

Women's Suffrage and Social Activism

5. The 19th Amendment to the U.S. Constitution granted:

A) Women the right to vote
B) Federal income tax
C) Direct election of Senators
D) Prohibition of alcohol

Answer: **A)**

6. Which prominent figures were leaders in the women's suffrage movement?

A) Elizabeth Cady Stanton & Susan B. Anthony
B) Ida Tarbell & Upton Sinclair
C) Theodore Roosevelt & Woodrow Wilson
D) W.E.B. Dubois & Booker T. Washington

Answer: **A)**

7. Margaret Sanger was a leading advocate for:

A) Birth control and reproductive rights
B) Labor union organizing
C) Temperance and prohibition of alcohol
D) Protecting endangered species

Answer: **A)**

8. The Temperance Movement, which ultimately led to Prohibition, crusaded against:

A) Child labor
B) Consumption of alcohol
C) Racial segregation and discrimination
D) Political corruption

Answer: **B)**

Government Reforms

9. Which Progressive reforms aimed to give citizens more direct power in government?

A) Referendum, Initiative, and Recall
B) Ratification of new constitutional amendments
C) Expansion of the spoils system
D) Establishment of political machines in cities

Answer: **A)**

10. The 17th Amendment to the U.S. Constitution established:

A) Direct election of Senators
B) Prohibition of alcohol
C) Women's right to vote
D) Government regulation of monopolies

Answer: **A)**

11. The rise of city managers and commissions signaled a change towards:

A) More professional and efficient city government
B) Increased power of political machines
C) Reduced government involvement in public services
D) Restricting the voting rights of immigrants

Answer: **A)**

12. Which government agency was established as a result of the publication of Upton Sinclair's "The Jungle"?

A) The Environmental Protection Agency (EPA)
B) The Food and Drug Administration (FDA)
C) The Federal Trade Commission (FTC)
D) The Occupational Safety and Health Administration (OSHA)

Answer: **B)**

Trust-Busting and Economic Regulation

13. President Theodore Roosevelt became known as a "trustbuster" for his actions to:

A) Enforce antitrust laws and break up monopolies
B) Promote cooperation between government and big business
C) Restrict immigration and protect jobs for American workers
D) Expand the U.S. military and acquire overseas territories

Answer: **A)**

14. The Clayton Antitrust Act strengthened earlier antitrust legislation (like the Sherman Antitrust Act) by:

A) Outlawing unfair business practices like price-fixing
B) Granting women the right to own property
C) Establishing a national park system
D) Creating the Federal Reserve banking system

Answer: **A)**

15. The Federal Reserve Act of 1913 was designed to:

A) Establish a central banking system to regulate the money supply.
B) Break up monopolies and promote competition in business.
C) Guarantee the right of workers to form unions.
D) Provide federal funding for conservation of natural resources.

Answer: **A)**

16. President Woodrow Wilson's "New Freedom" platform emphasized:

A) Smaller government and reduced regulation of business.
B) Expanded federal powers and social welfare reforms.
C) Greater regulation of business and banking to promote fairness.
D) U.S. neutrality in international affairs.

Answer: **C)**

Workers' Rights and Labor Unions

17. The Triangle Shirtwaist Factory fire was a pivotal event that led to:

A) Increased workplace safety regulations and labor reforms.
B) Creation of the National Park Service.
C) Passage of the 19th Amendment granting women's suffrage.
D) Restrictions on immigration and quotas for certain nationalities.

Answer: **A)**

18. Which labor union focused on organizing skilled workers and emphasized "bread and butter" issues like wages and working conditions?

A) Industrial Workers of the World (IWW)
B) American Federation of Labor (AFL)
C) The Knights of Labor
D) The Socialist Party of America

Answer: **B)**

19. The 1911 Supreme Court case Lochner v. New York is often cited as an example of:

A) Upholding government regulation of maximum work hours for bakers.
B) Supporting the right of workers to organize unions and bargain collectively.
C) The court favoring protection of business interests over workers' rights.
D) Ruling in favor of women's suffrage on constitutional grounds.

Answer: **C)**

Civil Rights and Racial Justice

20. W.E.B Du Bois was a prominent leader in the:

A) Labor union movement fighting for workers' rights.
B) Women's suffrage movement.
C) Civil rights movement and co-founded the NAACP.
D) Conservation movement protecting wilderness areas.

Answer: **C)**

21. Booker T. Washington advocated for:

A) Immediate and full social and political equality for African Americans.
B) African Americans focusing on economic self-sufficiency and vocational education.
C) Revolutionary overthrow of the capitalist system.
D) Restricting immigration to maintain American racial purity.

Answer: **B)**

22. The "Great Migration" during this period refers to:

A) Large-scale movement of African-Americans from the South to Northern cities.
B) Westward migration of white Americans seeking new land.
C) The influx of immigrants from Southern and Eastern Europe.
D) U.S. military interventions in Latin America.

Answer: **A)**

Conservation and Environmentalism

23. Which President is known for his commitment to conservation of natural resources and the creation of national parks?

A) Abraham Lincoln
B) William McKinley
C) William Howard Taft
D) Theodore Roosevelt

Answer: **D)**

24. The Sierra Club was founded by which prominent conservationist?

A) Theodore Roosevelt
B) Gifford Pinchot
C) John Muir
D) Rachel Carson

Answer: **C)**

25. The conflict between preservationists (like John Muir) and conservationists (like Gifford Pinchot) centered on:

A) Whether to fully protect nature from human use or manage resources wisely.
B) The role of government regulation versus business interests in development.
C) Granting women the right to vote.
D) Restricting immigration from Asia.

Answer: **A)**

U.S. Foreign Policy and World War I

26. Prior to entering World War I, President Wilson initially advocated for a policy of:

A) Neutrality and avoiding involvement in European conflicts.
B) Aggressive imperialism and expanding U.S. territory.
C) Building strong alliances with European powers.
D) Isolationism and reducing trade with other nations.

Answer: **A)**

27. The Zimmerman Telegram, which proposed an alliance between Germany and Mexico, was a factor in:

A) The U.S. declaring war on Germany and entering WWI.
B) The passage of the 19th Amendment granting women's suffrage.
C) The outbreak of the Spanish-American War.
D) The annexation of Hawaii as a U.S. territory.

Answer: **A)**

Women's Suffrage

Women's Suffrage in the United States was achieved nationally on August 18, 1920, with the ratification of the 19th Amendment to the Constitution. The amendment prohibits the denial of voting rights based on sex, granting women the right to vote. The women's suffrage movement began in the mid-19th century and gained momentum through the efforts of activists like Susan B. Anthony, Elizabeth Cady Stanton, and Alice Paul. The ratification of the 19th Amendment marked a significant milestone in the fight for gender equality and expanded the electorate, though many women of color continued to face barriers to voting due to discriminatory practices.

The Fight for the Vote

1. The 19th Amendment to the U.S. Constitution guaranteed:

    A) Equal pay for women
    B) Women the right to vote
    C) Prohibition of alcohol
    D) The right to own property for married women

Answer: **B)**

2. Which states were the FIRST to grant women full voting rights before the 19th Amendment?

A) New York, California, and Pennsylvania
B) Wyoming, Utah, and Colorado
C) Virginia, Massachusetts, and Rhode Island
D) Texas, Mississippi, and Georgia

Answer: **B)**

3. The Seneca Falls Convention in 1848 is considered a pivotal moment in women's suffrage history because it produced the:

A) 19th Amendment
B) Declaration of Sentiments
C) Founding of the National Woman's Party
D) Equal Rights Amendment

Answer: **B)**

4. Prominent women's suffrage leaders included:

A) Susan B. Anthony & Elizabeth Cady Stanton
B) Ida B. Wells & Mary McLeod Bethune
C) Carrie Chapman Catt & Alice Paul
D) All of the above

Answer: **D)**

5. The term "suffragist" is preferable to "suffragette" because:

A) Suffragettes were British, while suffragists were American.
B) Suffragettes were more radical, while suffragists favored peaceful methods.
C) "Suffragette" was a term used to belittle those fighting for the vote.
D) There is no practical difference between the terms.

Answer: **C)**

Strategies and Tactics

6. Which methods did suffragists use to advocate for their cause?

A) Lobbying politicians, organizing marches, and public speaking.
B) Civil disobedience, hunger strikes, and picketing the White House.
C) Guerilla warfare and acts of sabotage.
D) Both A and B

Answer: **D)**

7. The National Woman's Party, led by Alice Paul, favored a strategy focused on:

A) Lobbying state legislatures to pass suffrage laws.
B) A constitutional amendment for nationwide women's suffrage.
C) Educational campaigns and changing public opinion.
D) Cooperation with male-dominated political parties.

Answer: **B)**

8. Some opposition to women's suffrage was based on the belief that:

A) Women were not intelligent enough to understand politics.
B) Voting would distract women from their duties as wives and mothers.
C) It would disrupt the natural order and lead to societal chaos.
D) All of the above.

Answer: **D)**

Victory and Its Limitations

9. The 19th Amendment was ratified in:

A) 1848
B) 1870
C) 1920
D) 1965

Answer: **C)**

10. Which state's ratification was the final one needed to make the 19th Amendment official?

A) New York
B) Illinois
C) Tennessee
D) California

Answer: **C)**

World War I

The United States initially remained neutral during World War I, but eventually entered the conflict on April 6, 1917, on the side of the Allied Powers (France, Great Britain, and Russia) against the Central Powers (Germany, Austria-Hungary, and the Ottoman Empire). The U.S. decision to join the war was influenced by factors such as Germany's unrestricted submarine warfare, the Zimmermann Telegram, and the need to protect American economic and strategic interests. American troops, known as the American Expeditionary Forces (AEF), played a significant role in the later stages of the war, particularly in the Meuse-Argonne Offensive, which helped to tip the balance in favor of the Allies. The U.S. involvement was crucial in ending the war, with the Armistice of November 11, 1918, marking the end of hostilities and leading to the Treaty of Versailles in 1919.

The Road to War

1. The United States initially entered World War I with a policy of:

A) Immediate military intervention alongside the Allied Powers.
B) Isolationism and neutrality, avoiding involvement in the European conflict.
C) Supporting both sides of the war to maintain trade relations.
D) Forming an alliance with Germany and the Central Powers.

Answer: **B)**

2. The sinking of the Lusitania, a British passenger liner, by a German U-boat in 1915, is an example of:

A) A successful German naval strategy against Allied shipping.
B) An act that ultimately pushed the U.S. to join the war on the side of the Allies.
C) A violation of neutral American rights and a catalyst for anti-German sentiment.
D) A decisive naval battle that shifted the course of the war.

Answer: **C)**

3. The Zimmerman Telegram, intercepted by the British, revealed a secret plan by Germany to:

A) Develop a new generation of chemical weapons.
B) Launch a surprise attack on the Western Front.
C) Offer Mexico military support if they attacked the United States.
D) Form a peace treaty with Russia and withdraw from the war in the East.

Answer: **C)**

4. President Woodrow Wilson's rationale for entering World War I can be summarized by his belief in:

A) Protecting American economic interests and trade with Europe.
B) Spreading democracy and making the world "safe for democracy."
C) Gaining new territories and expanding American influence overseas.
D) Aiding Germany and the Central Powers to defeat communism.

Answer: **B)**

5. The declaration of war by the United States in 1917 officially ended the nation's policy of:

A) Manifest Destiny and westward expansion.
B) Isolationism and avoiding foreign entanglements.
C) Imperialism and acquiring overseas colonies.
D) Monroe Doctrine and protecting the Western Hemisphere.

Answer: **B)**

Mobilizing for War

6. The Selective Service Act of 1917 established a system of:

A) Universal conscription, drafting men for military service.
B) Volunteer recruitment for the U.S. armed forces.
C) Increased funding for war production and industrial mobilization.
D) Rationing of essential goods and supplies on the home front.

Answer: **A)**

7. The Committee on Public Information (CPI) was a U.S. government agency created to:

A) Provide objective war news and updates to the public.
B) Censor information and promote pro-war propaganda.
C) Coordinate military strategies with Allied commanders in Europe.
D) Negotiate peace treaties with the Central Powers after the war.

Answer: **B)**

8. The Liberty Loan drives were critical for the U.S. war effort by:

A) Raising money through the sale of government bonds to finance the war.
B) Encouraging rationing and conservation of essential resources.
C) Mobilizing American industry to produce war materials.
D) Recruiting volunteers for military service overseas.

Answer: **A)**

9. Women played a significant role on the American home front during World War I by:

A) Taking over jobs in factories and shipyards traditionally held by men.
B) Organizing volunteer efforts to support the troops and war relief.
C) Leading protests against the war and advocating for pacifism.
D) Enlisting in the U.S. military and serving overseas.

Answer: **A & B)**

10. The Espionage Act (1917) and Sedition Act (1918) were controversial because they:

A) Expanded conscription to include women in military service.
B) Established national parks to protect wilderness and natural resources.
C) Restricted freedom of expression and dissent against the war.
D) Promoted labor union organizing and workers' rights.

Answer: **C)**

The American Expeditionary Force on the Western Front

11. The nickname "doughboys" referred to:

A) Members of the American Red Cross working in Europe.
B) African American soldiers serving in segregated units.
C) American soldiers fighting in Europe under General Pershing.
D) German prisoners of war held by the United States.

Answer: **C)**

12. General John J. Pershing was the leader of the:

A) American Expeditionary Force in Europe during World War I.
B) Committee on Public Information, promoting war propaganda.
C) Food Administration, overseeing rationing on the home front.
D) U.S. Navy forces blockading German ports.

Answer: **A)**

13. The "Harlem Hellfighters," the 369th Infantry Regiment, were:

A) A segregated African American unit that earned recognition for bravery.
B) American pilots flying fighter planes against the German air force.
C) Labor activists protesting against the war and poor working conditions.
D) Volunteer nurses and medical personnel working on the European front lines.

Answer: **A)**

14. The Meuse-Argonne Offensive was a major Allied military campaign where:

A) A small number of American troops stopped the German advance at Verdun.
B) U.S. forces played a significant role in the final push that helped end the war.
C) The U.S. Navy defeated the German submarine fleet in the Atlantic.
D) American forces led a failed Allied invasion of the Ottoman Empire.

Answer: **B)**

The Armistice and the Treaty of Versailles

15. World War I officially ended on November 11, 1918, with the signing of the:

A) Armistice
B) Treaty of Versailles
C) Zimmerman Telegram
D) Lusitania Declaration

Answer: **A)**

16. The Treaty of Versailles, which formally ended World War I, included provisions that:

A) Imposed harsh reparations and territorial losses on Germany.
B) Established the League of Nations to promote international cooperation.
C) Granted independence to colonial territories in Africa and Asia.
D) Both A and B

Answer: **D)**

17. President Wilson's "Fourteen Points" outlined a plan for:

A) A postwar world with peace, self-determination, and collective security.
B) The immediate withdrawal of all U.S. forces from Europe.
C) An invasion of Germany to overthrow the Kaiser's government.
D) Punitive measures against Germany and her allies after the war.

Answer: **A)**

18. The U.S. Senate ultimately rejected ratification of the Treaty of Versailles and joining the League of Nations because of concerns about:

A) American isolationism and reluctance to enter into binding foreign alliances.
B) Public opposition to the harsh treatment of Germany in the Treaty.
C) Pro-war sentiment and calls to continue fighting until Germany's defeat.
D) Domestic opposition to President Wilson's leadership and political ideology.

Answer: **A)**

19. The aftermath of World War I for the United States saw:

A) A return to isolationism and less involvement in European affairs.
B) Rapid economic expansion and the rise of the "Roaring Twenties."
C) Labor strikes, social unrest, and the "Red Scare" fear of communism.
D) All of the above

Answer: **D)**

The Great Depression

The Great Depression was a severe economic downturn that began with the stock market crash in October 1929 and lasted until the late 1930s. It was characterized by widespread unemployment, poverty, and a significant decline in industrial output and economic activity. The causes of the Great Depression included the stock market crash, bank failures, a reduction in purchasing power, and a lack of government regulation and oversight. President Franklin D. Roosevelt's New Deal programs aimed to provide relief, recovery, and reform to the struggling nation, and while these programs helped alleviate some of the worst effects of the depression, it wasn't until World War II that the U.S. economy fully recovered.

The Stock Market Crash & Economic Collapse

1. The date that marked the start of the Great Depression is commonly known as:

A) Red Tuesday
B) Black Thursday
C) Blue Monday
D) White Wednesday

Answer: **B)**

2. Which factor was a major cause of the 1929 Stock Market Crash?

A) Overproduction and underconsumption of goods
B) Speculation and buying stocks "on margin"
C) Bank failures and a shrinking money supply
D) All of the above

Answer: **D)**

3. During the Great Depression, many banks failed, causing people to:

A) Lose their life savings
B) Invest more heavily in the stock market
C) Borrow more money and go into further debt
D) Become financially prosperous due to low interest rates

Answer: **A)**

4. The unemployment rate reached record highs during the Great Depression. Approximately what percentage of the workforce was unemployed at its peak?

A) 5%
B) 15%
C) 25%
D) 40%

Answer: **C)**

Hardships of the Era

5. The "Dust Bowl" was an environmental disaster that:

A) Devastated the Great Plains with drought and dust storms, displacing farmers.
B) Caused a massive oil spill along the Gulf Coast
C) Led to widespread forest fires in the Pacific Northwest
D) Caused major flooding of the Mississippi River

Answer: **A)**

6. "Hoovervilles" were:

A) Government-provided housing for the unemployed
B) Shantytowns of makeshift shelters built by the homeless
C) Work camps established by the New Deal
D) Suburbs developed for wealthy investors

Answer: **B)**

7. Many unemployed men became "hobos," which meant they:

A) Traveled by freight train in search of work
B) Stayed with relatives and relied on family support
C) Joined labor unions and organized strikes
D) Protested against government inaction and demanded welfare

Answer: **A)**

8. Families struggling during the Depression faced hardships, including:

A) Malnutrition and lack of basic necessities
B) Increased homelessness
C) Family separation as people sought work
D) All of the above

Answer: **D)**

President Roosevelt & the New Deal

9. President Herbert Hoover's approach to the Depression initially emphasized:

A) Large-scale government intervention and relief programs
B) Limited government action and reliance on private charities
C) Revolutionary restructuring of the U.S. economy
D) Nationalization of banks and industries

Answer: **B)**

10. President Franklin D. Roosevelt's "New Deal" refers to:

A) Reforms to the banking system to prevent future crashes.
B) His campaign promise for change during the 1932 election.
C) Programs created to address unemployment, stimulate the economy, and provide relief.
D) A plan to end the Depression within the first 100 days of his presidency.

Answer: **C)**

11. Which program provided jobs to young men in conservation projects like planting trees and building parks?

A) Works Progress Administration (WPA)
B) Civilian Conservation Corps (CCC)
C) Social Security Administration (SSA)
D) Federal Deposit Insurance Corporation (FDIC)

Answer: **B)**

12. The Social Security Act was designed to:

A) Provide pensions for the elderly and assistance to the disabled.
B) Insure bank deposits to protect people's savings.
C) Offer immediate cash payments to the unemployed
D) Regulate the stock market to prevent future crashes.

Answer: **A)**

New Deal

The New Deal was a series of programs, financial reforms, and public works projects introduced by President Franklin D. Roosevelt between 1933 and 1939 to combat the effects of the Great Depression in the United States. The New Deal aimed to provide relief for the unemployed, recovery of the economy, and reform of the financial system to prevent future depressions. Notable programs included the Civilian Conservation Corps (CCC), the Works Progress Administration (WPA), and the Social Security Act. While the New Deal did not end the Great Depression, it provided significant relief, helped modernize the U.S. economy, and laid the foundation for future social welfare programs.

The Basics

1. The New Deal was a response to:

A) The Stock Market Crash of 1929 and the Great Depression
B) The rise of fascism and threats to democracy in Europe
C) The end of World War I and calls for increased military spending
D) Demands for civil rights and racial equality legislation

Answer: **A)**

2. President Franklin D. Roosevelt's approach to the Depression focused on the three R's:

A) Reform, Recovery, and Redistribution
B) Reduce, Reuse, and Recycle
C) Relief, Recovery, and Reform
D) Reading, 'Riting, and 'Rithmetic

Answer: **C)**

3. The New Deal marked a shift in American politics because it:

A) Significantly expanded the role of the federal government in the economy.
B) Reduced federal involvement and emphasized state-level solutions.
C) Privatized banks and industries that were previously government-run.
D) Focused primarily on foreign policy and international affairs.

Answer: **A)**

Major New Deal Programs

4. The Tennessee Valley Authority (TVA) was designed to:

A) Provide flood control, electricity, and economic development in a rural region.
B) Regulate the stock market and prevent speculation.
C) Guarantee unemployment benefits and job training.
D) Break up monopolies and promote competition in business.

Answer: **A)**

5. Which New Deal program created jobs for young men in areas like reforestation and park construction?

A) Social Security Administration (SSA)
B) Works Progress Administration (WPA)
C) Agricultural Adjustment Administration (AAA)
D) Civilian Conservation Corps (CCC)

Answer: **D)**

6. The Federal Deposit Insurance Corporation (FDIC) aimed to:

A) Create jobs by building roads, bridges, and public buildings.
B) Restructure farm mortgages and assist struggling farmers.
C) Offer aid to the elderly and disabled through monthly pensions.
D) Restore confidence in banks by insuring people's deposits.

Answer: **D)**

7. The National Recovery Administration (NRA) was declared unconstitutional because it:

A) Gave the president too much legislative power and control over businesses.
B) Failed to effectively address the root causes of the Depression.
C) Was seen as favoring large corporations at the expense of workers.
D) Violated states' rights and interfered with interstate commerce.

Answer: **A)**

Debates and Criticisms

8. Some conservatives criticized the New Deal, arguing that it:

A) Made the government too powerful and stifled free enterprise.
B) Did not go far enough to help the poor and working class.
C) Increased the national debt and was financially unsustainable.
D) Both A and C

Answer: **D)**

9. The American Liberty League was formed by:

A) Industrialists and wealthy critics of the New Deal.
B) Supporters of Huey Long's "Share Our Wealth" plan.
C) Labor unions advocating for greater worker protections.
D) Civil rights leaders seeking equality legislation.

Answer: **A)**

10. The "court-packing plan" was President Roosevelt's controversial attempt to:

A) Lower the retirement age for Supreme Court justices.
B) Add more justices to the Supreme Court who supported the New Deal.
C) Impeach conservative judges who opposed New Deal legislation.
D) Move the Supreme Court hearings to a larger, more accessible building.

Answer: **B)**

World War II

The United States officially entered World War II on December 7, 1941, following the Japanese attack on Pearl Harbor. The U.S. fought on two major fronts, the European theater against Nazi Germany and the Pacific theater against Japan, while also providing crucial support to Allied nations through the Lend-Lease program. Key events included the D-Day invasion of Normandy, the Battle of Midway, and the atomic bombings of Hiroshima and Nagasaki. The war ended with the surrender of Germany in May 1945 and Japan in August 1945, with the United States emerging as a global superpower and playing a significant role in shaping the post-war world order.

The Basics

1. What event directly led to the US entry into World War II?

    A) The German invasion of Poland (1939)
    B) The bombing of Pearl Harbor by Japan (1941)
    C) The Battle of Britain (1940)
    D) The German invasion of the Soviet Union (1941)

Answer: **B)**

2. The Lend-Lease Act provided vital military aid to which Allied nation before the US officially entered the war?

A) France
B) Great Britain
C) China
D) The Soviet Union

Answer: **B)**

3. The surprise attack on Pearl Harbor targeted which US state?

A) California
B) Hawaii
C) Oregon
D) Alaska

Answer: **B)**

4. Who was the US President during World War II?

A) Franklin D. Roosevelt
B) Harry S. Truman
C) Dwight D. Eisenhower
D) Herbert Hoover

Answer: **A)**

5. The D-Day invasion, a turning point in the European theater, took place on which beaches in France?

A) Iwo Jima and Okinawa
B) Omaha, Utah, Juno, Gold, Sword
C) Midway and Guadalcanal
D) Stalingrad and Kursk

Answer: **B)**

6. The Manhattan Project was a top-secret US program that developed the world's first

A) Atomic bomb
B) Tank
C) Fighter plane
D) Antibiotic

Answer: **A)**

7. Dwight D. Eisenhower served as the Supreme Allied Commander during which crucial WWII operation?

A) The Battle of Britain
B) The Normandy invasion (D-Day)
C) The Manhattan Project
D) The Battle of Midway

Answer: **B)**

8. The bombing of Hiroshima and Nagasaki were controversial decisions made by the US to force Japan's surrender. What type of bombs were used?

A) Napalm bombs
B) Atomic bombs
C) Firebombs
D) Chemical weapons

Answer: **B)**

9. Which key naval battle in the Pacific theater decisively halted Japan's eastward expansion?

A) The Battle of the Atlantic
B) The Battle of Midway
C) The Battle of Coral Sea
D) The Battle of Leyte Gulf

Answer: **B)**

10. The iconic image of US Marines raising the American flag on Iwo Jima was captured by which photographer?

A) Robert Capa
B) Joe Rosenthal
C) Margaret Bourke-White
D) Dorothea Lange

Answer: **B)**

The War Effort and the Homefront

11. War bonds were a crucial way for the US government to do what?

A) Fund the war effort
B) Communicate with citizens about rationing
C) Recruit soldiers for military service
D) Maintain the neutrality of allied countries

Answer: **A)**

12. The Tuskegee Airmen were a historic group of African American pilots who played a vital role in which branch of the US armed forces?

A) Army Air Corps
B) Navy
C) Marines
D) Coast Guard

Answer: **A)**

13. Which US ship sunk in the attack on Pearl Harbor became a symbol of American sacrifice and a war memorial?

A) USS Lexington
B) USS Missouri
C) USS Enterprise
D) USS Arizona

Answer: **D)**

14. The "Rosie the Riveter" campaign symbolized women's expanded role in which sector during the war?

    A) Military Service
    B) The Workforce
    C) Politics
    D) Espionage

Answer: **B)**

15. Which government organization was responsible for coordinating wartime production on the home front?

    A) The United Service Organizations (USO)
    B) The Office of Strategic Services (OSS)
    C) The War Production Board
    D) The Office of War Information

Answer: **C)**

16. Which program resulted in the internment of thousands of Japanese Americans during WWII?

    A) Project Venona
    B) Operation Torch
    C) Executive Order 9066
    D) Executive Order 8802

Answer: **C)**

17. The Navajo Code Talkers contributed to the war effort by serving in the US Marine Corps and...

    A) ...developing a new form of cryptography for military transmissions.
    B) ...performing aerial reconnaissance missions.
    C) ...treating wounded soldiers on the battlefield.
    D) ...spearheading the Allied invasion of Italy.

Answer: **A)**

18. Rationing programs during the war forced many American families to do which of the following?

A) Limit their purchase of essential goods like food and fuel
B) Send all adult males in their household to fight in the war
C) Pay higher taxes to the federal government
D) Convert their homes into military barracks

Answer: **A)**

19. Which term describes a victory garden?

A) A military cemetery for casualties of the war
B) A private garden planted to help combat wartime food shortages.
C) A type of naval ship used in the North Atlantic
D) A government-sponsored morale-boosting campaign

Answer: **B)**

20. Famous posters featuring Uncle Sam saying, "I Want You for U.S. Army," were tools used for what purpose?

A) Promoting war bond purchases
B) Encouraging rationing
C) Military recruitment
D) Warning against German spies.

Answer: **C)**

Global Impact and Legacy

21. Which major Allied conference during the war included Roosevelt, Churchill, and Stalin discussing strategies?

A) The Potsdam Conference
B) The Yalta Conference
C) The Paris Peace Conference
D) The Munich Agreement

Answer: **B)**

22. Which battle in the Eastern Front is considered the largest in history and a turning point against the Germans?

A) The Battle of Midway
B) The Battle of Stalingrad
C) The Battle of Kursk
D) Operation Barbarossa

Answer: **B)**

23. Which two cities were targeted in the atomic bombings by the US?

A) Stalingrad and Leningrad
B) Dresden and Berlin
C) London and Paris
D) Hiroshima and Nagasaki

Answer: **D)**

24. The Holocaust refers to the genocide of approximately six million of what group by Nazi Germany?

A) Polish civilians
B) Soviet prisoners of war
C) European Jews
D) American soldiers

Answer: **C)**

25. Following the war, Nazi leaders were put on trial for war crimes in what city?

A) Nuremberg, Germany
B) Paris, France
C) Geneva, Switzerland
D) London, England

Answer: **A)**

26. What international organization was created after WWII with the aim of preventing future wars and promoting peace?

A) The League of Nations
B) The World Health Organization
C) The International Trade Organization
D) The United Nations

Answer: **D)**

27. The end of WWII ushered in a new era known as the Cold War, a period of tension between which two superpowers?

A) Soviet Union and United States
B) China and Japan
C) Great Britain and France
D) Japan and Germany

Answer: **A)**

28. The G.I. Bill, enacted in 1944, provided returning WWII veterans with benefits including which of the following?

A) Loans for homes and businesses
B) Reduced-cost healthcare
C) Education funding
D) All of the above

Answer: **D)**

29. Which term describes the post-WWII economic prosperity in the United States?

A) The Great Recession
B) The Baby Boom
C) The Gilded Age
D) The New Deal

Answer: **B)**

30. The wartime experiences of Black and female Americans at home and on the battlefield helped fuel the rise of which movement?

A) The Suffrage Movement
B) The Civil Rights Movement
C) The Anti-War Movement
D) The Temperance Movement

Answer: **B)**

The Cold War

The Cold War was a period of geopolitical tension and rivalry between the United States and the Soviet Union that lasted from the late 1940s until the collapse of the Soviet Union in 1991. The two superpowers engaged in an arms race, space race, and proxy wars, while also competing for global influence through political, economic, and ideological means. Key events during the Cold War included the Berlin Blockade, the Korean War, the Cuban Missile Crisis, and the Vietnam War. Although the United States and the Soviet Union never directly fought each other, the Cold War had a profound impact on international relations, shaping the world order for decades and leaving a lasting legacy on American society, politics, and culture.

1. The term "Cold War" refers to a period of geopolitical tension between which two superpowers?

A) Great Britain and France
B) The United States and the Soviet Union
C) Japan and China
D) Germany and Italy

Answer: **B)**

2. The Truman Doctrine, a cornerstone of early Cold War foreign policy, aimed to contain what?

A) The spread of fascism in Europe
B) The rise of decolonization movements
C) The proliferation of nuclear weapons
D) The expansion of communist influence

Answer: **D)**

3. The Marshall Plan was a US-led initiative that provided financial aid to which region after World War II?

A) Southeast Asia
B) Western Europe
C) The Middle East
D) Latin America

Answer: **B)**

4. The Berlin Airlift was a successful effort by the US and its allies to supply a blockaded city during the Cold War. Which city was blockaded?

A) Warsaw
B) Berlin
C) Leningrad
D) Prague

Answer: **B)**

5. The theory of "Mutually Assured Destruction" (MAD) during the Cold War relied on what concept to deter a full-scale nuclear war?

A) Nuclear disarmament treaties
B) The superiority of one nation's military
C) The threat of retaliation by both sides
D) A strong anti-war movement

Answer: **C)**

6. The Korean War (1950-1953) was a proxy war fought between which two ideologies?

A) Democracy and fascism
B) Communism and capitalism
C) Colonialism and independence movements
D) Monarchy and republicanism

Answer: **B)**

7. The development of the hydrogen bomb marked a new phase in the nuclear arms race. Who is credited with leading the Manhattan Project to create the atomic bomb in World War II?

A) Robert Oppenheimer
B) Dwight D. Eisenhower
C) Joseph Stalin
D) Winston Churchill

Answer: **A)**

8. The Warsaw Pact was a military alliance formed by which countries in 1955?

A) NATO member states
B) Soviet Union and Eastern European states
C) Southeast Asian nations
D) Latin American countries supported by the US

Answer: **B)**

9. The 1957 launch of Sputnik, the first artificial satellite, by the Soviet Union ushered in a new era of competition known as the...

A) Space Age
B) Vietnam War
C) Civil Rights Movement
D) Cuban Missile Crisis

Answer: **A)**

10. Senator Joseph McCarthy led a wave of accusations of communist infiltration in the US government during what period known for heightened fear of communism?

A) The Détente Era
B) The Second Red Scare
C) The Bay of Pigs Invasion
D) The SALT talks

Answer: **B)**

Civil Rights Movement

The Civil Rights Movement was a decades-long struggle by African Americans to end racial discrimination and gain equal rights under the law in the United States. The movement reached its peak in the 1950s and 1960s, with key events such as the Montgomery Bus Boycott (1955-1956), the Greensboro Sit-ins (1960), the March on Washington (1963), and the Selma to Montgomery Marches (1965). The movement led to significant legislation, including the Civil Rights Act of 1964 and the Voting Rights Act of 1965, which banned discrimination based on race, color, religion, sex, or national origin and protected the voting rights of African Americans. The Civil Rights Movement was marked by the leadership of figures such as Martin Luther King Jr., Rosa Parks, and Malcolm X, and while it achieved substantial progress, the fight for equality and justice continues to this day.

1. Which landmark Supreme Court case in 1954 declared racial segregation in public schools unconstitutional?

  A) Brown v. Board of Education
  B) Plessy v. Ferguson.
  C) Loving v. Virginia.
  D) Miranda v. Arizona.

Answer: **A)**

2. The Montgomery Bus Boycott, a pivotal moment in the Civil Rights Movement, was sparked by the arrest of:

A) Rosa Parks
B) Martin Luther King Jr.
C) Malcolm X.
D) Emmett Till.

Answer: A)

3. Which nonviolent protest tactic involved refusing to buy from or use businesses that discriminated?

A) Sit-in
B) Freedom Ride.
C) March on Washington.
D) Voter registration drive.

Answer: A)

4. The 1963 March on Washington for Jobs and Freedom was led by:

A) Rosa Parks
B) Malcolm X
C) Martin Luther King Jr.
D) Stokely Carmichael.

Answer: C)

5. The Voting Rights Act of 1965 outlawed discriminatory practices that prevented:

A) African Americans from voting
B) Women from voting
C) People under 21 from voting
D) All of the above

Answer: A)

6. The leader of the Nation of Islam, a prominent African American nationalist group, was:

A) Martin Luther King Jr.
B) Malcolm X
C) Rosa Parks
D) Thurgood Marshall

Answer: **B)**

7. The "Little Rock Nine" were a group of African American students who desegregated:

A) Montgomery bus system
B) Central High School in Little Rock, Arkansas
C) University of Mississippi
D) Selma, Alabama

Answer: **B)**

8. Which act of violence against Civil Rights workers in 1964 garnered national attention and helped lead to the passage of the Civil Rights Act of 1964?

A) The Montgomery Bus Boycott
B) The Birmingham Children's Crusade
C) The Freedom Summer
D) The Selma to Montgomery marches

Answer: **C)**

9. "I Have a Dream" is a famous speech delivered at the March on Washington by:

A) Malcolm X
B) Martin Luther King Jr
C) Rosa Parks
D) Stokely Carmichael

Answer: **B)**

10. The Selma to Montgomery marches of 1965 aimed to bring attention to:

A) Segregation in schools
B) Discrimination in hiring practices
C) Voting rights restrictions for African Americans
D) Police brutality

Answer: **C)**

11. The 24th Amendment to the U.S. Constitution, ratified in 1964, outlawed:

A) Poll taxes
B) Segregation in public accommodations
C) Literacy tests for voting
D) Discrimination in housing

Answer: **C)**

12. The tactic of riding interstate buses to challenge segregation laws in the South was known as:

A) Sit-in
B) Freedom Ride
C) March on Washington
D) Voter registration drive

Answer: **B)**

13. The Civil Rights Act of 1964 outlawed discrimination based on:

A) Race only
B) Race, color, religion, and national origin
C) Race and gender
D) All of the above

Answer: **B)**

14. The Student Nonviolent Coordinating Committee (SNCC) was a prominent Civil Rights organization led by:

A) Martin Luther King Jr.
B) John Lewis
C) Malcolm X
D) Thurgood Marshall

Answer: **B)**

15. The key figure in the Brown v. Board of Education case was:

A) Rosa Parks
B) Oliver Brown
C) Martin Luther King Jr.
D) Malcolm X

Answer: **B)**

17. Which young African American boy was brutally murdered in Mississippi in 1955, galvanizing the Civil Rights Movement?

A) Malcolm X
B) Medgar Evers
C) Emmett Till
D) James Meredith

Answer: **C)**

18. Who was the first African American student to attend the University of Mississippi, facing widespread opposition and violence?

A) James Meredith
B) Medgar Evers
C) Thurgood Marshall
D) Fred Shuttlesworth

Answer: **A)**

19. Which Civil Rights leader advocated for nonviolent resistance and led the Southern Christian Leadership Conference (SCLC)?

A) Martin Luther King Jr.
B) Malcolm X
C) Huey Newton
D) John Lewis

Answer: **A)**

20. The 16th Street Baptist Church bombing in Birmingham, Alabama, which killed four young girls, occurred in what year?

A) 1955
B) 1960
C) 1963
D) 1965

Answer: **C)**

21. Which Civil Rights Act prohibited discrimination in employment based on race, color, religion, sex, or national origin?

A) Civil Rights Act of 1964
B) Voting Rights Act of 1965
C) Fair Housing Act of 1968
D) Civil Rights Act of 1957

Answer: **A)**

22. "Bloody Sunday" refers to a violent confrontation between police and Civil Rights protestors during which march?

A) The March on Washington
B) The Selma to Montgomery march
C) The Freedom Rides
D) The Birmingham campaign

Answer: **B)**

23. Who founded the Black Panther Party in 1966, advocating for self-defense and community empowerment?

A) Martin Luther King Jr.
B) Malcolm X
C) Stokely Carmichael
D) Huey Newton and Bobby Seale

Answer: **D)**

24. Which Civil Rights leader promoted Black pride, self-reliance, and at times, Black separatism?

A) Martin Luther King Jr.
B) Malcolm X
C) Rosa Parks
D) Medgar Evers

Answer: **B)**

25. What 1968 federal legislation aimed to combat discrimination in the sale, rental, and financing of housing?

A) Civil Rights Act of 1964
B) Voting Rights Act of 1965
C) Fair Housing Act of 1968
D) Civil Rights Act of 1957

Answer: **C)**

26. The term "Jim Crow laws" refers to:

A) Laws enforcing racial segregation
B) Bans on religious freedoms
C) Restrictive gun control legislation
D) Unequal pay regulations

Answer: **A)**

27. Who was the first African American Supreme Court Justice?

A) Clarence Thomas
B) Colin Powell
C) Thurgood Marshall
D) Barack Obama

Answer: **C)**

28. The strategy of having Black and white activists ride together on buses in the South to challenge segregation was part of:

A) The Greensboro Sit-Ins
B) The Freedom Rides
C) The March on Washington
D) The Children's Crusade

Answer: **B)**

29. "We Shall Overcome" is known as:

A) An iconic protest song of the Civil Rights Movement
B) A Malcolm X speech
C) A key Supreme Court ruling on school desegregation
D) A Black Panther Party slogan

Answer: **A)**

30. Which Civil Right leader was assassinated in Memphis, Tennessee in 1968?

A) Malcolm X
B) Martin Luther King Jr
C) Medgar Evers
D) James Meredith

Answer: **B)**

Vietnam War (1955-1975)

The United States became involved in the Vietnam War to prevent the spread of communism in Southeast Asia, supporting South Vietnam against the communist North Vietnam and the Viet Cong. U.S. involvement escalated in the early 1960s with the deployment of ground troops and the commencement of a bombing campaign against North Vietnam. Despite the U.S. military's technological superiority, the war became increasingly unpopular at home as it dragged on and casualties mounted. In 1973, the U.S. withdrew its troops following the Paris Peace Accords, and South Vietnam eventually fell to the North in 1975, leading to the unification of Vietnam under communist rule.

1. The main reason the U.S. became involved in the Vietnam War was to:

A) Gain access to Vietnamese oil reserves
B) Contain the spread of communism in Southeast Asia
C) Support French colonial rule in Vietnam
D) Avert a global nuclear war

Answer: **B)**

2. Which theory influenced U.S. foreign policy during the Cold War, leading to involvement in Vietnam?

    A) Mutually Assured Destruction (MAD)
    B) Domino Theory
    C) Manifest Destiny
    D) Containment Policy

Answer: **B)**

3. The Viet Cong were:

    A) South Vietnamese communists fighting for reunification
    B) North Vietnamese regular army soldiers
    C) American anti-war protestors
    D) South Vietnamese nationalists

Answer: **A)**

4. The Gulf of Tonkin Resolution in 1964:

    A) Authorized a full-scale U.S. invasion of North Vietnam
    B) Granted the president broad war powers in Southeast Asia
    C) Ended U.S. involvement in the Vietnam War
    D) Marked official recognition of North Vietnam

Answer: **B)**

5. The Ho Chi Minh Trail was:

    A) A network of supply routes used by North Vietnam
    B) A series of heavily fortified North Vietnamese border defenses
    C) A location of major U.S. military bases in South Vietnam
    D) A peace negotiation held in Geneva, Switzerland

Answer: **A)**

6. Agent Orange was:

A) A powerful herbicide used to defoliate jungles
B) A type of North Vietnamese guerilla warfare tactic
C) A code name for a secret U.S. bombing campaign
D) A chemical weapon used by North Vietnam against South Vietnamese civilians

Answer: **A)**

7. The Tet Offensive of 1968:

A) Was a major North Vietnamese victory that turned public opinion against the war in the U.S.
B) Marked the beginning of peace talks between the U.S. and North Vietnam
C) Involved a successful U.S. invasion of North Vietnam
D) Was a large-scale anti-war protest in Washington D.C.

Answer: **A)**

8. Which strategy did U.S. forces primarily employ in Vietnam?

A) Blitzkrieg tactics with large armored divisions
B) Guerilla warfare using hit-and-run attacks
C) Focused air superiority with minimal ground troops
D) Defensive trench warfare along the Vietnamese border

Answer: **B)**

9. What was the main purpose of the Pentagon Papers?

A) To expose classified information about the Vietnam War
B) To outline plans for a U.S. withdrawal from Vietnam
C) To detail North Vietnamese military capabilities
D) To justify the escalation of U.S. involvement in the war

Answer: **A)**

10. The My Lai Massacre involved:

A) The use of Agent Orange by U.S. forces
B) The Vietnamese surprise attack during the Tet Offensive
C) The brutal killing of Vietnamese civilians by U.S. soldiers
D) A major North Vietnamese victory over a U.S. base

Answer: **C)**

11. The policy of "Vietnamization" aimed to:

A) Increase U.S. troop presence in Vietnam
B) Gradually transfer the war effort to South Vietnam
C) Negotiate a peace treaty with North Vietnam
D) Launch a full-scale invasion of North Vietnam

Answer: **B)**

12. The Paris Peace Accords of 1973:

A) Ended the war and resulted in a U.S. victory
B) Established a ceasefire but did not resolve the conflict
C) Led to a complete withdrawal of North Vietnamese troops
D) Marked the official start of U.S. involvement in the war

Answer: **B)**

13. The final U.S. evacuation from Vietnam in 1975 is known as:

A) Operation Rolling Thunder
B) The Ho Chi Minh Trail Withdrawal
C) Operation Frequent Wind
D) The Tet

Answer: **C)**

14. Which U.S. president began sending combat troops to Vietnam in significant numbers?

A) Dwight D. Eisenhower
B) John F. Kennedy
C) Lyndon B. Johnson
D) Richard Nixon

Answer: **C)**

15. Which U.S. president oversaw the majority of U.S. involvement and eventual withdrawal from Vietnam?

A) John F. Kennedy
B) Lyndon B. Johnson
C) Richard Nixon
D) Gerald Ford

Answer: **C)**

16. Opposition to the Vietnam War in the U.S. was particularly strong among:

A) Veterans of previous wars
B) College students
C) Senior citizens
D) Conservative politicians

Answer: **B)**

17. The draft system during the Vietnam War was seen by some as unfair because:

A) It only drafted men of a certain age
B) It allowed wealthier individuals to avoid service
C) It was based on racial quotas
D) It drafted those unwilling to support the war effort

Answer: **B)**

18. One of the most iconic and disturbing images of the war, the "Napalm Girl" photograph, shows:

A) A North Vietnamese soldier killed in battle
B) Vietnamese villagers fleeing an American bombing raid
C) A young Vietnamese girl burned by a napalm attack
D) American prisoners of war

Answer: **C)**

19. The Kent State Massacre occurred on a college campus in 1970 when:

A) Anti-war demonstrations escalated into violence with foreign students
B) National Guard troops opened fire on student protestors
C) A student protest turned into a riot and destruction of the campus
D) North Vietnamese sympathizers infiltrated a protest march

Answer: **B)**

20. The 1971 publication of the Pentagon Papers by the New York Times led to:

A) Immediate withdrawal of U.S. troops from Vietnam
B) Public outrage over government deception regarding the war
C) New restrictions on journalistic freedom
D) An intensification of U.S. bombing campaigns in Vietnam

Answer: **B)**

21. Which of the following was NOT a country in Southeast Asia to which the U.S. expanded its military intervention during the Vietnam War?

A) Laos
B) Cambodia
C) Thailand
D) North Vietnam

Answer: **C)**

22. "Search and destroy" missions were a tactic used by the U.S. military in Vietnam that primarily targeted:

A) Enemy villages and suspected Viet Cong hideouts
B) Large military bases and concentrations of North Vietnamese troops
C) Tunnels used by the Viet Cong
D) Farms and rice fields supplying the North Vietnamese

Answer: **A)**

23. Morale among U.S. troops in Vietnam tended to be low due to factors like:

A) Lack of a clear objective and shifting war aims
B) Unfamiliarity with the hot, humid climate
C) Ineffective military leadership
D) All of the above

Answer: **A)**

24. The U.S. bombing campaign of North Vietnam under President Johnson was called:

A) Operation Linebacker II
B) Operation Rolling Thunder
C) Operation Desert Shield
D) Operation Enduring Freedom

Answer: **B)**

25. The Fall of Saigon in 1975 marked:

A) The beginning of the Vietnam War
B) The communist victory and unification of Vietnam
C) The start of U.S. invasion of North Vietnam
D) The signing of the Paris Peace Accords

Answer: **B)**

Central Intelligence Agency (CIA)

Origins and Purpose

1. In what year was the Central Intelligence Agency formed?

A) 1918
B) 1945
C) 1947
D) 1963

Answer: **C)**

2. Which government act established the CIA?

A) The Homeland Security Act
B) The Patriot Act
C) The National Security Act of 1947
D) The Espionage Act

Answer: **C)**

3. The primary mission of the CIA is to:

A) Conduct domestic surveillance and investigations
B) Collect and analyze foreign intelligence
C) Prosecute cases of espionage
D) Enforce international sanctions

Answer: **C)**

Key Activities and Roles

4. Which of the following is NOT a major directorate (division) within the CIA?

A) Directorate of Operations
B) Directorate of Analysis
C) Directorate of Science and Technology
D) Directorate of Internal Investigations

Answer: **D)**

5. Covert operations carried out by the CIA can include:

A) Paramilitary actions
B) Propaganda campaigns
C) Supporting foreign political groups
D) All of the above

Answer: **D)**

6. Which world event is considered one of the CIA's greatest intelligence failures?

A) The Cuban Missile Crisis
B) The fall of the Berlin Wall
C) The 9/11 attacks
D) The Iranian Revolution

Answer: **C)**

Controversies and Criticisms

7. During the Cold War, the CIA was involved in overthrowing democratically elected governments in countries like:

    A) Iran and Guatemala
    B) North Korea and China
    C) Cuba and Venezuela
    D) Egypt and Syria

Answer: **A)**

8. The CIA's use of "enhanced interrogation techniques" after 9/11 is considered by many to be:

    A) Justified in the pursuit of national security
    B) Examples of torture
    C) Ineffective at producing valuable information
    D) Authorized under the Geneva Conventions

Answer: **B)**

9. Which government program leaked by Edward Snowden revealed the CIA's global surveillance activities?

    A) Wikileaks
    B) Panama Papers
    C) PRISM
    D) Pentagon Papers

Answer: **C)**

Historical Events

10. The Bay of Pigs invasion was a failed CIA operation to overthrow:

    A) Muammar Gaddafi in Libya
    B) Fidel Castro in Cuba
    C) Saddam Hussein in Iraq
    D) Kim Il-sung in North Korea

Answer: **B)**

11. Which CIA program involved illegal experiments with mind control and chemical interrogation?

A) Project Stargate
B) Operation Condor
C) Project MKUltra
D) Operation Paperclip

Answer: **C)**

12. The Church Committee in the 1970s investigated and exposed a range of CIA abuses and illegal activities, including:

A) Domestic surveillance on U.S. citizens
B) Assassination plots against foreign leaders
C) Unauthorized covert operations
D) All of the above

Answer: **D)**

CIA in Popular Culture

13. Which fictional character is a popular CIA agent in books and movies?

A) Sherlock Holmes
B) James Bond
C) Jack Ryan
D) Harry Potter

Answer: **C)**

14. Which American television series centers around a young CIA recruit?

A) Homeland
B) 24
C) NCIS
D) The Blacklist

Answer: **A)**

15. Which film won the Academy Award for Best Picture and depicts a CIA operation to rescue hostages in Iran?

    A) Zero Dark Thirty
    B) The Hurt Locker
    C) Argo
    D) American Sniper

Answer: **C)**

Federal Bureau of Investigation (FBI)

Establishment and Mission

1. When was the FBI founded?

    A) 1908
    B) 1924
    C) 1941
    D) 1953

Answer: **A)**

2. What was the original name of the FBI?

    A) Department of Justice (DOJ)
    B) Bureau of Investigation (BOI)
    C) Federal Criminal Intelligence Bureau (FCIB)
    D) Special Investigations Unit (SIU)

Answer: **B)**

3. The FBI's primary responsibility is to:

A) Enforce international treaties
B) Conduct foreign espionage operations
C) Uphold federal law and protect the United States
D) Patrol U.S. borders

Answer: **C)**

Jurisdiction and Investigations

4. Which of these crimes does the FBI investigate?

A) Cybercrime
B) Terrorism
C) Organized crime
D) All of the above

Answer: **D)**

5. The FBI has jurisdiction over violations of how many federal laws?

A) Around 50
B) Over 200
C) Around 1,000
D) Over 5,000

Answer: **B)**

6. Which type of crime is NOT primarily investigated by the FBI?

A) Bank robbery
B) Human trafficking
C) Traffic violations
D) Kidnapping

Answer: **C)**

Organization and Operations

7. Where is the FBI headquarters located?

    A) New York City, NY
    B) Los Angeles, CA
    C) Washington, D.C.
    D) Miami, FL

Answer: **C)**

8. What is the name of the FBI's main laboratory that provides forensic services?

    A) CSI Division
    B) Quantico Laboratory
    C) National Criminal Analysis Center
    D) Evidence Response Team

Answer: **B)**

9. The FBI's Ten Most Wanted Fugitives list is designed to:

    A) Raise money for crime victims
    B) Deter criminal activity
    C) Apprehend dangerous criminals with public assistance
    D) Increase FBI staffing levels

Answer: **C)**

Special Agents and Training

10. The FBI Academy, where agents undergo rigorous training, is located in:

    A) Langley, Virginia
    B) Quantico, Virginia
    C) Washington, D.C.
    D) New York City, New York

Answer: **B)**

11. What is the minimum age to become an FBI Special Agent?

    A) 18
    B) 21
    C) 23
    D) 25

Answer: **C)**

12. Which of the following is NOT a typical requirement for FBI Special Agents?

    A) US citizenship
    B) Bachelor's degree
    C) Military service
    D) Excellent physical condition

Answer: **C)**

Historical Events and Figures

13. Who was the FBI's longest-serving Director?

    A) J. Edgar Hoover
    B) Robert Mueller
    C) Louis Freeh
    D) James Comey

Answer: **A)**

14. Which 1930s gangster was dubbed "Public Enemy No. 1" by the FBI?

    A) Al Capone
    B) Bonnie Parker
    C) John Dillinger
    D) Charles "Lucky" Luciano

Answer: **C)**

15. The FBI played a key role in investigating which major terrorist attack?

A) Oklahoma City bombing
B) 9/11 attacks
C) Boston Marathon bombing
D) All of the above

Answer: **A)**

16. J. Edgar Hoover's long tenure as FBI Director was controversial due to allegations of:

A) Abuse of power and surveillance of political figures
B) Corruption and financial misconduct
C) Ineffective handling of organized crime threats
D) Leaking classified information to foreign powers

Answer: **A)**

17. The COINTELPRO program was a controversial FBI counterintelligence program that targeted:

A) Domestic dissident groups
B) Foreign espionage networks
C) Organized crime syndicates
D) International terrorist cells

Answer: **A)**

18. Which government body is primarily responsible for providing oversight of the FBI?

A) The Supreme Court
B) The Department of Justice
C) The White House
D) The Senate Intelligence Committee

Answer: **B)**

FBI in the 21st Century

19. After the 9/11 attacks, a top priority of the FBI has been:

A) Counterterrorism
B) Narcotics trafficking
C) White-collar crime
D) Immigration enforcement

Answer: **A)**

20. Which technological advancement has posed new challenges for FBI investigations?

A) Encryption
B) DNA analysis
C) Satellite surveillance
D) Fingerprint databases

Answer: **A)**

21. SWAT teams (Special Weapons and Tactics) are elite units within the FBI's:

A) Hostage Rescue Team (HRT)
B) Behavioral Analysis Unit (BAU)
C) National Center for the Analysis of Violent Crime (NCAVC)
D) Evidence Response Team (ERT)

Answer: **A)**

FBI in Popular Culture

22. Which fictional FBI Special Agent famously profiled serial killers in the books and film "The Silence of the Lambs"?

A) Fox Mulder
B) Clarice Starling
C) Dana Scully
D) Will Graham

Answer: **B)**

23. Which long-running television series focused on the FBI's investigation of paranormal events?

A) CSI
B) The X-Files
C) Criminal Minds
D) Law & Order

Answer: **B)**

24. Which film depicts the FBI's effort to infiltrate the mafia, starring Johnny Depp?

A) The Departed
B) Donnie Brasco
C) Goodfellas
D) The Untouchables

Answer: **B)**

More Challenging Questions

25. What is the USA PATRIOT Act, and what impact did it have on FBI powers?

A) Legislation expanding surveillance and investigative powers after 9/11
B) A law criminalizing hate speech
C) Federal protection for whistleblowers
D) Gun control legislation

Answer: **A)**

26. What does the acronym FISA stand for, and how is it related to the FBI?

A) Federal Intelligence Surveillance Agency
B) Foreign Intelligence Surveillance Act
C) Financial Institutions Security Authority
D) Federal Investigations Standards Agency

Answer: **B)**

Here's another set of FBI quiz questions to round out your collection:

More Challenging Questions (cont.)

28. What are National Security Letters (NSLs), and why are they controversial?

A) Classified documents sent by the FBI to Congress on intelligence matters
B) Official FBI reports detailing criminal investigations
C) Subpoena-like demands for information with gag orders
D) Diplomatic messages between the FBI and foreign law enforcement agencies

Answer: **C)**

31. Which historical outlaw duo were pursued and ultimately killed in an FBI-led manhunt in the 1930s?

A) Jesse James and Billy the Kid
B) Butch Cassidy and the Sundance Kid
C) Bonnie and Clyde
D) Al Capone and John Dillinger

Answer: **C)**

32. Who was the first female FBI Special Agent?

A) Sally Ride
B) Amelia Earhart
C) Marie Curie
D) None of the above – women could not initially be agents

Answer: **D)**

33. In the 1920s, what notorious event was linked to the agency then known as the Bureau of Investigation?

A) The Scopes Monkey Trial
B) The Teapot Dome Scandal
C) The Lindbergh baby kidnapping
D) The St. Valentine's Day Massacre

Answer: **B)**

34. The FBI maintains a massive database of fingerprints. What is it called?

A) National Fingerprint File (NFF)
B) Integrated Automated Fingerprint Identification System (IAFIS)
C) Criminal Identification Network (CIN)
D) Biometric Identification System (BIS)

Answer: **B)**

Supreme Court

The Supreme Court of the United States is the highest federal court in the country, established by Article III of the U.S. Constitution. It consists of nine justices, including a Chief Justice, who are nominated by the President and confirmed by the Senate. The Supreme Court has the power of judicial review, allowing it to interpret the Constitution and rule on the constitutionality of laws and government actions. As the ultimate arbiter of legal disputes, the Supreme Court's decisions are final and binding, making it a crucial branch of the U.S. government that shapes the nation's legal landscape.

Structure and Powers

1. How many justices serve on the Supreme Court?

    A) 5
    B) 8
    C) 9
    D) 12

Answer: **C)**

2. Federal judges are appointed by the president and:

A) Elected by the people
B) Confirmed by the Senate
C) Appointed by Congress
D) Hereditary positions

Answer: **B)**

3. The power of judicial review allows the Supreme Court to:

A) Veto laws passed by Congress
B) Declare laws unconstitutional
C) Rewrite laws deemed unfair
D) Appoint lower court judges

Answer: **B)**

4. What is the term for a legal precedent set by a Supreme Court decision?

A) Stare decisis
B) Amicus curiae
C) Writ of certiorari
D) Habeas corpus

Answer: **A)**

Types of Cases and Jurisdiction

5. Which type of case does the Supreme Court have original jurisdiction over?

A) Criminal trials involving federal crimes
B) Disputes between states
C) Appeals from lower federal courts
D) Patent law disputes

Answer: **B)**

6. In most cases, how does a case reach the Supreme Court?

A) Trial by jury
B) Public vote
C) Writ of certiorari (granted review)
D) Automatic appeal

Answer: **C)**

7. What is an amicus curiae brief?

A) A legal argument from a friend of the court
B) A summary of the case presented by each side
C) A dissenting opinion written by a Supreme Court justice
D) A law requiring a new trial

Answer: **A)**

Landmark Cases and Decisions

8. The landmark Brown v. Board of Education (1954) decision:

A) Desegregated public schools
B) Upheld the poll tax as a voting requirement
C) Established Miranda rights for criminal suspects
D) Granted women the right to vote

Answer: **A)**

9. Which Supreme Court case legalized abortion nationwide?

A) Roe v. Wade (1973)
B) Plessy v. Ferguson (1896)
C) Gideon v. Wainwright (1963)
D) Marbury v. Madison (1803)

Answer: **A)**

10. Miranda v. Arizona (1966) established the right to:

A) An attorney during police questioning
B) A fair and speedy trial
C) Remain silent and have an attorney appointed
D) All of the above

Answer: **A)**

The Judicial Process and Legal Terms

11. A jury trial is guaranteed by the Constitution in:

A) All criminal cases
B) All civil cases
C) Only federal court cases
D) Only serious criminal cases

Answer: **D)**

12. The burden of proof in a criminal case lies with:

A) The defendant
B) The judge
C) The jury
D) The prosecution

Answer: **D)**

13. A plea bargain involves a defendant:

A) Appealing the verdict directly to the Supreme Court
B) Pleading guilty to a lesser charge in exchange for leniency
C) Demanding a trial by jury
D) Hiring a new attorney

Answer: **B)**

14. In the American court system, a precedent refers to:

A) A legal challenge to a law
B) A previous legal decision serving as an example
C) A law passed by both houses of Congress
D) A type of punishment for a crime

Answer: **B)**

Lower Courts and the Federal System

15. The federal court system below the Supreme Court consists of:

A) District courts and circuit courts of appeals
B) State trial courts and federal appellate courts
C) Only criminal courts
D) Only

Answer: **A)**

16. The vast majority of court cases in the United States are heard in:

A) The U.S Supreme Court
B) State and local courts
C) Federal district courts
D) Military courts

Answer: **B)**

17. The principle that the Supreme Court should defer to decisions made by elected representatives (Congress, President) is known as:

A) Judicial activism
B) Original jurisdiction
C) Judicial restraint
D) Constitutional supremacy

Answer: **C)**

Philosophy of Law and Interpretation

18. Which theory of constitutional interpretation believes judges should strictly adhere to the original intent of the framers of the Constitution?

A) Judicial activism
B) Originalism
C) Judicial restraint
D) Living Constitution

Answer: **B)**

19. Justices who believe the Constitution should be interpreted in light of modern-day values and societal changes adhere to:

A) Judicial restraint
B) Living Constitution
C) Originalism
D) Common law

Answer: **B)**

20. Which of these rights is protected by the First Amendment?

A) Freedom of speech
B) Right to a grand jury
C) Protection from self-incrimination
D) Right to bear arms

Answer: **A)**

Checks and Balances

21. How can Congress check the power of the Supreme Court?

A) Impeach justices
B) Veto Supreme Court decisions
C) Appoint new judges
D) Overturn judicial precedents

Answer: **A)**

22. The President can check the power of the judicial branch by:

A) Appointing judges
B) Passing laws overturning court decisions
C) Impeaching Supreme Court justices
D) Setting court budgets

Answer: **A)**

Current Issues and Debates

23. A controversial debate surrounding the Supreme Court involves whether:

A) Court terms should be extended
B) Justices should be elected rather than appointed
C) Courts should be filmed for transparency
D) Justices should have to retire at a certain age

Answer: **D)**

24. The process of changing the number of justices on the Supreme Court is known as:

A) Impeachment
B) Gerrymandering
C) Court-packing
D) Filibuster

Answer: **C)**

25. A Supreme Court decision that receives a 5-4 vote is considered:

A) Likely to be overturned in the future
B) A strong legal precedent
C) A sign of a divided court
D) Unconstitutional

Answer: **C)**

More Challenging Questions

26. What does the doctrine of "separation of powers" ensure?

A) A balance of power between branches of government
B) Equal power between federal and state governments
C) Protections for individual liberties
D) The independence of the judiciary

Answer: **A)**

27. The Exclusionary Rule prohibits:

A) Discrimination during jury selection
B) Using illegally obtained evidence in court
C) Cruel and unusual punishment
D) Unfair business practices

Answer: **B)**

28. Which type of law is created by legislative bodies (like Congress)?

A) Constitutional law
B) Common law
C) Statutory law
D) Case law

Answer: **C)**

29. The concept of due process, guaranteed by the Constitution, ensures:

A) Legal cases move efficiently
B) Fair procedures and respect for individual rights in legal proceedings
C) Unanimous jury verdicts
D) Equal outcomes under the law

Answer: **B)**

30. Which landmark Supreme Court case established the power of judicial review?

A) Miranda v. Arizona (1966)
B) Brown v. Board of Education (1954)
C) Marbury v. Madison (1803)
D) Roe v. Wade (1973)

Answer: **C)**

31. What is the difference between criminal law and civil law?

A) Criminal law involves crimes against society; civil law involves disputes between individuals or groups
B) Criminal law uses the "beyond a reasonable doubt" standard; civil law uses "preponderance of the evidence"
C) Criminal law is only heard in state courts; civil law is only heard in federal courts
D) Criminal law involves law enforcement; civil law involves attorneys filing lawsuits

Answer: **A)**

32. What is habeas corpus?

A) A right prohibiting unlawful imprisonment
B) A type of court order
C) A principle of double jeopardy
D) A legal term for a hung jury

Answer: **A)**

33. Which recent Supreme Court decision overturned Roe v. Wade, significantly impacting abortion rights in the U.S.?

A) Dobbs v. Jackson Women's Health Organization
B) Obergefell v. Hodges
C) Citizens United v. FEC
D) Heller v. District of Columbia

Answer: **A)**

34. The practice of judicial activism refers to:

A) Judges who strictly follow prior case law
B) Judges who seek to overturn existing laws and establish new precedents
C) The power of a president to nominate judges.
D) The process of Congress overriding a presidential veto

Answer: **B)**

35. Which current U.S. Supreme Court justice is considered the leader of the court's conservative wing?

A) Elena Kagan
B) Ruth Bader Ginsburg
C) Clarence Thomas
D) Sonia Sotomayor

Answer: **C)**

36. The term "swing vote" on the Supreme Court refers to a justice who:

A) Often changes their rulings based on the issue
B) Can tip the balance between liberal and conservative rulings
C) Regularly releases dissenting opinions
D) Never votes with the majority

Answer: **B)**

37. Which branch of government is responsible for enforcing laws?

A) Legislative Branch
B) Judicial Branch
C) Executive Branch
D) Bureaucracy

Answer: **C)**

38. What is the highest level of the federal court system?

A) State Supreme Court
B) U.S. District Courts
C) U.S. Courts of Appeals
D) U.S. Supreme Court

Answer: **D)**

39. The principle that prohibits trying the same person from being tried twice for the same crime is known as:

A) Habeas corpus
B) Due process
C) Double jeopardy
D) The exclusionary rule

Answer: **C)**

40. Which landmark Supreme Court case established the principle of "separate but equal"?

A) Brown v. Board of Education
B) Roe v. Wade
C) Marbury v. Madison
D) Plessy v. Ferguson

Answer: **D)**

Congress

The Congress of the United States is the bicameral legislative branch of the federal government, consisting of the Senate and the House of Representatives. The Senate includes 100 members, two from each state, serving six-year terms, while the House has 435 members apportioned based on state populations, each serving two-year terms. Congress is responsible for making federal laws, approving the federal budget, and overseeing the executive branch. It also has the power to declare war, confirm presidential appointments, and ratify treaties.

General Structure

1. What is the main legislative body of the United States?

A) Congress
B) Senate
C) House of Representatives
D) Supreme Court

Answer: **A)**

2. How many chambers does the United States Congress have?

    A) One
    B) Two
    C) Three
    D) Four

Answer: **B)**

3. What are the two chambers of Congress called?

    A) House of Commons and House of Lords
    B) Senate and House of Representatives
    C) House of Delegates and Senate
    D) Council and Assembly

Answer: **B)**

4. Who is the presiding officer of the House of Representatives?

    A) President
    B) Vice President
    C) Speaker of the House
    D) Majority Leader

Answer: **C)**

5. How many members are there in the House of Representatives?

    A) 100
    B) 435
    C) 200
    D) 150

Answer: **B)**

6. What is the term length for a member of the House of Representatives?

    A) 2 years
    B) 4 years
    C) 6 years
    D) 8 years

Answer: **A)**

7. How many Senators does each state have?

    A) One
    B) Two
    C) Three
    D) Four

Answer: **B)**

8. What is the term length for a U.S. Senator?

    A) 2 years
    B) 4 years
    C) 6 years
    D) 8 years

Answer: **C)**

9. Who is the presiding officer of the Senate?

    A) President
    B) Speaker of the House
    C) Vice President
    D) Majority Leader

Answer: **C)**

10. If the Vice President is absent, who presides over the Senate?

A) President
B) President pro tempore
C) Majority Leader
D) Speaker of the House

Answer: **B)**

Powers and Functions

11. Which article of the U.S. Constitution outlines the powers of Congress?

A) Article I
B) Article II
C) Article III
D) Article IV

Answer: **A)**

12. What power does Congress have concerning war?

A) Declare war
B) Command the armed forces
C) Negotiate peace treaties
D) Deploy troops

Answer: **A)**

13. Who has the power to impeach the President?

A) Senate
B) Supreme Court
C) House of Representatives
D) Vice President

Answer: **C)**

14. Who conducts the trial in an impeachment proceeding?

A) House of Representatives
B) Senate
C) Supreme Court
D) President

Answer: **B)**

15. What majority is needed in the Senate to convict and remove a President?

A) Simple majority
B) Three-fifths majority
C) Two-thirds majority
D) Three-fourths majority

Answer: **C)**

16. Which chamber of Congress confirms presidential appointments?

A) House of Representatives
B) Senate
C) Both chambers
D) Neither chamber

Answer: **B)**

17. Which chamber of Congress ratifies treaties?

A) House of Representatives
B) Senate
C) Both chambers
D) Neither chamber

Answer: **B)**

18. What power does Congress have over the federal budget?

A) None
B) Approve and amend it
C) Draft it
D) Veto it

Answer: **B)**

19. Which chamber initiates revenue-raising bills?

A) House of Representatives
B) Senate
C) Both chambers
D) Supreme Court

Answer: **A)**

20. Which committee is responsible for tax legislation in the House of Representatives?

A) Appropriations Committee
B) Ways and Means Committee
C) Budget Committee
D) Finance Committee

Answer: **B)**

Membership and Elections

21. What is the minimum age requirement for a U.S. Representative?

A) 25 years
B) 30 years
C) 35 years
D) 40 years

Answer: **A)**

22. What is the minimum age requirement for a U.S. Senator?

A) 25 years
B) 30 years
C) 35 years
D) 40 years

Answer: **B)**

23. How long must a U.S. Representative have been a citizen to be eligible for office?

A) 7 years
B) 9 years
C) 10 years
D) 14 years

Answer: **A)**

24. How long must a U.S. Senator have been a citizen to be eligible for office?

A) 7 years
B) 9 years
C) 10 years
D) 14 years

Answer: **B)**

25. Who has the power to regulate congressional elections?

A) Congress
B) President
C) Supreme Court
D) States

Answer: **D)**

26. What is the term length for a member of the House of Representatives?

A) 2 years
B) 4 years
C) 6 years
D) 8 years

Answer: **A)**

27. What is the term length for a U.S. Senator?

A) 2 years
B) 4 years
C) 6 years
D) 8 years

Answer: **C)**

28. How often are congressional elections held?

A) Every year
B) Every two years
C) Every four years
D) Every six years

Answer: **B)**

29. Which amendment to the U.S. Constitution provides for the direct election of Senators?

A) 16th Amendment
B) 17th Amendment
C) 18th Amendment
D) 19th Amendment

Answer: **B)**

30. Who has the power to expel a member of Congress?

A) President
B) Supreme Court
C) The respective chamber (House or Senate)
D) Vice President

Answer: **C)**

Committees and Procedures

31. What is a standing committee in Congress?

A) A temporary committee
B) A permanent committee
C) A joint committee
D) An investigative committee

Answer: **B)**

32. What is a conference committee?

A) A temporary committee to resolve differences in House and Senate versions of a bill
B) A permanent committee
C) A joint committee for budget matters
D) An investigative committee

Answer: **A)**

33. What is a filibuster?

A) A vote to end debate in the Senate
B) A prolonged speech to delay legislative action in the Senate
C) A type of committee hearing
D) A method of voting in Congress

Answer: **B)**

34. How can a filibuster be ended?

A) Majority vote
B) Cloture vote
C) Presidential veto
D) Supreme Court ruling

Answer: **B)**

35. What majority is needed for a cloture vote to end a filibuster?

A) Simple majority
B) Three-fifths majority
C) Two-thirds majority
D) Three-fourths majority

Answer: **B)**

36. What is the role of the House Rules Committee?

A) Oversee the budget
B) Set the rules for debate and amendments on the floor
C) Conduct investigations
D) Draft tax legislation

Answer: **B)**

37. What is a discharge petition in the House of Representatives?

A) A method to remove a member from office
B) A procedure to bring a bill out of committee for a floor vote
C) A way to end debate
D) A tool to amend a bill

Answer: **B)**

38. What is a quorum in the context of Congress?

A) The number of votes needed to pass a bill
B) The number of members needed to conduct business
C) The majority party's leadership team
D) The process of ending a filibuster

Answer: **B)**

39. What is a veto override?

A) Presidential power to reject a bill
B) Congressional power to overturn a presidential veto
C) Supreme Court power to nullify a law
D) Senate power to end debate

Answer: **B)**

40. What majority is needed to override a presidential veto?

A) Simple majority
B) Three-fifths majority
C) Two-thirds majority
D) Three-fourths majority

Answer: **C)**

Special Functions and Powers

41. What is the role of the Appropriations Committee?

A) Drafts tax legislation
B) Manages government spending and budgeting
C) Oversees the judiciary
D) Conducts foreign relations

Answer: **B)**

42. What is the purpose of a joint session of Congress?

A) To pass legislation
B) To conduct investigations
C) To hear the President's State of the Union address
D) To elect congressional leadership

Answer: **C)**

43. Who has the power to approve the federal budget?

A) President
B) Supreme Court
C) Congress
D) Vice President

Answer: **C)**

44. What is a pocket veto?

A) A President's formal rejection of a bill
B) A President's indirect veto by not signing a bill while Congress is adjourned
C) A Senate procedure to end debate
D) A House procedure to discharge a bill from committee

Answer: **B)**

45. Who has the power to declare war?

A) President
B) Congress
C) Supreme Court
D) Joint Chiefs of Staff

Answer: **B)**

46. What is the purpose of congressional oversight?

A) To draft legislation
B) To monitor and supervise federal agencies and programs
C) To conduct elections
D) To amend the Constitution

Answer: **B)**

47. What is the role of the Senate Judiciary Committee?

A) Drafts criminal legislation
B) Confirms federal judges and Supreme Court justices
C) Conducts impeachment trials
D) Oversees the federal budget

Answer: **B)**

48. What is a continuing resolution?

A) A law that funds the government temporarily when the regular budget process is not complete
B) A vote to end a filibuster
C) An amendment to the Constitution
D) A procedure to bring a bill out of committee

Answer: **A)**

49. What is the role of the Senate Foreign Relations Committee?

A) Oversees domestic policy
B) Manages foreign policy and international relations
C) Confirms judicial appointments
D) Oversees government spending

Answer: **B)**

50. What is a select committee?

A) A permanent committee
B) A temporary committee established for a specific purpose
C) A joint committee
D) A standing committee

Answer: **B)**

Legislative Process

51. What is the first step in the legislative process?

A) Committee hearing
B) Floor debate
C) Introduction of a bill
D) Presidential signature

Answer: **C)**

52. Where can a bill be introduced in Congress?

A) Only in the House of Representatives
B) Only in the Senate
C) In either the House or the Senate
D) Only by the President

Answer: **C)**

53. What happens to a bill after it is introduced?

A) It goes directly to the President
B) It is debated on the floor
C) It is sent to a committee for review
D) It becomes law immediately

Answer: **C)**

54. What can happen to a bill in committee?

A) It can be amended, rejected, or approved
B) It goes directly to the floor for a vote
C) It is sent to the President for approval
D) It is put to a public vote

Answer: **A)**

55. What happens if a bill is approved by committee?

A) It becomes law
B) It is sent to the other chamber for consideration
C) It is sent to the President
D) It is put to a public vote

Answer: **B)**

56. What is a markup session?

A) A committee meeting to amend and rewrite a bill
B) A floor debate session
C) A presidential review process
D) A budget planning session

Answer: **A)**

57. What is a bill called after it passes both the House and Senate?

A) A resolution
B) A law
C) A joint resolution
D) An act

Answer: **D)**

58. What must happen for a bill to become law after passing both chambers?

    A) It must be signed by the President
    B) It must be approved by the Supreme Court
    C) It must be voted on by the public
    D) It must be signed by the Vice President

Answer: **A)**

59. What happens if the President vetoes a bill?

    A) It is sent back to Congress
    B) It becomes law anyway
    C) It goes to the Supreme Court
    D) It is put to a public vote

Answer: **A)**

60. What is the purpose of a conference committee?

    A) To draft new legislation
    B) To reconcile differences between House and Senate versions of a bill
    C) To conduct investigations
    D) To approve presidential appointments

Answer: **B)**

Historical and Current Context

61. When was the first United States Congress convened?

    A) 1776
    B) 1781
    C) 1789
    D) 1791

Answer: **C)**

62. Who was the first Speaker of the House?

A) John Adams
B) Thomas Jefferson
C) James Madison
D) Frederick Muhlenberg

Answer: **D)**

63. Which act established the structure of the federal judiciary?

A) Judiciary Act of 1789
B) Judiciary Act of 1801
C) Judicial Procedures Reform Act
D) Judiciary Reorganization Act

Answer: **A)**

64. What landmark legislation did Congress pass in 1964?

A) Social Security Act
B) Civil Rights Act
C) Voting Rights Act
D) Affordable Care Act

Answer: **B)**

65. Which amendment gave Congress the power to levy income taxes?

A) 15th Amendment
B) 16th Amendment
C) 17th Amendment
D) 19th Amendment

Answer: **B)**

66. What is the primary purpose of the War Powers Resolution of 1973?

A) To grant the President unlimited war-making powers
B) To limit the President's ability to engage in military action without congressional approval
C) To establish the Department of Defense
D) To regulate arms sales

Answer: **B)**

67. Which congressional act created the Medicare program?

A) Social Security Act
B) Medicare Act of 1965
C) Affordable Care Act
D) Health Insurance Act

Answer: **B)**

68. What was the main purpose of the Patriot Act?

A) To reform the healthcare system
B) To enhance national security and combat terrorism
C) To regulate immigration
D) To establish new tax policies

Answer: **B)**

69. Which amendment to the Constitution abolished slavery?

A) 13th Amendment
B) 14th Amendment
C) 15th Amendment
D) 16th Amendment

Answer: **A)**

70. What significant legislation was passed in 2010 regarding healthcare?

A) Social Security Act
B) Medicare Act
C) Affordable Care Act
D) Health Insurance Act

Answer: **C)**

Congressional Leadership and Organization

71. Who is the current Speaker of the House (as of 2024)?

A) Nancy Pelosi
B) Kevin McCarthy
C) John Boehner
D) Paul Ryan

Answer: **B)**

72. Who is the current Senate Majority Leader (as of 2024)?

A) Mitch McConnell
B) Chuck Schumer
C) Harry Reid
D) Nancy Pelosi

Answer: **B)**

73. What is the role of the House Minority Leader?

A) Preside over the House
B) Lead the majority party
C) Lead the minority party
D) Confirm presidential appointments

Answer: **C)**

74. What is the role of the Senate Minority Leader?

A) Preside over the Senate
B) Lead the majority party
C) Lead the minority party
D) Confirm presidential appointments

Answer: **C)**

75. What is the purpose of the Congressional Black Caucus?

A) To draft tax legislation
B) To advocate for the interests of African Americans and minorities in Congress
C) To oversee the budget
D) To confirm judicial appointments

Answer: **B)**

76. What is the role of the Whips in Congress?

A) Preside over sessions
B) Manage party discipline and secure votes
C) Draft legislation
D) Confirm presidential appointments

Answer: **B)**

77. Who is the President pro tempore of the Senate?

A) Vice President
B) Majority Leader
C) Senior-most member of the majority party
D) Speaker of the House

Answer: **C)**

78. What is the primary function of the Congressional Budget Office (CBO)?

A) Drafts tax legislation
B) Provides nonpartisan budget and economic information to Congress
C) Oversees the judiciary
D) Manages foreign policy

Answer: **B)**

79. What is the purpose of the House Ethics Committee?

A) Drafts criminal legislation
B) Investigates and enforces standards of conduct for House members
C) Confirms judicial appointments
D) Oversees government spending

Answer: **B)**

80. What is the primary function of the Senate Armed Services Committee?

A) Drafts tax legislation
B) Oversees the Department of Defense and the armed forces
C) Manages foreign policy
D) Confirms judicial appointments

Answer: **B)**

Constitutional Amendments and Congress

81. Which amendment limits the number of terms a President can serve?

A) 20th Amendment
B) 22nd Amendment
C) 25th Amendment
D) 27th Amendment

Answer: **B)**

82. Which amendment lowered the voting age to 18?

A) 19th Amendment
B) 23rd Amendment
C) 24th Amendment
D) 26th Amendment

Answer: **D)**

83. Which amendment abolished poll taxes in federal elections?

A) 15th Amendment
B) 19th Amendment
C) 24th Amendment
D) 25th Amendment

Answer: **C)**

84. Which amendment provided for the direct election of Senators?

A) 16th Amendment
B) 17th Amendment
C) 18th Amendment
D) 19th Amendment

Answer: **B)**

85. Which amendment granted women the right to vote?

A) 15th Amendment
B) 18th Amendment
C) 19th Amendment
D) 21st Amendment

Answer: **C)**

86. Which amendment established the procedures for presidential succession?

A) 20th Amendment
B) 22nd Amendment
C) 25th Amendment
D) 27th Amendment

Answer: **C)**

87. Which amendment prohibits Congress from giving itself a pay raise during the current session?

A) 20th Amendment
B) 22nd Amendment
C) 25th Amendment
D) 27th Amendment

Answer: **D)**

88. Which amendment addresses the rights of citizens to be free from discrimination in voting based on race, color, or previous condition of servitude?

A) 13th Amendment
B) 14th Amendment
C) 15th Amendment
D) 16th Amendment

Answer: **C)**

89. Which amendment guarantees the right to a speedy and public trial?

A) 4th Amendment
B) 5th Amendment
C) 6th Amendment
D) 8th Amendment

Answer: **C)**

90. Which amendment provides the right to bear arms?

A) 1st Amendment
B) 2nd Amendment
C) 3rd Amendment
D) 4th Amendment

Answer: **B)**

Congressional Sessions and Operations

91. How often must Congress meet according to the Constitution?

A) Annually
B) Biannually
C) Quarterly
D) Monthly

Answer: **A)**

92. What is a lame-duck session of Congress?

A) A session held after a new President is elected but before they take office
B) A session held before elections
C) A session held during recess
D) A session focused on passing emergency legislation

Answer: **A)**

93. Who has the power to call a special session of Congress?

A) Speaker of the House
B) Senate Majority Leader
C) President
D) Supreme Court

Answer: **C)**

94. What is the official record of the proceedings and debates of Congress?

A) Congressional Record
B) Federal Register
C) House Journal
D) Senate Journal

Answer: **A)**

95. What is the purpose of a congressional caucus?

A) To elect the Speaker of the House
B) To draft legislation
C) To meet and pursue common legislative objectives among members
D) To confirm presidential appointments

Answer: **C)**

96. What is a recess in Congress?

A) A period during which Congress is not in session
B) A special legislative session
C) A break during committee meetings
D) An emergency session

Answer: **A)**

97. What is the purpose of a congressional hearing?

A) To pass legislation
B) To investigate and gather information on specific issues
C) To confirm judicial appointments
D) To approve the federal budget

Answer: **B)**

98. What is a bill of attainder?

A) A law that declares a person guilty of a crime without a trial
B) A tax legislation
C) A budget resolution
D) An impeachment article

Answer: **A)**

99. What is the purpose of a rider in legislative terms?

A) An amendment attached to a bill that is not related to the bill's subject
B) A primary clause of a bill
C) A procedural rule
D) A type of filibuster

Answer: **A)**

100. What is the purpose of a sunset provision in legislation?

A) To establish a permanent law
B) To set an expiration date for a law unless it is reauthorized
C) To confirm presidential appointments
D) To create a tax policy

Answer: **B)**

The Executive Branch

The Executive Branch of the United States Government is responsible for enforcing and implementing federal laws. It is headed by the President, who also serves as the Commander-in-Chief of the Armed Forces and the chief diplomat. This branch includes the Vice President and the President's Cabinet, which consists of the heads of federal departments and key advisors. Additionally, numerous federal agencies and commissions operate under the Executive Branch, managing specific governmental functions and services.

General Structure

1. Who is the head of the Executive Branch of the United States Government?

A) Chief Justice
B) Speaker of the House
C) President
D) Senate Majority Leader

Answer: **C)**

2. How long is the term for the President of the United States?

   A) 2 years
   B) 4 years
   C) 6 years
   D) 8 years

Answer: **B)**

3. Who is the second-highest official in the Executive Branch?

   A) Chief Justice
   B) Speaker of the House
   C) Vice President
   D) Secretary of State

Answer: **C)**

4. Which amendment limits the President to two terms in office?

   A) 19th Amendment
   B) 20th Amendment
   C) 22nd Amendment
   D) 25th Amendment

Answer: **C)**

5. What is the official residence of the President?

   A) Capitol Building
   B) White House
   C) Camp David
   D) Pentagon

Answer: **B)**

Powers and Duties

6. Which power allows the President to reject a bill passed by Congress?

A) Filibuster
B) Veto
C) Override
D) Cloture

Answer: **B)**

7. Who has the authority to negotiate treaties with foreign nations?

A) Congress
B) Supreme Court
C) Vice President
D) President

Answer: **D)**

8. Who confirms the President's appointments to the Supreme Court?

A) House of Representatives
B) Senate
C) Vice President
D) Supreme Court

Answer: **B)**

9. What is the President's role as Commander-in-Chief?

A) Head of the judiciary
B) Leader of the armed forces
C) Head of Congress
D) Chief diplomat

Answer: **B)**

10. What is the purpose of the State of the Union Address?

A) To veto legislation
B) To appoint judges
C) To inform Congress and the nation about the President's agenda and national priorities
D) To declare war

Answer: **C)**

The Vice President

11. What is one of the primary constitutional duties of the Vice President?

A) Veto legislation
B) Serve as Speaker of the House
C) Preside over the Senate
D) Serve as Chief Justice

Answer: **C)**

12. Who becomes President if both the President and Vice President can no longer serve?

A) Secretary of State
B) Speaker of the House
C) Senate Majority Leader
D) Attorney General

Answer: **B)**

13. Which amendment addresses presidential succession and disability?

A) 20th Amendment
B) 22nd Amendment
C) 25th Amendment
D) 27th Amendment

Answer: **C)**

14. What role does the Vice President play in the event of a tie vote in the Senate?

A) No role
B) Casts the deciding vote
C) Vetoes the tie
D) Refers the vote to the Supreme Court

Answer: **B)**

15. What is the Vice President's official residence?

A) Camp David
B) White House
C) Number One Observatory Circle
D) Blair House

Answer: **C)**

Executive Departments and Agencies

16. Which department is responsible for foreign policy and international relations?

A) Department of Defense
B) Department of Homeland Security
C) Department of State
D) Department of Commerce

Answer: **C)**

17. Which department oversees the nation's military?

A) Department of State
B) Department of Homeland Security
C) Department of Defense
D) Department of Justice

Answer: **C)**

18. Which department is responsible for the nation's finances, including managing federal revenue and the economy?

A) Department of Commerce
B) Department of Treasury
C) Department of Labor
D) Department of the Interior

Answer: **B)**

19. Which department is in charge of natural resources and public lands?

A) Department of Agriculture
B) Department of Energy
C) Department of Commerce
D) Department of the Interior

Answer: **D)**

20. What is the role of the Department of Justice?

A) Oversee the military
B) Manage the economy
C) Enforce federal laws and administer justice
D) Conduct foreign policy

Answer: **C)**

21. Which executive agency is responsible for space exploration?

A) Department of Transportation
B) Federal Aviation Administration (FA**A)**
C) National Aeronautics and Space Administration (NAS**A)**
D) Environmental Protection Agency (EP**A)**

Answer: **C)**

22. Which department administers programs for veterans?

A) Department of Health and Human Services
B) Department of Defense
C) Department of Veterans Affairs
D) Department of Labor

Answer: **C)**

23. Which department is tasked with securing the nation from terrorist attacks and managing disaster response?

A) Department of Defense
B) Department of Homeland Security
C) Department of Justice
D) Department of State

Answer: **B)**

24. Which department oversees public health and social services?

A) Department of Education
B) Department of Health and Human Services
C) Department of Housing and Urban Development
D) Department of Commerce

Answer: **B)**

25. Which executive office assists the President in preparing the federal budget?

A) Office of Management and Budget (OM**B)**
B) Council of Economic Advisers
C) Department of Treasury
D) Federal Reserve

Answer: **A)**

Presidential Powers

26. What is an executive order?

A) A legislative act passed by Congress
B) A directive issued by the President to manage operations of the federal government
C) A Supreme Court ruling
D) A budgetary amendment

Answer: **B)**

27. What is the purpose of a presidential pardon?

A) To amend the Constitution
B) To forgive a person for a crime and eliminate the associated penalties
C) To veto legislation
D) To appoint federal judges

Answer: **B)**

28. Who has the power to declare war?

A) President
B) Congress
C) Secretary of Defense
D) Vice President

Answer: **B)**

29. What is a presidential veto?

A) Approval of a bill
B) Rejection of a bill passed by Congress
C) Amendment to a bill
D) Signing of a treaty

Answer: **B)**

30. Which office is responsible for advising the President on national security issues?

A) Department of Defense
B) Central Intelligence Agency (CIA)
C) National Security Council (NSC)
D) Department of State

Answer: **C)**

Presidential Elections

31. How is the President of the United States elected?

A) By popular vote
B) By Congress
C) By the Electoral College
D) By the Supreme Court

Answer: **C)**

32. How many electoral votes are needed to win the Presidency?

A) 200
B) 270
C) 300
D) 350

Answer: **B)**

33. When is the Presidential Inauguration held?

A) January 1
B) January 20
C) December 25
D) July 4

Answer: **B)**

34. Who administers the oath of office to the President?

A) Speaker of the House
B) Vice President
C) Chief Justice of the Supreme Court
D) Secretary of State

Answer: **C)**

35. Which amendment changed the start date of the Presidential term from March 4 to January 20?

A) 19th Amendment
B) 20th Amendment
C) 22nd Amendment
D) 25th Amendment

Answer: **B)**

Checks and Balances

36. What is the primary check the President has on the legislative branch?

A) Judicial review
B) Veto power
C) Appointment power
D) Budget control

Answer: **B)**

37. Which branch of government has the power to impeach the President?

A) Judicial branch
B) Executive branch
C) Legislative branch
D) Military

Answer: **C)**

38. What role does the Senate play in the impeachment process?

A) Initiates the impeachment
B) Conducts the impeachment trial
C) Drafts articles of impeachment
D) Vetoes the impeachment

Answer: **B)**

39. Who has the power to interpret the constitutionality of executive actions?

A) President
B) Congress
C) Supreme Court
D) Vice President

Answer: **C)**

40. What is the term used for the President's advisory group composed of the heads of the executive departments?

A) Senate
B) Supreme Court
C) Cabinet
D) Congress

Answer: **C)**

Historical Context and Current Issues

41. Who was the first President of the United States?

A) Thomas Jefferson
B) John Adams
C) George Washington
D) James Madison

Answer: **C)**

42. Which President issued the Emancipation Proclamation?

A) Thomas Jefferson
B) Abraham Lincoln
C) Ulysses S. Grant
D) Andrew Jackson

Answer: **B)**

43. Who was the first President to resign from office?

A) John F. Kennedy
B) Richard Nixon
C) Jimmy Carter
D) Gerald Ford

Answer: **B)**

44. Which President signed the Civil Rights Act of 1964 into law?

A) John F. Kennedy
B) Lyndon B. Johnson
C) Dwight D. Eisenhower
D) Richard Nixon

Answer: **B)**

45. Who was the only President to serve more than two terms?

A) Franklin D. Roosevelt
B) Harry S. Truman
C) Woodrow Wilson
D) Theodore Roosevelt

Answer: **A)**

Presidential Succession

46. What is the line of succession after the Vice President?

A) Secretary of State
B) Speaker of the House
C) Senate Majority Leader
D) Attorney General

Answer: **B)**

47. Who follows the Speaker of the House in the line of presidential succession?

A) Secretary of Defense
B) Senate Majority Leader
C) President pro tempore of the Senate
D) Secretary of State

Answer: **C)**

48. Who follows the President pro tempore of the Senate in the line of succession?

A) Secretary of Defense
B) Secretary of State
C) Attorney General
D) Secretary of Treasury

Answer: **B)**

49. Which law established the current order of presidential succession?

A) Presidential Succession Act of 1792
B) Presidential Succession Act of 1886
C) Presidential Succession Act of 1947
D) Presidential Succession Act of 1967

Answer: **C)**

50. Who has the authority to determine the President's inability to discharge the powers and duties of the office under the 25th Amendment?

A) Vice President and majority of the Cabinet
B) Congress
C) Supreme Court
D) President pro tempore of the Senate

Answer: **A)**

Federal Electoral System

The Federal Electoral system of the United States is designed to elect the President, Vice President, and members of Congress. Presidential elections use the Electoral College, where electors from each state, based on the state's congressional representation, cast votes for the candidates. Congressional elections are held every two years, with all seats in the House of Representatives and approximately one-third of the Senate seats up for election. The system allows for direct voting by citizens, with various state laws governing voter registration, voting procedures, and the counting of votes.

General Overview

1. What is the primary method used to elect the President of the United States?

A) Popular vote
B) Congressional vote
C) Electoral College
D) Supreme Court decision

Answer: **C)**

2. How many total electoral votes are there in the Electoral College?

    A) 435
    B) 538
    C) 270
    D) 100

Answer: **B)**

3. How many electoral votes are needed to win the presidency?

    A) 200
    B) 270
    C) 300
    D) 350

Answer: **B)**

4. Which constitutional amendment established the Electoral College?

    A) 10th Amendment
    B) 12th Amendment
    C) 15th Amendment
    D) 19th Amendment

Answer: **B)**

5. Who formally elects the President if no candidate receives a majority of electoral votes?

    A) Senate
    B) Supreme Court
    C) House of Representatives
    D) Vice President

Answer: **C)**

Electoral College

6. How are the number of electoral votes per state determined?

A) Population size
B) Number of registered voters
C) Number of Senators and Representatives
D) Geographic size

Answer: **C)**

7. Which state has the most electoral votes?

A) Texas
B) Florida
C) New York
D) California

Answer: **D)**

8. What is the minimum number of electoral votes a state can have?

A) One
B) Two
C) Three
D) Four

Answer: **C)**

9. Who are the electors in the Electoral College?

A) Members of Congress
B) Appointed officials
C) Party representatives chosen by the states
D) Supreme Court Justices

Answer: **C)**

10. When do electors cast their official votes for President?

A) Election Day in November
B) Inauguration Day in January
C) December after the general election
D) July before the general election

Answer: **C)**

Presidential Primaries and Caucuses

11. What is the purpose of presidential primaries and caucuses?

A) To elect the President directly
B) To select delegates for the national party conventions
C) To determine electoral votes
D) To pass legislation

Answer: **B)**

12. Which state traditionally holds the first primary in the nation?

A) Iowa
B) New Hampshire
C) South Carolina
D) Nevada

Answer: **B)**

13. Which state traditionally holds the first caucus in the nation?

A) Iowa
B) New Hampshire
C) South Carolina
D) Nevada

Answer: **A)**

14. What is a "Super Tuesday"?

A) The day of the general election
B) The day of the electoral vote count
C) A day when multiple states hold primaries or caucuses
D) The day of the presidential inauguration

Answer: **C)**

15. What is the role of delegates at the national party conventions?

A) To elect the President
B) To vote on the party platform
C) To select the party's presidential nominee
D) To pass national legislation

Answer: **C)**

Voting and Elections

16. What is the minimum voting age in the United States?

A) 16 years
B) 18 years
C) 21 years
D) 25 years

Answer: **B)**

17. Which amendment granted women the right to vote?

A) 15th Amendment
B) 19th Amendment
C) 22nd Amendment
D) 26th Amendment

Answer: **B)**

18. Which amendment lowered the voting age from 21 to 18?

    A) 15th Amendment
    B) 19th Amendment
    C) 22nd Amendment
    D) 26th Amendment

Answer: **D)**

19. What is absentee voting?

    A) Voting in person on Election Day
    B) Voting by mail before Election Day
    C) Voting by proxy
    D) Voting at a polling place

Answer: **B)**

20. What is a primary election?

    A) The first election held in the year
    B) An election to select a party's candidate for the general election
    C) An election to determine state legislation
    D) An election to pass constitutional amendments

Answer: **B)**

Campaigns and Financing

21. What is the main purpose of a political campaign?

    A) To raise taxes
    B) To promote candidates and their policies
    C) To draft legislation
    D) To conduct judicial reviews

Answer: **B)**

22. Which federal body regulates campaign finance?

A) Federal Reserve
B) Federal Communications Commission (FCC)
C) Federal Election Commission (FEC)
D) Internal Revenue Service (IRS)

Answer: **C)**

23. What is a Political Action Committee (PAC)?

A) A group that raises and spends money to influence elections
B) A government agency
C) A legislative body
D) A judicial committee

Answer: **A)**

24. What is the maximum amount an individual can contribute to a candidate per election cycle (as of 2024)?

A) $1,000
B) $2,900
C) $5,000
D) $10,000

Answer: **B)**

25. What is a "Super PAC"?

A) A type of PAC that can raise unlimited sums of money from corporations, unions, and individuals
B) A legislative committee
C) A state government body
D) A judicial review board

Answer: **A)**

Voting Rights and Regulations

26. Which act aimed to eliminate racial discrimination in voting?

A) Voting Rights Act of 1965
B) Civil Rights Act of 1964
C) Immigration and Nationality Act
D) Social Security Act

Answer: **A)**

27. Which amendment prohibited poll taxes in federal elections?

A) 19th Amendment
B) 24th Amendment
C) 26th Amendment
D) 15th Amendment

Answer: **B)**

28. What is the purpose of voter registration?

A) To track tax payments
B) To ensure eligible voters are on the electoral roll
C) To allocate electoral votes
D) To confirm citizenship

Answer: **B)**

29. What is gerrymandering?

A) The process of voting by mail
B) Drawing electoral district boundaries to favor a political party
C) The procedure for presidential impeachment
D) Campaign fundraising

Answer: **B)**

30. Which body typically administers elections at the local level?

A) Federal Election Commission (FEC)
B) State government
C) County or municipal election boards
D) Supreme Court

Answer: **C)**

Presidential Elections

31. What is the general election day for federal offices?

A) First Tuesday in November
B) Second Monday in October
C) First Thursday in December
D) Last Friday in September

Answer: **A)**

32. Who certifies the electoral votes?

A) President
B) Supreme Court
C) Congress
D) Federal Election Commission (FEC)

Answer: **C)**

33. What is the "winner-takes-all" system in the Electoral College?

A) The candidate who wins the popular vote in a state wins all its electoral votes
B) The candidate who wins the popular vote nationwide wins all the electoral votes
C) The candidate who raises the most funds wins
D) The candidate with the most endorsements wins

Answer: **A)**

34. Which two states do not use the "winner-takes-all" system?

A) Texas and California
B) Florida and New York
C) Maine and Nebraska
D) Ohio and Pennsylvania

Answer: **C)**

35. What happens if no presidential candidate receives a majority of electoral votes?

A) The Supreme Court decides
B) The House of Representatives elects the President
C) The Senate elects the President
D) The election is held again

Answer: **B)**

Voting Systems and Methods

36. What is a "provisional ballot"?

A) A ballot used for absentee voting
B) A ballot used when there are questions about a voter's eligibility
C) A ballot used in early voting
D) A ballot used for military personnel

Answer: **B)**

37. What is "early voting"?

A) Voting on Election Day
B) Voting by mail after Election Day
C) Voting before Election Day in person or by mail
D) Voting by absentee ballot

Answer: **C)**

38. What is the purpose of a "polling place"?

A) To collect tax payments
B) To serve as a location where voters cast their ballots in person
C) To draft legislation
D) To administer justice

Answer: **B)**

39. What is a "runoff election"?

A) An election held to break a tie
B) An election held when no candidate wins a majority in the initial election
C) An election held during the primary season
D) An election held for special referendums

Answer: **B)**

40. Which amendment granted residents of Washington, D.C., the right to vote in presidential elections?

A) 22nd Amendment
B) 23rd Amendment
C) 24th Amendment
D) 25th Amendment

Answer: **B)**

Post World War II Presidents

Following World War II, the United States experienced a period of economic growth and political change under several presidents. Harry S. Truman (1945-1953) oversaw the end of the war, the beginning of the Cold War, and the desegregation of the military. Dwight D. Eisenhower (1953-1961) focused on domestic issues, such as infrastructure and civil rights, while also dealing with the Cold War tensions. John F. Kennedy (1961-1963) faced the Cuban Missile Crisis and initiated the Apollo space program before his assassination, which led to Lyndon B. Johnson (1963-1969) taking office and signing landmark civil rights legislation and expanding social welfare programs, but also escalating U.S. involvement in the Vietnam War.

Harry S. Truman (1945-1953)

1. Before becoming President, Harry S. Truman served as:

A) Governor of Missouri
B) U.S. Senator from Missouri
C) Secretary of State
D) A five-star general

Answer: **B)**

2. Which World War did Truman serve in as an artillery captain?

A) World War I
B) World War II
C) The Korean War
D) The Vietnam War

Answer: **A)**

3. Truman's middle name was simply the letter "S." and didn't stand for anything.

A) True
B) False

Answer: **A)**

4. What was the name of the men's clothing store Truman operated before entering politics?

A) Truman and Jacobson
B) Truman's Haberdashery
C) Sharp Suits
D) The Presidential Tailor

Answer: **A)**

5. Harry S. Truman became president after the death of:

A) Dwight D. Eisenhower
B) Herbert Hoover
C) Franklin D. Roosevelt
D) John F. Kennedy

Answer: **C)**

6. Which famous post-WWII economic aid program to rebuild Europe was initiated by Truman?

    A) The New Deal
    B) The Marshall Plan
    C) The Great Society
    D) The Truman Doctrine

Answer: **B)**

7. What term did Truman use to describe his domestic policy initiatives?

    A) The New Deal
    B) The New Frontier
    C) The Fair Deal
    D) The Great Society

Answer: **C)**

8. Truman famously ordered the desegregation of the U.S. Armed Forces in 1948.

    A) True
    B) False

Answer: **A)**

9. The Truman Doctrine was designed to:

    A) Expand nuclear weapons development
    B) Contain the spread of communism
    C) Rebuild Europe after the war
    D) Establish peace with the Soviet Union

Answer: **B)**

10. Which international organization was formed in 1949 during Truman's presidency as a defensive alliance?

    A) League of Nations
    B) United Nations
    C) NATO
    D) Warsaw Pact

Answer: **C)**

11. Which major conflict involving North and South Korea began during Truman's presidency?

    A) World War II
    B) The Vietnam War
    C) The Korean War
    D) The Cold War

Answer: **C)**

12. The controversial decision to drop atomic bombs on Japan was made during Truman's presidency.

    A) True
    B) False

Answer: **A)**

13. The "buck stops here" was a famous phrase signifying:

    A) Truman's strong support for big business
    B) Truman's decisive foreign policy stance
    C) Truman's commitment to ending segregation
    D) Truman's ultimate responsibility as President

Answer: **D)**

14. Truman's approval ratings were very low when he left office.

A) True
B) False

Answer: A)

15. Which major post-war economic boom in the U.S. occurred partly during Truman's presidency?

A) Roaring Twenties
B) 1950s economic expansion
C) Dot-Com Bubble
D) Great Recession

Answer: B)

Dwight D. Eisenhower (1953-1961)

1. Which small Kansas town was Eisenhower's hometown?

A) Abilene
B) Topeka
C) Wichita
D) Leavenworth

Answer: A)

2. Eisenhower attended the United States Military Academy at:

A) Annapolis
B) West Point
C) Colorado Springs
D) Kings Point

Answer: B)

3. Eisenhower achieved the rank of five-star general and served as Supreme Allied Commander in which war?

    A) World War I
    B) World War II
    C) The Korean War
    D) The Vietnam War

Answer: **B)**

4. Before becoming President, Eisenhower served as the president of which prestigious university?

    A) Harvard University
    B) Yale University
    C) Columbia University
    D) Stanford University

Answer: **C)**

5. Dwight D. Eisenhower was a member of the:

    A) Democratic Party
    B) Republican Party
    C) Whig Party
    D) Independent Party

Answer: **B)**

6. Which Civil Rights landmark was signed into law during Eisenhower's presidency?

    A) The Brown v Board of Education ruling
    B) The Civil Rights Act of 1964
    C) The Voting Rights Act of 1965
    D) The Civil Rights Act of 1957

Answer: **D)**

7. Which massive infrastructure project was initiated under Eisenhower?

A) The Transcontinental Railroad
B) The Panama Canal
C) The Interstate Highway System
D) The Hoover Dam

Answer: **C)**

8. The state of Alaska was admitted to the Union during Eisenhower's presidency.

A) True
B) False

Answer: **A)**

9. Eisenhower's policy emphasizing the threat and possible use of nuclear weapons was known as:

A) Mutually Assured Destruction (MAD)
B) Brinkmanship
C) Detente
D) Massive Retaliation

Answer: **D)**

10. Which international organization aimed at space exploration was created during Eisenhower's presidency?

A) NASA
B) SpaceX
C) United Nations
D) NATO

Answer: **A)**

11. The U-2 incident, involving an American spy plane shot down over the Soviet Union, occurred during Eisenhower's presidency.

A) True
B) False

Answer: **A)**

12. The Suez Crisis, a confrontation over control of the Suez Canal, occurred during Eisenhower's administration.

A) True
B) False

Answer: **A)**

13. One of Eisenhower's most famous warnings in his farewell address was about the growing power of:

A) China
B) The military-industrial complex
C) Big tech companies
D) Environmentalists

Answer: **B)**

John F. Kennedy (1961–1963)

1. John F. Kennedy was born in:

A) Boston, Massachusetts
B) Brookline, Massachusetts
C) New York City, New York
D) Washington, D.C.

Answer: **B)**

2. Kennedy served in which branch of the U.S. military during World War II?

A) Army
B) Navy
C) Air Force
D) Marines

Answer: **B)**

3. Which Ivy League university did Kennedy attend?

A) Yale University
B) Princeton University
C) Harvard University
D) Columbia University

Answer: **C)**

4. Before becoming President, Kennedy served as a U.S. Representative and then Senator from which state?

A) New York
B) California
C) Massachusetts
D) Texas

Answer: **C)**

5. John F. Kennedy was the first and only president to be:

A) A military veteran
B) Born outside the mainland U.S.
C) A Roman Catholic
D) An Ivy League graduate

Answer: **C)**

6. Which program initiated by Kennedy sent young Americans to help developing nations?

A) AmeriCorps
B) Peace Corps
C) Teach for America
D) Alliance for Progress

Answer: **B)**

7. Kennedy's ambitious domestic policy program was called:

A) The New Frontier
B) The Fair Deal
C) The Great Society
D) The New Deal

Answer: **A)**

8. Which major Civil Rights event occurred during Kennedy's presidency?

A) The Selma to Montgomery marches
B) The Civil Rights Act of 1964
C) March on Washington
D) The Voting Rights Act of 1965

Answer: **C)**

9. The failed CIA-backed invasion of Cuba is historically known as:

A) Operation Overlord
B) The Tet Offensive
C) The Bay of Pigs Invasion
D) The Cuban Missile Crisis

Answer: **C)**

10. Which landmark space program did Kennedy vow to achieve before the end of the 1960s?

A) Creating the International Space Station
B) Landing a man on the moon
C) Launching the first satellite into orbit
D) Sending a probe to Mars

Answer: **B)**

11. The construction of the Berlin Wall, a symbol of Cold War division, began in 1961 during Kennedy's term.

A) True
B) False

Answer: **A)**

12. The Cuban Missile Crisis brought the U.S. and the Soviet Union to the brink of nuclear war.

A) True
B) False

Answer: **A)**

13. John F. Kennedy was assassinated in:

A) Washington, D.C.
B) Dallas, Texas
C) New York City, New York
D) Los Angeles, California

Answer: **B)**

14. Which government investigation concluded Lee Harvey Oswald acted alone in Kennedy's assassination?

A) The FBI Report
B) The Mueller Report
C) The Warren Commission
D) The Church Committee

Answer: **C)**

Lyndon B. Johnson (1963-1969)

1. Lyndon B. Johnson was born in which region of Texas known for its poverty and hardship?

A) Hill Country
B) Gulf Coast
C) Panhandle
D) Rio Grande Valley

Answer: **A)**

2. Before his political career, LBJ worked as a:

A) Lawyer
B) Farmer
C) Teacher
D) Journalist

Answer: **C)**

3. Which prestigious university did LBJ briefly attend as a law student?

A) Yale University
B) Georgetown University
C) Stanford University
D) Harvard University

Answer: **B)**

4. How did Lyndon B. Johnson first enter national politics?

A) He was appointed to the U.S. Senate
B) He was elected to the U.S. House of Representatives
C) He was appointed a cabinet secretary
D) He served as a state governor

Answer: **B)**

5. LBJ gained significant power within the U.S. Senate by becoming:

A) Senate Minority Leader
B) Speaker of the Senate
C) Chairman of the Foreign Relations committee
D) Senate Majority Leader

Answer: **D)**

6. LBJ became president upon the assassination of:

A) Franklin D. Roosevelt
B) Dwight D. Eisenhower
C) John F. Kennedy
D) Harry S. Truman

Answer: **C)**

7. The "Great Society" was LBJ's ambitious program focusing on:

A) Infrastructure and urban renewal
B) Foreign policy and military expansion
C) Fighting poverty and social inequality
D) Space exploration and scientific advancement

Answer: **C)**

8. Which federal programs were created as part of the Great Society?

A) Medicare and Medicaid
B) The Environmental Protection Agency (EPA)
C) The Department of Homeland Security
D) The Social Security Administration

Answer: **A)**

9. The 1964 legislation signed by LBJ that outlawed racial discrimination in public spaces was called:

A) Brown v. Board of Education
B) The Voting Rights Act
C) The Civil Rights Act
D) The Emancipation Proclamation

Answer: **C)**

10. The Vietnam War significantly intensified during LBJ's presidency, fueled by concerns about:

A) Middle Eastern oil reserves
B) Communist expansion in Southeast Asia
C) Nuclear proliferation
D) The rise of fascism in Europe

Answer: **B)**

11. Which event in the Vietnam War became a symbol of North Vietnamese military strength and weakened U.S. public support?

A) The Gulf of Tonkin incident
B) The Battle of Khe Sanh
C) The Tet Offensive
D) The Fall of Saigon

Answer: **C)**

12. Which policy change made by LBJ resulted in a major escalation of U.S. troops in Vietnam?

A) The policy of containment
B) The Truman Doctrine
C) The Gulf of Tonkin Resolution
D) The policy of détente

Answer: **C)**

13. Growing protests and unrest against what issue contributed to LBJ's declining popularity?

A) The Vietnam War
B) The Space Race
C) Civil Rights legislation
D) Economic recession

Answer: **A)**

14. What decision announced by LBJ in 1968 surprised the nation and signaled his political decline?

A) Declaring war on North Vietnam
B) Impeachment proceedings against him
C) Not seeking reelection as president
D) Sending troops into Cambodia

Answer: **C)**

15. Which U.S. president succeeded Lyndon B. Johnson?

A) Jimmy Carter
B) Gerald Ford
C) Ronald Reagan
D) Richard Nixon

Answer: **D)**

Richard Nixon (1969–1974)

1. Richard Nixon was born and raised in which U.S. state?

A) New York
B) Ohio
C) Texas
D) California

Answer: **D)**

2. Nixon earned a law degree from which university?

A) Harvard University
B) Duke University
C) Yale University
D) Columbia University

Answer: **B)**

3. Before becoming president, Nixon served as a U.S. Senator from California and as Vice President under:

A) Harry S. Truman
B) Lyndon B. Johnson
C) Dwight D. Eisenhower
D) John F. Kennedy

Answer: **C)**

4. Nixon gained early political notoriety as a member of which congressional committee investigating communist infiltration?

A) House Foreign Affairs Committee
B) House Un-American Activities Committee (HUAC)
C) Senate Judiciary Committee
D) Warren Commission

Answer: **B)**

5. Nixon narrowly lost the 1960 presidential election to:

A) Dwight D. Eisenhower
B) Harry S. Truman
C) John F. Kennedy
D) Lyndon B. Johnson

Answer: **C)**

6. Nixon finally won the presidency in what year?

A) 1964
B) 1968
C) 1972
D) 1976

Answer: **B)**

7. Which federal agency dedicated to environmental protection was established during Nixon's presidency?

A) Department of Energy
B) Occupational Safety and Health Administration (OSHA)
C) Environmental Protection Agency (EPA)
D) Department of the Interior

Answer: **B)**

8. Nixon's economic strategy included imposing temporary:

A) High tariffs on foreign goods
B) Wage and price controls
C) Tax cuts for the wealthy
D) Strict environmental regulations

Answer: **B)**

9. Nixon implemented a social policy known as "New Federalism," which aimed to:

A) Expand the role of the federal government
B) Decentralize power and give more authority to states
C) Provide a universal basic income for all citizens
D) Nationalize major industries

Answer: **B)**

10. Which foreign policy approach emphasized a reduction of Cold War tensions with the Soviet Union?

A) Containment
B) Détente
C) Appeasement
D) Brinkmanship

Answer: **B)**

11. Nixon made a historic visit to which communist nation in 1972, beginning the process of normalization?

A) North Korea
B) Cuba
C) China
D) Vietnam

Answer: **C)**

12. The Vietnam War continued during Nixon's presidency, and his administration's policy included:

A) Immediate withdrawal of U.S. troops
B) Expansion of the war into Cambodia
C) Increased bombing campaigns in North Vietnam
D) Sending ground troops into North Vietnam

Answer: **B)**

13. The Watergate scandal involved the break-in at the headquarters of which political party?

A) Republican Party
B) Democratic Party
C) Libertarian Party
D) Green Party

Answer: **B)**

14. Nixon's involvement in the attempted cover-up of the Watergate scandal led to:

A) His successful impeachment and removal from office
B) Him being censured by Congress
C) His resignation from the presidency
D) No legal consequences

Answer: **C)**

15. Which president pardoned Richard Nixon for any federal crimes he may have committed?

A) Lyndon B. Johnson
B) Jimmy Carter
C) Gerald Ford
D) Ronald Reagan

Answer: **C)**

Gerald Ford (1974-1977)

1. Gerald Ford was born with a different name. What was his birth name?

A) John Smith
B) William Miller
C) Leslie Lynch King Jr.
D) Robert Johnson

Answer: **C)**

2. Ford was a star athlete in college, playing what sport at the University of Michigan?

A) Basketball
B) Baseball
C) Football
D) Track & Field

Answer: C)

3. Before entering politics, Ford served in the U.S. Navy during which major conflict?

A) World War I
B) World War II
C) The Korean War
D) The Vietnam War

Answer: B)

4. Ford entered politics by being elected to the U.S. House of Representatives from which state?

A) Michigan
B) Ohio
C) New York
D) California

Answer: A)

5. Ford became the Minority Leader of the U.S. House of Representatives. Which political party did he represent?

A) Democratic Party
B) Republican Party
C) Libertarian Party
D) Green Party

Answer: B)

6. How did Gerald Ford become Vice President under Richard Nixon?

A) Elected alongside Nixon in the 1972 election
B) He was Nixon's original VP, but Nixon resigned
C) Appointed after the resignation of VP Spiro Agnew
D) Chosen by Congress after Nixon's impeachment

Answer: **C)**

7. Gerald Ford became president following:

A) Winning the 1974 presidential election.
B) The assassination of Richard Nixon.
C) The resignation of Richard Nixon
D) The death of Richard Nixon.

Answer: **C)**

8. One of Ford's most controversial acts as president was:

A) Launching an invasion of North Vietnam
B) Pardoning Richard Nixon
C) Enacting sweeping environmental regulations
D) Establishing a national healthcare system

Answer: **B)**

9. Ford's abbreviated presidency lasted less than:

A) One year
B) Two years
C) Three years
D) Four years

Answer: **C)**

10. Ford's economic plan called "Whip Inflation Now" (WIN) aimed to address what primary issue?

A) Declining wages
B) High inflation
C) Stock market crash
D) Rising unemployment

Answer: **B)**

11. The fall of Saigon and the end of the Vietnam War occurred during Ford's presidency.

A) True
B) False

Answer: **A)**

12. What was the name of the domestic crisis involving a serial killer terrorizing New York City during Ford's presidency?

A) Night Stalker
B) Zodiac Killer
C) Son of Sam
D) BTK Killer

Answer: **C)**

13. Which international accords aimed at easing tensions with the Soviet Union were signed by Ford?

A) The SALT Treaties
B) The Helsinki Accords
C) The Camp David Accords
D) The Paris Peace Accords

Answer: **B)**

14. Ford faced criticism for his handling of which incident involving the seizure of a U.S. merchant ship by Cambodian forces?

A) The Gulf of Tonkin Incident
B) The Pueblo Incident
C) The Mayaguez Incident
D) The Iran Hostage Crisis

Answer: **C)**

15. Which U.S. president defeated Gerald Ford in the 1976 presidential election?

A) Ronald Reagan
B) Jimmy Carter
C) George H.W Bush
D) Bill Clinton

Answer: **B)**

Jimmy Carter (1977 1981)

1. What was Jimmy Carter's full name?

A) James Earl Carter Jr.
B) John Edward Carter
C) Joseph Edgar Carter
D) Jacob Ethan Carter

Answer: **A)**

2. In which state was Jimmy Carter born?

A) Georgia
B) Alabama
C) Mississippi
D) Texas

Answer: **A)**

3. Before becoming President, what was Jimmy Carter's profession?

A) Lawyer
B) Farmer
C) Teacher
D) Doctor

Answer: **B)**

4. Which political party did Jimmy Carter represent?

A) Republican Party
B) Democratic Party
C) Libertarian Party
D) Green Party

Answer: **B)**

5. What was Jimmy Carter's rank in the U.S. Navy?

A) Lieutenant
B) Captain
C) Admiral
D) Commander

Answer: **D)**

6. Which year did Jimmy Carter win the Nobel Peace Prize?

A) 1976
B) 1980
C) 1992
D) 2002

Answer: **B)**

7. Who was Jimmy Carter's Vice President during his presidency?

A) George H.W. Bush
B) Gerald Ford
C) Walter Mondale
D) Ronald Reagan

Answer: **C)**

8. Which international conflict was mediated by Jimmy Carter resulting in the Camp David Accords?

A) Israeli-Palestinian Conflict
B) Korean War
C) Gulf War
D) Vietnam War

Answer: **A)**

9. What was the name of Jimmy Carter's wife?

A) Barbara
B) Nancy
C) Rosalynn
D) Hillary

Answer: **C)**

10. Which university did Jimmy Carter attend for his undergraduate degree?

A) Harvard University
B) Yale University
C) Princeton University
D) Georgia Institute of Technology

Answer: **D)**

11. What was the nickname of Jimmy Carter's presidential campaign?

A) "A New Beginning"
B) "Hope and Change"
C) "Make America Great Again"
D) "Yes We Can

Answer: **A)**

12. Which government agency did Jimmy Carter create during his presidency to address energy issues?

A) Environmental Protection Agency (EPA)
B) Department of Energy (DOE)
C) National Aeronautics and Space Administration (NASA)
D) Federal Emergency Management Agency (FEMA)

Answer: **B)**

13. What was Jimmy Carter's occupation after leaving the presidency?

A) Diplomat
B) Humanitarian
C) Author
D) All of the above

Answer: **D)**

14. What significant event happened during Jimmy Carter's presidency in 1979?

A) Berlin Wall fell
B) Iran Hostage Crisis began
C) Vietnam War ended
D) Cuban Missile Crisis occurred

Answer: **B)**

15. What major piece of legislation did Jimmy Carter sign into law in 1978, aimed at reducing discrimination in housing?

A) Civil Rights Act
B) Voting Rights Act
C) Fair Housing Act
D) Equal Rights Amendment

Answer: **C)**

16. Which treaty was signed by Jimmy Carter and Soviet leader Leonid Brezhnev in 1979?

A) Treaty of Versailles
B) Strategic Arms Limitation Treaty (SALT II)
C) Treaty of Paris
D) North Atlantic Treaty

Answer: **B)**

17. What was Jimmy Carter's nickname during his presidency?

A) Honest Abe
B) Silent Cal
C) Peanut Man
D) The Great Communicator

Answer: **C)**

18. Which significant event in space exploration occurred during Jimmy Carter's presidency?

A) First Moon Landing
B) Launch of the Hubble Space Telescope
C) Apollo-Soyuz Test Project
D) Voyager 2 reaching Jupiter

Answer: **C)**

19. What was the name of Jimmy Carter's presidential campaign autobiography?

A) "A Full Life"
B) "Why Not the Best?"
C) "An Hour Before Daylight"
D) "Faith in the Future"

Answer: **B)**

20. What significant event happened on January 20, 1977, regarding Jimmy Carter?

A) Inauguration as President
B) Nobel Peace Prize Award Ceremony
C) Birthday Celebration
D) Wedding Anniversary

Answer: **A)**

21. Which religious denomination did Jimmy Carter belong to?

A) Catholic
B) Baptist
C) Methodist
D) Presbyterian

Answer: **D)**

22. What was the name of Jimmy Carter's peanut business?

A) Carter's Nuts & Co.
B) Peanut Paradise
C) Carter Peanut Farm
D) Carter's Peanuts

Answer: **C)**

23. Who was Jimmy Carter's opponent in the 1980 presidential election?

A) Ronald Reagan
B) Gerald Ford
C) George H.W. Bush
D) Richard Nixon

Answer: **A)**

24. Which country did Jimmy Carter boycott the 1980 Summer Olympics in protest of?

A) Soviet Union
B) China
C) North Korea
D) South Africa

Answer: **A)**

25. What was the name of the initiative launched by Jimmy Carter aimed at promoting energy conservation?

A) Operation Energy
B) Energy for All
C) Project Green
D) National Energy Plan

Answer: **D)**

26. Who did Jimmy Carter defeat in the 1976 presidential election to become President?

A) Gerald Ford
B) Richard Nixon
C) Ronald Reagan
D) Lyndon B. Johnson

Answer: **A)**

27. Which African country did Jimmy Carter play a significant role in mediating a peace agreement in the late 1970s?

A) Egypt
B) South Africa
C) Nigeria
D) Sudan

Answer: **A)**

28. What was the name of the space mission launched during Jimmy Carter's presidency that aimed to explore the outer solar system?

A) Apollo 11
B) Space Shuttle Challenger
C) Voyager 1
D) Skylab

Answer: **C)**

29. Which U.S. state did Jimmy Carter represent as Governor before becoming President?

A) Alabama
B) Florida
C) Georgia
D) Tennessee

Answer: **C)**

30. What was the name of the organization founded by Jimmy Carter to promote peace, human rights, and alleviate suffering worldwide?

A) Carter Foundation
B) Carter Center
C) Peace Initiative International
D) Global Harmony Organization

Answer: **B)**

Ronald Reagan (1981-1989)

1. Which political party did Ronald Reagan belong to during his presidency?

A) Democratic Party
B) Libertarian Party
C) Republican Party
D) Green Party

Answer: **C)**

2. Prior to serving as President, Ronald Reagan held which position?

A) Vice President
B) Governor of California
C) Secretary of State
D) Speaker of the House

Answer: **B)**

3. Ronald Reagan was inaugurated as the _____ President of the United States.

A) 38th
B) 39th
C) 40th
D) 41st

Answer: **C)**

4. What was Ronald Reagan's nickname, often associated with his political ideology?

A) The Gipper
B) The Great Communicator
C) The Iron Horse
D) The Maverick

Answer: **A)**

5. During Reagan's presidency, which major economic policy was implemented to reduce inflation and stimulate economic growth?

A) New Deal
B) Great Society
C) Reaganomics
D) New Frontier

Answer: **C)**

6. What was the name of Ronald Reagan's signature domestic initiative aimed at reducing federal government influence in the economy?

A) Medicare
B) Medicaid
C) Social Security Reform
D) Reagan Revolution

Answer: **D)**

7. Ronald Reagan survived an assassination attempt in 1981 by whom?

A) Lee Harvey Oswald
B) John Hinckley Jr.
C) Sirhan Sirhan
D) Timothy McVeigh

Answer: **B)**

8. What was the name of the policy initiated by Reagan aimed at countering Soviet influence and expanding U.S. military capabilities?

A) Détente
B) Strategic Arms Limitation Talks (SALT)
C) Star Wars Initiative
D) Helsinki Accords

Answer: **C)**

9. Reagan famously called for which country to "tear down this wall" during a speech in Berlin?

A) France
B) Germany
C) Soviet Union
D) United Kingdom

Answer: C)

10. What scandal during Reagan's presidency involved the covert sale of weapons to Iran in exchange for hostages and funds to support Nicaraguan Contras?

A) Watergate Scandal
B) Iran-Contra Affair
C) Teapot Dome Scandal
D) Lewinsky Scandal

Answer: B)

11. Which U.S. state did Ronald Reagan represent as Governor before becoming President?

A) Illinois
B) Texas
C) California
D) New York

Answer: C)

12. What was the name of Reagan's first wife, an actress whom he married in 1940?

A) Marilyn Monroe
B) Nancy Reagan
C) Jane Wyman
D) Betty Ford

Answer: C)

13. What famous phrase did Reagan use to describe the Soviet Union as an "evil empire"?

A) Axis of Evil
B) Iron Curtain
C) Evil Empire
D) Big Brother

Answer: **C)**

14. Ronald Reagan appointed the first female justice to the Supreme Court. What was her name?

A) Sandra Day O'Connor
B) Ruth Bader Ginsburg
C) Sonia Sotomayor
D) Elena Kagan

Answer: **A)**

15. What was the name of the tax cut legislation signed into law by Reagan in 1981, aimed at stimulating economic growth?

A) Tax Cuts and Jobs Act
B) Economic Recovery Tax Act
C) Tax Reform Act
D) Budget Reconciliation Act

Answer: **B)**

16. Which country did Reagan order to invade in 1983, citing concerns about the spread of communism in the Western Hemisphere?

A) Nicaragua
B) Cuba
C) Panama
D) Grenada

Answer: **D)**

17. What major event occurred in the Reagan presidency that helped bring an end to the Cold War?

A) Fall of the Berlin Wall
B) Cuban Missile Crisis
C) Korean War Armistice
D) Vietnam War Ceasefire

Answer: **A)**

18. Which disease did Ronald Reagan publicly battle during his presidency, raising awareness and funding for research?

A) Cancer
B) Alzheimer's disease
C) Diabetes
D) AIDS

Answer: **B)**

19. What was the name of the Soviet leader with whom Reagan negotiated arms reduction agreements during the late 1980s?

A) Nikita Khrushchev
B) Mikhail Gorbachev
C) Leonid Brezhnev
D) Joseph Stalin

Answer: **B)**

20. What was the title of Ronald Reagan's autobiography, published in 1990?

A) An American Life
B) My American Journey
C) The Reagan Diaries
D) Time for Choosing

Answer: **A)**

21. Which landmark tax reform legislation, aimed at simplifying the tax code, did Reagan sign into law in 1986?

    A) Tax Cuts and Jobs Act
    B) Economic Recovery Tax Act
    C) Tax Reform Act
    D) Budget Reconciliation Act

Answer: **C)**

22. Ronald Reagan's economic policy emphasized reducing government regulation and promoting free market principles. What term was coined to describe this policy?

    A) Reaganomics
    B) New Deal
    C) Great Society
    D) Fair Deal

Answer: **A)**

23. What was the name of the scandal involving covert arms sales to Iran and the diversion of profits to Nicaraguan Contra rebels?

    A) Watergate Scandal
    B) Iran-Contra Affair
    C) Teapot Dome Scandal
    D) Lewinsky Scandal

Answer: **B)**

24. Which major economic indicator experienced significant improvement during Reagan's presidency, contributing to his popularity?

    A) Inflation rate
    B) Unemployment rate
    C) Poverty rate
    D) National debt

Answer: **A)**

25. What was the name of Reagan's economic policy adviser and later Secretary of the Treasury, known for advocating supply-side economics?

A) Alan Greenspan
B) Milton Friedman
C) Paul Volcker
D) David Stockman

Answer: **D)**

26. During Reagan's presidency, which crisis led to a showdown between his administration and the air traffic controllers' union?

A) Oil Crisis
B) Steel Crisis
C) Air Traffic Controllers' Strike
D) Farm Crisis

Answer: **C)**

27. What was the name of the U.S. space program initiative proposed by Reagan in 1983 to protect against nuclear missile attacks?

A) Star Wars Initiative
B) Space Race
C) Apollo Program
D) Mercury Project

Answer: **A)**

28. Ronald Reagan famously quipped "Mr. Gorbachev, tear down this wall!" in a speech delivered in which city?

A) Paris
B) London
C) Berlin
D) Moscow

Answer: **C)**

29. What was the primary focus of Reagan's foreign policy approach towards the Soviet Union?

A) Détente
B) Containment
C) Diplomatic isolation
D) Regime change

Answer: **B)**

30. What was the name of the bipartisan commission established to investigate the Iran-Contra Affair during Reagan's presidency?

A) Watergate Commission
B) Iran-Contra Investigative Committee
C) Tower Commission
D) Reagan-Gorbachev Commission

Answer: **C)**

George H. W. Bush (1989 1993)

1. What was George H. W. Bush's middle name?

A) Henry
B) Herbert
C) Harold
D) Howard

Answer: **B)**

2. Which political party did George H. W. Bush represent?

A) Democratic Party
B) Republican Party
C) Libertarian Party
D) Green Party

Answer: **B)**

3. What position did George H. W. Bush hold before becoming President?

A) Vice President
B) Secretary of State
C) Governor
D) Ambassador

Answer: **A)**

4. Which state was George H. W. Bush from?

A) Texas
B) Massachusetts
C) New York
D) Connecticut

Answer: **A)**

5. What was George H. W. Bush's role in the U.S. Navy during World War II?

A) Fighter pilot
B) Submarine captain
C) Destroyer commander
D) Aircraft carrier officer

Answer: **A)**

6. Who was George H. W. Bush's Vice President during his presidency?

A) Dan Quayle
B) Ronald Reagan
C) Dick Cheney
D) Al Gore

Answer: **A)**

7. Which international conflict occurred during George H. W. Bush's presidency?

A) Persian Gulf War
B) Korean War
C) Vietnam War
D) Cold War

Answer: **A)**

8. What was George H. W. Bush's nickname during his presidency?

A) Gentleman George
B) Compassionate Conservative
C) Old Hickory
D) Bush Sr.

Answer: **D)**

9. Which major piece of environmental legislation did George H. W. Bush sign into law?

A) Clean Air Act
B) Endangered Species Act
C) Clean Water Act
D) National Environmental Policy Act

Answer: **A)**

10. What was the name of George H. W. Bush's wife?

A) Barbara
B) Nancy
C) Laura
D) Hillary

Answer: **A)**

11. Which political office did George H. W. Bush hold before becoming Vice President?

A) Governor of Texas
B) Senator from Texas
C) Congressman from Texas
D) Mayor of Houston

Answer: **C)**

12. What significant event happened in 1989, the year George H. W. Bush took office?

A) Fall of the Berlin Wall
B) Apollo 11 Moon Landing
C) Challenger Space Shuttle disaster
D) Exxon Valdez oil spill

Answer: **A)**

13. Which economic term did George H. W. Bush famously use to describe an economic downturn during his presidency?

A) Recession
B) Inflation
C) Stagflation
D) Depression

Answer: **A)**

14. What was the name of George H. W. Bush's presidential campaign slogan in 1988?

A) "A Thousand Points of Light"
B) "Read My Lips: No New Taxes"
C) "Morning in America"
D) "Hope and Change"

Answer: **B)**

15. Which country did George H. W. Bush send troops to liberate during his presidency?

A) Kuwait
B) Iraq
C) Afghanistan
D) Panama

Answer: **A)**

16. Who was George H. W. Bush's opponent in the 1992 presidential election?

A) Bill Clinton
B) Ronald Reagan
C) Ross Perot
D) Bob Dole

Answer: **A)**

17. What was the name of the international coalition assembled by George H. W. Bush to oppose Iraqi aggression in the Persian Gulf War?

A) Coalition of the Willing
B) North Atlantic Treaty Organization (NATO)
C) United Nations Security Council
D) Coalition of Desert Storm

Answer: **D)**

18. Which economic agreement did George H. W. Bush negotiate with Canada and Mexico, signed in 1992?

A) North American Free Trade Agreement (NAFTA)
B) Trans-Pacific Partnership (TPP)
C) General Agreement on Tariffs and Trade (GATT)
D) World Trade Organization (WTO)

Answer: **A)**

19. What was the name of George H. W. Bush's son who later became President?

A) George W. Bush
B) Jeb Bush
C) Neil Bush
D) Marvin Bush

Answer: **A)**

20. Which major international summit did George H. W. Bush host in 1990 to discuss global environmental issues?

A) Earth Summit
B) G7 Summit
C) Rio Summit
D) Kyoto Protocol Summit

Answer: **A)**

Absolutely!

More Quiz Questions on George H. W. Bush

21. Which war did George H. W. Bush famously describe as "the mother of all battles"?

A) Persian Gulf War
B) Vietnam War
C) Korean War
D) World War II

Answer: **A)**

22. What was the name of George H. W. Bush's vice president during his second term in office?

A) Dick Cheney
B) Dan Quayle
C) Al Gore
D) George W. Bush

Answer: **B)**

23. What was the name of the domestic policy initiative introduced by George H. W. Bush aimed at promoting volunteerism?

A) Operation Compassion
B) Volunteer America
C) Points of Light
D) Community Action Network

Answer: **C)**

24. Which country was invaded by the United States under George H. W. Bush's presidency in 1989 to oust Manuel Noriega?

A) Panama
B) Nicaragua
C) Cuba
D) Grenada

Answer: **A)**

25. What was the name of the economic plan proposed by George H. W. Bush during his presidential campaign in 1988?

A) Reaganomics
B) Trickle-down Economics
C) Bush Boom
D) Economic Recovery Plan

Answer: **D)**

26. Which major event did George H. W. Bush attend representing the U.S. shortly after taking office in 1989?

A) Olympics in Seoul
B) UN Climate Change Conference
C) NATO Summit in Brussels
D) G7 Summit in Paris

Answer: **A)**

27. What was the name of the scandal involving the sale of arms to Iran and the diversion of proceeds to fund Nicaraguan rebels during George H. W. Bush's presidency?

A) Watergate Scandal
B) Iran-Contra Affair
C) Whitewater Controversy
D) Lewinsky Scandal

Answer: **B)**

28. Which space program did George H. W. Bush announce during his presidency, aimed at sending humans to Mars?

A) Apollo Program
B) Mars Exploration Program
C) Space Shuttle Program
D) Space Exploration Initiative

Answer: **D)**

29. What was the name of the agreement signed by George H. W. Bush and Soviet leader Mikhail Gorbachev in 1991, reducing both countries' nuclear arsenals?

A) START I Treaty
B) INF Treaty
C) SALT II Treaty
D) Helsinki Accords

Answer: **A)**

30. Which Supreme Court Justice did George H. W. Bush nominate to the bench, who later became the first African American Justice on the Court?

A) Sandra Day O'Connor
B) Ruth Bader Ginsburg
C) Clarence Thomas
D) Antonin Scalia

Answer: **C)**

Bill Clinton (1993-2001)

1. What was Bill Clinton's full name?

A) William Jefferson Clinton
B) John William Clinton
C) Robert William Clinton
D) William Henry Clinton

Answer: **A)**

2. In which state was Bill Clinton born?

A) Arkansas
B) New York
C) Illinois
D) Texas

Answer: **A)**

3. Which political party did Bill Clinton represent?

A) Republican Party
B) Democratic Party
C) Libertarian Party
D) Green Party

Answer: **B)**

4. What position did Bill Clinton hold before becoming President?

A) Governor
B) Senator
C) Mayor
D) Secretary of State

Answer: **A)**

5. Who was Bill Clinton's Vice President during his presidency?

A) Al Gore
B) Joe Biden
C) Dick Cheney
D) George H.W. Bush

Answer: **A)**

6. Which international conflict occurred during Bill Clinton's presidency?

A) Gulf War
B) Korean War
C) Vietnam War
D) Bosnian War

Answer: **D)**

7. What was the nickname of Bill Clinton's economic plan that aimed to balance the federal budget?

A) New Deal
B) Great Society
C) New Covenant
D) Economic Recovery Plan

Answer: **C)**

8. What was the name of the health care reform plan proposed by Bill Clinton's administration?

A) Healthy America Initiative
B) Obamacare
C) Medicare for All
D) Hillarycare

Answer: **D)**

9. Who did Bill Clinton defeat in the 1992 presidential election?

A) George H.W. Bush
B) Ronald Reagan
C) Bob Dole
D) Ross Perot

Answer: **A)**

10. Which major trade agreement did Bill Clinton sign into law, reducing trade barriers among the United States, Canada, and Mexico?

A) NAFTA
B) TPP
C) GATT
D) WTO

Answer: **A)**

11. What was the name of the scandal involving Bill Clinton's affair with White House intern Monica Lewinsky?

A) Watergate Scandal
B) Iran-Contra Affair
C) Whitewater Controversy
D) Lewinsky Scandal

Answer: **D)**

12. What was the name of Bill Clinton's wife, who later became a prominent political figure?

A) Barbara
B) Nancy
C) Laura
D) Hillary

Answer: **D)**

13. Which major terrorist attack occurred during Bill Clinton's presidency in 1993?

A) 9/11
B) Oklahoma City bombing
C) World Trade Center bombing
D) Embassy bombings in Africa

Answer: **C)**

14. What was the name of Bill Clinton's economic plan that aimed to stimulate job growth and reduce the deficit?

A) Economic Recovery Act
B) Jobs and Growth Initiative
C) Economic Opportunity Act
D) Economic Growth and Tax Relief Reconciliation Act

Answer: **C)**

15. What was the name of the welfare reform legislation signed by Bill Clinton in 1996?

A) Welfare to Work Act
B) Social Security Act
C) Medicare Act
D) Medicaid Expansion Act

Answer: **A)**

16. Which government agency did Bill Clinton create to address the threat of domestic terrorism?

A) Department of Homeland Security
B) Federal Bureau of Investigation (FBI)
C) Central Intelligence Agency (CIA)
D) Department of Justice

Answer: **A)**

17. What was the name of the international peace agreement brokered by Bill Clinton between Israel and the Palestine Liberation Organization (PLO)?

A) Oslo Accords
B) Camp David Accords
C) Dayton Accords
D) Madrid Peace Conference

Answer: **A)**

18. What was the name of the initiative launched by Bill Clinton to encourage young people to participate in community service?

A) Youth Corps
B) AmeriCorps
C) Serve America
D) Volunteers of America

Answer: **B)**

19. Which foreign leader did Bill Clinton negotiate with to normalize diplomatic relations between the United States and Vietnam?

A) Fidel Castro
B) Kim Jong-il
C) Mikhail Gorbachev
D) Ho Chi Minh

Answer: **A)**

20. What was the name of the agreement signed by Bill Clinton and Russian President Boris Yeltsin, aimed at reducing both countries' nuclear arsenals?

A) START I Treaty
B) INF Treaty
C) SALT II Treaty
D) Helsinki Accords

Answer: **A)**

21. What was the name of the federal program initiated by Bill Clinton aimed at providing health coverage to low-income children?

A) Medicare
B) Medicaid
C) SCHIP
D) Obamacare

Answer: **C)**

22. Which country did Bill Clinton authorize military intervention in to stop ethnic cleansing during the Balkan Wars?

A) Bosnia
B) Serbia
C) Croatia
D) Kosovo

Answer: **D)**

23. What was the name of Bill Clinton's economic plan that aimed to stimulate economic growth through tax cuts?

A) Economic Growth and Tax Relief Reconciliation Act
B) Economic Recovery Act
C) Jobs and Growth Initiative
D) Economic Freedom Plan

Answer: **A)**

24. Which Supreme Court Justice did Bill Clinton nominate, who was confirmed despite a contentious confirmation process?

A) Ruth Bader Ginsburg
B) Antonin Scalia
C) Clarence Thomas
D) Sonia Sotomayor

Answer: A)

25. What was the name of the military operation led by Bill Clinton aimed at capturing Somali warlords and providing humanitarian relief?

A) Operation Desert Storm
B) Operation Restore Hope
C) Operation Enduring Freedom
D) Operation Iraqi Freedom

Answer: **B)**

26. Which country did Bill Clinton sign a historic peace agreement with in 1994, ending decades of conflict?

A) Israel
B) South Africa
C) North Korea
D) Ireland

Answer: **D)**

27. What was the name of the budget bill passed by Bill Clinton in 1993, which aimed to reduce the federal deficit?

A) Balanced Budget Act
B) Budget Control Act
C) Omnibus Budget Reconciliation Act
D) Budget Reconciliation Act

Answer: **C)**

28. What was the name of the scandal involving illegal fundraising for Bill Clinton's reelection campaign?

A) Whitewater Scandal
B) Travelgate Scandal
C) Chinagate Scandal
D) Filegate Scandal

Answer: C)

29. Which trade agreement did Bill Clinton negotiate and sign into law, reducing trade barriers among the United States, Canada, and Mexico?

A) NAFTA
B) GATT
C) TPP
D) WTO

Answer: A)

30. What was the name of the 1994 legislation signed by Bill Clinton that banned assault weapons in the United States?

A) Brady Bill
B) Crime Bill
C) Gun Control Act
D) Assault Weapons Ban

Answer: D)

George W. Bush (2001-2009)

1. What is George W. Bush's full name?

A) George William Bush
B) George Walker Bush
C) George Washington Bush
D) George Wesley Bush

Answer: B)

2. In which state was George W. Bush born?

A) New York
B) California
C) Texas
D) Florida

Answer: **C)**

3. Which political party did George W. Bush represent?

A) Democratic Party
B) Republican Party
C) Libertarian Party
D) Green Party

Answer: **B)**

4. What position did George W. Bush hold before becoming President?

A) Governor
B) Senator
C) Congressman
D) Secretary of State

Answer: **A)**

5. Who was George W. Bush's Vice President during his presidency?

A) Dick Cheney
B) Joe Biden
C) Al Gore
D) Mike Pence

Answer: **A)**

6. Which major terrorist attack occurred during George W. Bush's presidency?

A) 9/11
B) Oklahoma City bombing
C) World Trade Center bombing
D) Embassy bombings in Africa

Answer: **A)**

7. What was the name of the military operation initiated by George W. Bush in response to the 9/11 attacks?

A) Operation Enduring Freedom
B) Operation Iraqi Freedom
C) Operation Desert Storm
D) Operation Infinite Reach

Answer: **A)**

8. What was the name of the controversial detention facility established by George W. Bush for suspected terrorists?

A) Guantanamo Bay
B) Abu Ghraib
C) Alcatraz Island
D) Rikers Island

Answer: **A)**

9. Who did George W. Bush defeat in the 2000 presidential election?

A) Al Gore
B) Bill Clinton
C) John Kerry
D) George H.W. Bush

Answer: **A)**

10. Which country did George W. Bush invade in 2003, leading to a prolonged conflict?

A) Afghanistan
B) Iraq
C) Syria
D) Iran

Answer: **B)**

11. What was the name of the education reform bill signed into law by George W. Bush in 2002?

A) No Child Left Behind Act
B) Every Student Succeeds Act
C) Race to the Top Act
D) Education for All Act

Answer: **A)**

12. Which major hurricane devastated the Gulf Coast during George W. Bush's presidency in 2005?

A) Hurricane Sandy
B) Hurricane Katrina
C) Hurricane Rita
D) Hurricane Andrew

Answer: **B)**

13. What was the name of George W. Bush's domestic policy initiative aimed at providing prescription drug coverage to seniors?

A) Medicaid Expansion
B) Medicare Part D
C) Affordable Care Act
D) Health Insurance Portability and Accountability Act (HIPAA)

Answer: **B)**

14. Which major financial crisis occurred during George W. Bush's presidency in 2008?

A) Dot-com Bubble Burst
B) Savings and Loan Crisis
C) Subprime Mortgage Crisis
D) Great Depression

Answer: **C)**

15. What was the name of the doctrine introduced by George W. Bush that stated the United States would preemptively strike against perceived threats?

A) Monroe Doctrine
B) Bush Doctrine
C) Truman Doctrine
D) Eisenhower Doctrine

Answer: **B)**

16. What was the name of the tax cut legislation signed into law by George W. Bush in 2001?

A) Tax Relief Act
B) Taxpayer Protection Act
C) Economic Growth and Tax Relief Reconciliation Act
D) Tax Fairness Act

Answer: **C)**

17. What was the name of the controversial interrogation technique used by the CIA during George W. Bush's presidency?

A) Waterboarding
B) Sleep deprivation
C) Solitary confinement
D) Sensory deprivation

Answer: **A)**

18. Which major U.S. city experienced a terrorist attack in 2001?

A) Los Angeles
B) Washington D.C.
C) New York City
D) Chicago

Answer: **C)**

19. What was the name of the federal program initiated by George W. Bush aimed at combating the spread of HIV/AIDS in Africa?

A) PEPFAR
B) CDC
C) WHO
D) UNAIDS

Answer: **A)**

20. What was the name of the international coalition assembled by George W. Bush to support the War on Terror?

A) Coalition of the Willing
B) North Atlantic Treaty Organization (NATO)
C) United Nations Security Council
D) Warsaw Pact

Answer: **A)**

Barack Obama (2009-2017)

1. What is Barack Obama's full name?

A) Barack Hussein Obama Jr.
B) Barack Malik Obama
C) Barack Obama Sr.
D) Barack Hussein Obama II

Answer: **A)**

2. In which state was Barack Obama born?

A) Hawaii
B) Illinois
C) New York
D) California

Answer: **A)**

3. Which political party did Barack Obama represent?

A) Republican Party
B) Democratic Party
C) Libertarian Party
D) Green Party

Answer: **B)**

4. What position did Barack Obama hold before becoming President?

A) Governor
B) Senator
C) Congressman
D) Mayor

Answer: **B)**

5. Who was Barack Obama's Vice President during his presidency?

A) Joe Biden
B) Hillary Clinton
C) Al Gore
D) John McCain

Answer: **A)**

6. Which major healthcare reform legislation did Barack Obama sign into law in 2010?

A) Affordable Care Act
B) Medicare for All Act
C) Medicaid Expansion Act
D) Health Insurance Portability and Accountability Act (HIPAA)

Answer: **A)**

7. What was the name of the economic stimulus package signed into law by Barack Obama in response to the 2008 financial crisis?

A) American Recovery and Reinvestment Act
B) Economic Growth and Tax Relief Reconciliation Act
C) Jobs and Growth Tax Relief Reconciliation Act
D) Economic Opportunity Act

Answer: **A)**

8. What was the name of the mission that resulted in the death of Osama bin Laden during Barack Obama's presidency?

A) Operation Enduring Freedom
B) Operation Iraqi Freedom
C) Operation Neptune Spear
D) Operation Inherent Resolve

Answer: **C)**

9. Who did Barack Obama defeat in the 2008 presidential election?

A) John McCain
B) Mitt Romney
C) George W. Bush
D) Donald Trump

Answer: **A)**

10. What was the name of the international agreement aimed at combating climate change, negotiated by Barack Obama?

A) Paris Agreement
B) Kyoto Protocol
C) Copenhagen Accord
D) Montreal Protocol

Answer: **A)**

11. What was the name of the federal program initiated by Barack Obama aimed at providing financial assistance to homeowners facing foreclosure?

A) Housing Recovery Program
B) Home Affordable Modification Program (HAMP)
C) Mortgage Assistance Initiative
D) Foreclosure Prevention Act

Answer: **B)**

12. Which major piece of financial regulation legislation did Barack Obama sign into law in 2010?

A) Dodd-Frank Wall Street Reform and Consumer Protection Act
B) Glass-Steagall Act
C) Sarbanes-Oxley Act
D) Gramm-Leach-Bliley Act

Answer: **A)**

13. What was the name of the controversial immigration policy implemented by Barack Obama aimed at deferring deportation for certain undocumented immigrants brought to the U.S. as children?

A) Dream Act
B) DACA (Deferred Action for Childhood Arrivals)
C) Comprehensive Immigration Reform Act
D) Secure Fence Act

Answer: **B)**

301

14. Which country did Barack Obama normalize diplomatic relations with in 2015 after decades of hostility?

A) Iran
B) Cuba
C) North Korea
D) Venezuela

Answer: **B)**

15. What was the name of the federal program initiated by Barack Obama aimed at investing in infrastructure projects to stimulate economic growth and create jobs?

A) New Deal
B) Economic Stimulus Plan
C) American Jobs Act
D) Infrastructure Investment Program

Answer: **C)**

16. Which major trade agreement negotiated by Barack Obama aimed to reduce trade barriers among the United States and Pacific Rim countries?

A) NAFTA
B) TPP (Trans-Pacific Partnership)
C) TTIP (Transatlantic Trade and Investment Partnership)
D) USMCA (United States-Mexico-Canada Agreement)

Answer: **B)**

17. What was the name of the federal program initiated by Barack Obama aimed at providing student loan forgiveness for individuals working in public service jobs?

A) Student Loan Relief Program
B) Public Service Loan Forgiveness Program
C) Education Opportunity Act
D) College Affordability Act

Answer: **B)**

18. Which U.S. military operation authorized by Barack Obama aimed to capture or kill Osama bin Laden in Pakistan?

A) Operation Enduring Freedom
B) Operation Iraqi Freedom
C) Operation Neptune Spear
D) Operation Inherent Resolve

Answer: **C)**

19. What was the name of the international agreement aimed at preventing Iran from developing nuclear weapons, negotiated by Barack Obama?

A) Iran Nuclear Deal
B) Tehran Accord
C) Iran Nuclear Non-Proliferation Agreement
D) Iran Sanctions Relief Act

Answer: **A)**

20. Which major environmental regulation did Barack Obama implement to reduce carbon emissions from power plants?

A) Clean Power Plan
B) Carbon Emission Reduction Act
C) Environmental Protection Act
D) Climate Change Mitigation Plan

Answer: **A)**

21. What was the name of the federal program initiated by Barack Obama aimed at providing assistance to struggling homeowners to refinance their mortgages?

A) Housing Recovery Plan
B) Mortgage Relief Program
C) Home Affordable Refinance Program (HARP)
D) Foreclosure Prevention Initiative

Answer: **C)**

22. Which major U.S. healthcare reform legislation did Barack Obama sign into law in 2010, aiming to increase access to healthcare and regulate insurance practices?

A) Medicare for All Act
B) Medicaid Expansion Act
C) Affordable Care Act
D) Healthcare Equality Act

Answer: C)

23. What was the name of the federal program initiated by Barack Obama aimed at providing financial assistance to states and local governments to prevent layoffs of teachers and first responders?

A) Jobs for America Act
B) Teacher and First Responder Relief Fund
C) State and Local Government Assistance Program
D) Education Jobs Fund

Answer: D)

24. Which major financial institution did Barack Obama oversee the government bailout of during the 2008 financial crisis?

A) JPMorgan Chase
B) Bank of America
C) Citigroup
D) Goldman Sachs

Answer: C)

25. What was the name of the federal program initiated by Barack Obama aimed at providing financial assistance to automakers during the 2008 financial crisis?

A) Auto Industry Recovery Program
B) Automotive Bailout Initiative
C) Detroit Recovery Fund
D) Car Manufacturer Assistance Plan

Answer: A)

26. Which U.S. military operation authorized by Barack Obama aimed to eliminate the threat posed by ISIS in Iraq and Syria?

A) Operation Enduring Freedom
B) Operation Iraqi Freedom
C) Operation Inherent Resolve
D) Operation Freedom's Sentinel

Answer: **C)**

27. What was the name of the federal program initiated by Barack Obama aimed at providing broadband internet access to underserved communities?

A) Connect America Program
B) Digital Divide Initiative
C) Broadband Expansion Project
D) Internet for All Program

Answer: **A)**

28. Which major trade agreement negotiated by Barack Obama aimed to reduce trade barriers among the United States, Canada, and Mexico?

A) NAFTA
B) TPP (Trans-Pacific Partnership)
C) TTIP (Transatlantic Trade and Investment Partnership)
D) USMCA (United States-Mexico-Canada Agreement)

Answer: **D)**

29. What was the name of the federal program initiated by Barack Obama aimed at providing financial assistance to struggling homeowners to modify their mortgages and avoid foreclosure?

A) Home Affordable Modification Program (HAMP)
B) Foreclosure Prevention Initiative
C) Mortgage Relief Program
D) Housing Recovery Plan

Answer: **A)**

30. Which major international agreement negotiated by Barack Obama aimed to limit global warming by reducing greenhouse gas emissions?

A) Paris Agreement
B) Kyoto Protocol
C) Copenhagen Accord
D) Montreal Protocol

Answer: **A)**

Donald Trump (2017-2021)

1. What is Donald Trump's middle name?

A) John
B) James
C) Joseph
D) Jules

Answer: **B)**

2. In which state was Donald Trump born?

A) New York
B) Florida
C) New Jersey
D) Pennsylvania

Answer: **A)**

3. Which political party did Donald Trump represent during his presidency?

A) Democratic Party
B) Republican Party
C) Libertarian Party
D) Green Party

Answer: **B)**

4. What position did Donald Trump hold before becoming President?

A) Governor
B) Senator
C) Congressman
D) Businessman

Answer: **D)**

5. Who was Donald Trump's Vice President during his presidency?

A) Joe Biden
B) Mike Pence
C) Hillary Clinton
D) Barack Obama

Answer: **B)**

6. Which major tax reform legislation did Donald Trump sign into law in 2017?

A) Tax Cuts and Jobs Act
B) Taxpayer Protection Act
C) Tax Fairness Act
D) Tax Relief and Economic Growth Act

Answer: **A)**

7. What was the name of the controversial immigration policy implemented by Donald Trump aimed at restricting entry to the U.S. from certain countries?

A) Safe Travel Ban
B) Refugee Ban
C) Border Security Act
D) Travel Ban

Answer: **D)**

8. What was the name of the diplomatic initiative led by Donald Trump aimed at achieving peace between Israel and Arab countries?

A) Oslo Accords
B) Camp David Accords
C) Abraham Accords
D) Madrid Peace Conference

Answer: **C)**

9. Who did Donald Trump defeat in the 2016 presidential election?

A) Hillary Clinton
B) Joe Biden
C) Bernie Sanders
D) Ted Cruz

Answer: **A)**

10. Which major international trade agreement did Donald Trump withdraw the United States from?

A) NAFTA
B) TPP (Trans-Pacific Partnership)
C) TTIP (Transatlantic Trade and Investment Partnership)
D) USMCA (United States-Mexico-Canada Agreement)

Answer: **B)**

11. What was the name of the federal program initiated by Donald Trump aimed at reducing illegal immigration by constructing a barrier along the U.S.-Mexico border?

A) Secure Border Initiative
B) Border Security Act
C) Border Wall Project
D) Border Security and Immigration Enforcement Fund

Answer: **A)**

12. Which major healthcare reform legislation did Donald Trump and the Republican-controlled Congress attempt to repeal and replace?

A) Affordable Care Act
B) Medicaid Expansion Act
C) Medicare for All Act
D) Children's Health Insurance Program (CHIP)

Answer: **A)**

13. What was the name of the summit between Donald Trump and North Korean leader Kim Jong-un in 2018?

A) Singapore Summit
B) Hanoi Summit
C) Pyongyang Summit
D) Seoul Summit

Answer: **A)**

14. What was the name of the federal program initiated by Donald Trump aimed at revitalizing urban communities through tax incentives for investment?

A) Urban Renewal Initiative
B) Opportunity Zone Program
C) Inner City Revitalization Act
D) Urban Development Fund

Answer: **B)**

15. Which major environmental regulation did Donald Trump roll back to loosen restrictions on coal-fired power plants?

A) Clean Power Plan
B) Carbon Emission Reduction Act
C) Environmental Protection Act
D) Climate Change Mitigation Plan

Answer: **A)**

16. What was the name of the federal program initiated by Donald Trump aimed at increasing military spending and modernizing the armed forces?

A) Military Modernization Initiative
B) Defense Enhancement Program
C) Military Strength Act
D) National Defense Authorization Act

Answer: **D)**

17. Which major international agreement did Donald Trump withdraw the United States from, citing concerns about unfair trade practices?

A) Paris Agreement
B) NAFTA
C) TPP (Trans-Pacific Partnership)
D) WTO (World Trade Organization)

Answer: **D)**

18. What was the name of the federal program initiated by Donald Trump aimed at promoting job creation and economic growth through tax incentives for businesses?

A) American Jobs Act
B) Economic Stimulus Plan
C) Tax Relief and Job Creation Act
D) Tax Cuts and Jobs Act

Answer: **D)**

19. Which major terrorist leader was killed in a U.S. military operation authorized by Donald Trump in 2019?

A) Osama bin Laden
B) Abu Bakr al-Baghdadi
C) Ayman al-Zawahiri
D) Khalid Sheikh Mohammed

Answer: **B)**

20. What was the name of the federal program initiated by Donald Trump aimed at providing financial assistance to farmers affected by tariffs and trade disputes?

A) Agricultural Relief Program
B) Farm Subsidy Initiative
C) Trade Adjustment Assistance Program
D) Market Facilitation Program

Answer: **D)**

21. What was the name of the federal program initiated by Donald Trump aimed at providing financial assistance to businesses and individuals affected by the COVID-19 pandemic?

A) CARES Act
B) Pandemic Relief Program
C) Economic Stimulus Package
D) Recovery and Assistance Fund

Answer: **A)**

22. Which major international agreement did Donald Trump withdraw the United States from, citing concerns about Iran's nuclear program?

A) Paris Agreement
B) NAFTA
C) TPP (Trans-Pacific Partnership)
D) Iran Nuclear Deal

Answer: **D)**

23. What was the name of the federal program initiated by Donald Trump aimed at reducing prescription drug prices by promoting price transparency and competition?

A) Prescription Drug Affordability Act
B) Pharmaceutical Price Reduction Initiative
C) Drug Pricing Executive Order
D) Prescription Drug Plan

Answer: **C)**

24. Which major international organization did Donald Trump criticize and threaten to withdraw funding from, accusing it of bias against Israel?

A) United Nations (UN)
B) World Health Organization (WHO)
C) International Monetary Fund (IMF)
D) World Trade Organization (WTO)

Answer: A)

25. What was the name of the federal program initiated by Donald Trump aimed at reducing opioid addiction and overdose deaths?

A) Opioid Crisis Response Program
B) Drug Abuse Prevention Act
C) Opioid Addiction Treatment Initiative
D) Opioid Epidemic Response Plan

Answer: A)

26. Which major diplomatic initiative did Donald Trump undertake, resulting in a series of agreements between Israel and several Arab countries?

A) Oslo Accords
B) Camp David Accords
C) Abraham Accords
D) Tehran Accords

Answer: C)

27. What was the name of the federal program initiated by Donald Trump aimed at providing financial assistance to small businesses affected by the COVID-19 pandemic?

A) Small Business Relief Program
B) Paycheck Protection Program (PPP)
C) Economic Recovery Fund
D) Business Assistance Initiative

Answer: B)

28. Which major international trade agreement did Donald Trump renegotiate to replace NAFTA?

A) TPP (Trans-Pacific Partnership)
B) USMCA (United States-Mexico-Canada Agreement)
C) TTIP (Transatlantic Trade and Investment Partnership)
D) WTO (World Trade Organization)

Answer: **B)**

29. What was the name of the federal program initiated by Donald Trump aimed at increasing investment in infrastructure projects across the United States?

A) Infrastructure Investment Plan
B) Build Back Better Initiative
C) National Infrastructure Program
D) Infrastructure Investment and Jobs Act

Answer: **D)**

30. Which major U.S. city experienced widespread protests and civil unrest during Donald Trump's presidency following the killing of George Floyd by police officers?

A) New York City
B) Los Angeles
C) Chicago
D) Minneapolis

Answer: **D)**

31. What was the name of the federal program initiated by Donald Trump aimed at restricting travel and immigration from several predominantly Muslim countries?

A) Safe Travel Initiative
B) Refugee Ban
C) Border Security Act
D) Travel Ban

Answer: **D)**

32. Which major international agreement did Donald Trump withdraw the United States from, citing concerns about climate change and unfair economic burdens?

A) Paris Agreement
B) Kyoto Protocol
C) Copenhagen Accord
D) Montreal Protocol

Answer: **A)**

33. What was the name of the federal program initiated by Donald Trump aimed at supporting American farmers affected by retaliatory tariffs imposed by other countries?

A) Farm Aid Program
B) Agricultural Relief Initiative
C) Trade Adjustment Assistance Program
D) Market Facilitation Program

Answer: **D)**

34. Which major healthcare reform legislation did Donald Trump and the Republican-controlled Congress attempt to repeal and replace?

A) Affordable Care Act
B) Medicaid Expansion Act
C) Medicare for All Act
D) Children's Health Insurance Program (CHIP)

Answer: **A)**

35. What was the name of the federal program initiated by Donald Trump aimed at reducing regulations on businesses to promote economic growth?

A) Business Deregulation Initiative
B) Economic Freedom Program
C) Regulatory Relief for Businesses Act
D) Cutting Red Tape Initiative

Answer: **A)**

36. Which major international organization did Donald Trump announce the withdrawal of the United States from, citing concerns about unfair trade practices and sovereignty?

    A) United Nations (UN)
    B) World Health Organization (WHO)
    C) North Atlantic Treaty Organization (NATO)
    D) World Trade Organization (WTO)

Answer: **D)**

37. What was the name of the federal program initiated by Donald Trump aimed at reducing drug prices by allowing importation of prescription drugs from other countries?

    A) Prescription Drug Importation Program
    B) Drug Price Competition Initiative
    C) Safe Drug Reimportation Plan
    D) Prescription Drug Importation Act

Answer: **A)**

38. Which major immigration policy did Donald Trump implement to end the Deferred Action for Childhood Arrivals (DACA) program?

    A) Dream Act Repeal
    B) DACA Termination Order
    C) Executive Action on Immigration
    D) Immigration Reform Act

Answer: **B)**

39. What was the name of the federal program initiated by Donald Trump aimed at reducing prescription drug prices by promoting competition and negotiation?

    A) Prescription Drug Affordability Act
    B) Drug Pricing Executive Order
    C) Pharmaceutical Price Reduction Initiative
    D) Prescription Drug Plan

Answer: **B)**

40. Which major international agreement did Donald Trump withdraw the United States from, citing concerns about national sovereignty and immigration control?

A) Paris Agreement
B) NAFTA
C) TPP (Trans-Pacific Partnership)
D) UN Refugee Compact

Answer: **D)**

Joe Biden (2021–2025)

1. What is Joe Biden's middle name?

A) Robinette
B) Robert
C) Randolph
D) Ronald

Answer: **A)**

2. In which state was Joe Biden born?

A) Pennsylvania
B) Delaware
C) New York
D) New Jersey

Answer: **B)**

3. Which political party does Joe Biden represent?

A) Republican Party
B) Democratic Party
C) Libertarian Party
D) Green Party

Answer: **B)**

4. What position did Joe Biden hold before becoming President?

A) Governor
B) Senator
C) Congressman
D) Vice President

Answer: **D)**

5. Who was Joe Biden's Vice President during his presidency?

A) Kamala Harris
B) Barack Obama
C) Hillary Clinton
D) Mike Pence

Answer: **A)**

6. Which major healthcare reform legislation did Joe Biden support during his time as Vice President?

A) Affordable Care Act
B) Medicare for All Act
C) Medicaid Expansion Act
D) CHIP (Children's Health Insurance Program)

Answer: **A)**

7. What was the name of the federal program initiated by Joe Biden aimed at providing financial assistance to Americans during the COVID-19 pandemic?

A) CARES Act
B) American Rescue Plan
C) Economic Stimulus Package
D) Relief for Americans Act

Answer: **B)**

8. Which major infrastructure proposal did Joe Biden announce with the aim of rebuilding American infrastructure and creating jobs?

    A) Build Back Better Plan
    B) American Jobs Plan
    C) Infrastructure Investment Initiative
    D) Economic Recovery Program

Answer: **B)**

9. Who did Joe Biden defeat in the 2020 presidential election?

    A) Donald Trump
    B) Bernie Sanders
    C) Hillary Clinton
    D) Mike Pence

Answer: **A)**

10. What was the name of the international climate agreement that Joe Biden recommitted the United States to after taking office?

    A) Kyoto Protocol
    B) Copenhagen Accord
    C) Paris Agreement
    D) Montreal Protocol

Answer: **C)**

11. Which major tax credit did Joe Biden expand as part of his economic relief measures?

    A) Child Tax Credit
    B) Earned Income Tax Credit
    C) Capital Gains Tax Credit
    D) Corporate Tax Credit

Answer: **A)**

12. What was the name of the federal program initiated by Joe Biden aimed at accelerating COVID-19 vaccine distribution?

A) Operation Warp Speed
B) Vaccinate America Initiative
C) Operation Enduring Freedom
D) Vaccine Equity Task Force

Answer: **D)**

13. Which major immigration policy did Joe Biden reverse, allowing Deferred Action for Childhood Arrivals (DACA) recipients to stay in the U.S.?

A) Dream Act Repeal
B) DACA Termination Order
C) Executive Action on Immigration
D) Immigration Reform Act

Answer: **B)**

14. What was the name of the federal program initiated by Joe Biden aimed at providing financial assistance to state and local governments during the COVID-19 pandemic?

A) State and Local Relief Fund
B) Municipal Aid Program
C) CARES Act Extension
D) American Rescue Plan

Answer: **D)**

15. Which major international organization did Joe Biden announce the return of the United States to, reversing the withdrawal initiated by the previous administration?

A) United Nations (UN)
B) World Health Organization (WHO)
C) North Atlantic Treaty Organization (NATO)
D) World Trade Organization (WTO)

Answer: **B)**

16. What was the name of the federal program initiated by Joe Biden aimed at expanding access to healthcare and lowering costs?

A) Medicare for All Act
B) Public Option Program
C) Affordable Care Enhancement Act
D) Health Security Plan

Answer: **C)**

17. Which major federal agency did Joe Biden appoint the first female director to lead?

A) Federal Bureau of Investigation (FBI)
B) Central Intelligence Agency (CIA)
C) Department of Homeland Security (DHS)
D) National Aeronautics and Space Administration (NASA)

Answer: **B)**

18. What was the name of the federal program initiated by Joe Biden aimed at expanding access to COVID-19 testing and treatment for uninsured Americans?

A) COVID-19 Relief Fund
B) Pandemic Response Program
C) Uninsured Americans Coverage Initiative
D) COVID-19 Uninsured Program

Answer: **D)**

19. What was the name of the major legislative proposal by Joe Biden aimed at reforming the U.S. immigration system and providing a pathway to citizenship for undocumented immigrants?

A) Immigration Reform Act
B) Dream Act
C) Secure Border Initiative
D) Comprehensive Immigration Reform Bill

Answer: **A)**

20. Which executive order did Joe Biden issue on his first day in office to rejoin the Paris Agreement on climate change?

A) Executive Order 13990
B) Executive Order 14005
C) Executive Order 13768
D) Executive Order 13848

Answer: **B)**

21. What was the name of the federal program initiated by Joe Biden aimed at providing financial assistance to renters affected by the COVID-19 pandemic?

A) Rental Relief Program
B) Housing Assistance Initiative
C) Eviction Moratorium Extension
D) Emergency Rental Assistance Program

Answer: **D)**

22. Which major international agreement did Joe Biden rejoin, aimed at preventing Iran from developing nuclear weapons?

A) Paris Agreement
B) JCPOA (Joint Comprehensive Plan of Action)
C) NAFTA (North American Free Trade Agreement)
D) TPP (Trans-Pacific Partnership)

Answer: **B)**

23. What was the name of the federal program initiated by Joe Biden aimed at increasing access to affordable childcare and expanding the childcare workforce?

A) Childcare Expansion Act
B) Universal Childcare Program
C) American Families Plan
D) Early Childhood Development Initiative

Answer: **C)**

24. Which major international summit did Joe Biden attend in June 2021, where he met with leaders of G7 nations?

A) G20 Summit
B) NATO Summit
C) UN General Assembly
D) G7 Summit

Answer: **D)**

25. What was the name of the federal program initiated by Joe Biden aimed at providing financial assistance to small businesses affected by the COVID-19 pandemic?

A) Small Business Recovery Fund
B) Paycheck Protection Program (PPP)
C) Economic Injury Disaster Loan (EIDL) Program
D) Restaurant Revitalization Fund

Answer: **D)**

26. Which major federal agency did Joe Biden appoint the first Native American cabinet secretary to lead?

A) Department of the Interior
B) Department of Health and Human Services
C) Environmental Protection Agency
D) Department of Education

Answer: **A)**

27. What was the name of the federal program initiated by Joe Biden aimed at increasing access to broadband internet in rural and underserved areas?

A) Digital Connectivity Initiative
B) Rural Broadband Expansion Program
C) Connect America Fund
D) Broadband Infrastructure Plan

Answer: **A)**

28. Which executive order did Joe Biden issue to revoke the Keystone XL pipeline permit, citing environmental concerns?

A) Executive Order 13990
B) Executive Order 14005
C) Executive Order 13768
D) Executive Order 13848

Answer: **B)**

29. What was the name of the federal program initiated by Joe Biden aimed at providing support to state and local governments for COVID-19 vaccine distribution?

A) Vaccine Distribution Fund
B) Operation Warp Speed
C) COVID-19 Vaccination Assistance Program
D) Vaccinate America Plan

Answer: **D)**

30. Which major federal agency did Joe Biden appoint the first transgender person to lead?

A) Department of Health and Human Services
B) Environmental Protection Agency
C) Department of Housing and Urban Development
D) Small Business Administration

Answer: **C)**

American Foreign Policy

American foreign policy has undergone significant changes throughout history, reflecting shifts in national interests and global dynamics. Initially focused on non-intervention and isolationism, as exemplified by the Monroe Doctrine, it shifted towards more active engagement and interventionism by the late 19th and early 20th centuries, with actions like the Spanish-American War and the establishment of the Open Door Policy in China. Post-World War II, the policy was dominated by Cold War dynamics, leading to a strategy of containment against the Soviet Union and involvement in numerous proxy wars. In the post-Cold War era, American foreign policy has grappled with global terrorism, the rise of China, and complex issues in the Middle East, emphasizing a mix of military intervention and diplomatic engagement.

Part 1

1. Who was the U.S. Secretary of State during the signing of the Treaty of Paris in 1783?

A) Thomas Jefferson
B) John Jay
C) Alexander Hamilton
D) Benjamin Franklin

Answer: **B)**

2. The Monroe Doctrine, a key element of U.S. foreign policy, was primarily authored by which Secretary of State?

A) James Monroe
B) John Quincy Adams
C) Henry Clay
D) Andrew Jackson

Answer: **B)**

3. Which Secretary of State negotiated the purchase of Alaska from Russia?

A) William H. Seward
B) James G. Blaine
C) Daniel Webster
D) John Sherman

Answer: **A)**

4. Who served as Secretary of State under President Lincoln and was known for his efforts to prevent European support for the Confederacy?

A) William Seward
B) Salmon P. Chase
C) Edward Bates
D) Gideon Welles

Answer: **A)**

5. The Good Neighbor Policy, aimed at improving U.S. relations with Latin America, was a hallmark of which President's administration?

A) Franklin D. Roosevelt
B) Herbert Hoover
C) Harry S. Truman
D) Dwight D. Eisenhower

Answer: **A)**

6. Which Secretary of State is known for the "Marshall Plan" to rebuild Europe after World War II?

A) George C. Marshall
B) Dean Acheson
C) John Foster Dulles
D) Henry Kissinger

Answer: A)

7. The "Open Door Policy" in China was primarily advocated by which U.S. Secretary of State?

A) William McKinley
B) John Hay
C) William Jennings Bryan
D) Elihu Root

Answer: B)

8. Who was the U.S. Secretary of State who initiated the eponymous "Doctrine" opposing European colonialism in the Americas?

A) James Monroe
B) John Quincy Adams
C) James Madison
D) Thomas Jefferson

Answer: A)

9. During the Cuban Missile Crisis, who was the U.S. Secretary of State?

A) Dean Rusk
B) Christian Herter
C) Alexander Haig
D) Cyrus Vance

Answer: A)

10. The "Ping-Pong Diplomacy" that led to the reopening of relations between the U.S. and China was under which Secretary of State?

A) Henry Kissinger
B) William P. Rogers
C) Cyrus Vance
D) Dean Acheson

Answer: A)

11. Who was the first African American Secretary of State?

A) Colin Powell
B) Condoleezza Rice
C) Madeleine Albright
D) Cyrus Vance

Answer: A)

12. The Treaty of Portsmouth, which ended the Russo-Japanese War, was mediated by which U.S. President?

A) Theodore Roosevelt
B) William Howard Taft
C) Woodrow Wilson
D) Franklin D. Roosevelt

Answer: A)

13. Which U.S. Secretary of State was in office during the signing of the Camp David Accords?

A) Cyrus Vance
B) Henry Kissinger
C) Warren Christopher
D) Madeleine Albright

Answer: A)

14. The "XYZ Affair" involved diplomats from the U.S. and which other country?

    A) Britain
    B) France
    C) Spain
    D) Germany

Answer: **B)**

15. Which Secretary of State was known for his role in the acquisition of the Panama Canal Zone?

    A) John Hay
    B) Elihu Root
    C) William Jennings Bryan
    D) Cordell Hull

Answer: **A)**

16. The Kellogg-Briand Pact of 1928, which aimed to outlaw war, was signed under which Secretary of State?

    A) Charles Evans Hughes
    B) Frank B. Kellogg
    C) Henry L. Stimson
    D) Cordell Hull

Answer: **B)**

17. Who was the U.S. Secretary of State during the Iran hostage crisis?

    A) Henry Kissinger
    B) Alexander Haig
    C) Cyrus Vance
    D) Edmund Muskie

Answer: **C)**

18. Which Secretary of State played a pivotal role in the negotiations of the Treaty of Guadalupe Hidalgo?

A) James Buchanan
B) John C. Calhoun
C) Daniel Webster
D) Lewis Cass

Answer: **A)**

19. The Strategic Arms Limitation Talks (SALT I) were conducted under which Secretary of State?

A) Henry Kissinger
B) William P. Rogers
C) Dean Rusk
D) Cyrus Vance

Answer: **B)**

20. Who was Secretary of State during the "Six-Day War" between Israel and its Arab neighbors?

A) Dean Rusk
B) Henry Kissinger
C) William P. Rogers
D) Cyrus Vance

Answer: **A)**

21. Which U.S. Secretary of State was instrumental in the development of the United Nations?

A) Edward Stettinius Jr.
B) Cordell Hull
C) Dean Acheson
D) George C. Marshall

Answer: **A)**

22. Who was Secretary of State when the U.S. formally recognized the People's Republic of China in 1979?

A) Henry Kissinger
B) Cyrus Vance
C) Alexander Haig
D) Dean Rusk

Answer: **B)**

23. The "Kitchen Debate" occurred during the tenure of which U.S. Secretary of State?

A) John Foster Dulles
B) Dean Acheson
C) Christian Herter
D) Henry Kissinger

Answer: **C)**

24. Which Secretary of State helped negotiate the end of the Bosnian War with the Dayton Accords?

A) Warren Christopher
B) Madeleine Albright
C) Colin Powell
D) Hillary Clinton

Answer: **A)**

25. The "Fourteen Points" speech, proposing a basis for peace after World War I, was delivered by which U.S. President?

A) Theodore Roosevelt
B) Woodrow Wilson
C) Franklin D. Roosevelt
D) Harry S. Truman

Answer: **B)**

26. Which Secretary of State was a leading figure in the detente policy with the Soviet Union during the 1970s?

A) Henry Kissinger
B) Dean Rusk
C) Cyrus Vance
D) Alexander Haig

Answer: **A)**

27. Who was U.S. Secretary of State when NATO was founded in 1949?

A) George C. Marshall
B) Dean Acheson
C) John Foster Dulles
D) Christian Herter

Answer: **B)**

28. The Platt Amendment, which affected U.S. relations with Cuba, was enforced under which Secretary of State?

A) John Hay
B) Elihu Root
C) William Jennings Bryan
D) Philander C. Knox

Answer: **A)**

29. Which Secretary of State is credited with the "Dollar Diplomacy" policy?

A) William Jennings Bryan
B) Philander C. Knox
C) Robert Lansing
D) Charles Evans Hughes

Answer: **B)**

30. The "Potsdam Declaration," which outlined the terms for Japanese surrender in WWII, was issued under which President?

A) Franklin D. Roosevelt
B) Harry S. Truman
C) Dwight D. Eisenhower
D) John F. Kennedy

Answer: **B)**

31. Who was Secretary of State during the 1956 Suez Crisis?

A) John Foster Dulles
B) Dean Acheson
C) Christian Herter
D) Henry Kissinger

Answer: **A)**

32. The "Reset" strategy with Russia was proposed during the tenure of which Secretary of State?

A) Condoleezza Rice
B) Hillary Clinton
C) John Kerry
D) Rex Tillerson

Answer: **B)**

33. Which U.S. President introduced the policy of "Big Stick Diplomacy"?

A) Theodore Roosevelt
B) William Howard Taft
C) Woodrow Wilson
D) Franklin D. Roosevelt

Answer: **A)**

34. The "Lend-Lease Act," crucial during WWII, was signed under which Secretary of State?

A) Cordell Hull
B) Henry Stimson
C) Frank Knox
D) George C. Marshall

Answer: **A)**

35. Who was the U.S. Secretary of State during the Iranian Revolution of 1979?

A) Cyrus Vance
B) Henry Kissinger
C) Alexander Haig
D) Warren Christopher

Answer: **A)**

36. The "Truman Doctrine" was a key policy under which Secretary of State?

A) Dean Acheson
B) George C. Marshall
C) John Foster Dulles
D) Christian Herter

Answer: **A)**

37. Which Secretary of State negotiated the Antarctic Treaty, which set aside Antarctica as a scientific preserve?

A) Christian Herter
B) Dean Rusk
C) Henry Kissinger
D) William P. Rogers

Answer: **B)**

38. Who was the Secretary of State during the liberation of Kuwait in the Gulf War?

A) James Baker
B) Lawrence Eagleburger
C) Colin Powell
D) Madeleine Albright

Answer: **A)**

39. Which Secretary of State played a key role in the signing of the Intermediate-Range Nuclear Forces (INF) Treaty?

A) George Shultz
B) Caspar Weinberger
C) Colin Powell
D) Madeleine Albright

Answer: **A)**

40. Who was the first woman to serve as U.S. Secretary of State?

A) Condoleezza Rice
B) Madeleine Albright
C) Hillary Clinton
D) Janet Reno

Answer: **B)**

41. The Oslo Accords, a pivotal moment in the Israeli-Palestinian peace process, were signed during the tenure of which Secretary of State?

A) Warren Christopher
B) Madeleine Albright
C) Colin Powell
D) Hillary Clinton

Answer: **A)**

42. Which Secretary of State was in office during the U.S. invasion of Panama in 1989?

A) George Shultz
B) James Baker
C) Lawrence Eagleburger
D) Colin Powell

Answer: **B)**

43. Who was the U.S. Secretary of State during the "Tet Offensive" in Vietnam?

A) Dean Rusk
B) Henry Kissinger
C) William P. Rogers
D) Cyrus Vance

Answer: **A)**

44. Which Secretary of State was known for the "Shuttle Diplomacy" strategy during the Middle East peace process?

A) Henry Kissinger
B) Cyrus Vance
C) James Baker
D) Madeleine Albright

Answer: **A)**

45. The Treaty of Versailles was negotiated under the guidance of which U.S. President?

A) Woodrow Wilson
B) Franklin D. Roosevelt
C) Harry S. Truman
D) Dwight D. Eisenhower

Answer: **A)**

46. Which Secretary of State was a key figure in the development of the "Pivot to Asia" strategy?

A) Condoleezza Rice
B) Hillary Clinton
C) John Kerry
D) Rex Tillerson

Answer: **B)**

47. Who was Secretary of State when the Berlin Wall fell in 1989?

A) George Shultz
B) James Baker
C) Lawrence Eagleburger
D) Colin Powell

Answer: **B)**

48. The "Roosevelt Corollary" to the Monroe Doctrine was articulated during the administration of which President?

A) Theodore Roosevelt
B) William McKinley
C) Woodrow Wilson
D) Franklin D. Roosevelt

Answer: **A)**

49. Which Secretary of State served the longest term under President Franklin D. Roosevelt?

A) Cordell Hull
B) Henry Stimson
C) Dean Acheson
D) George C. Marshall

Answer: **A)**

50. The "Bricker Amendment," concerning the executive power in treaty-making, was proposed during which Secretary of State's tenure?

A) Dean Acheson
B) John Foster Dulles
C) Christian Herter
D) Henry Kissinger

Answer: **A)**

51. Which Secretary of State was in office during the signing of the North American Free Trade Agreement (NAFTA)?

A) Warren Christopher
B) Madeleine Albright
C) Colin Powell
D) Hillary Clinton

Answer: **A)**

52. Who was the Secretary of State during the Bay of Pigs invasion?

A) Dean Rusk
B) Henry Kissinger
C) William P. Rogers
D) Cyrus Vance

Answer: **A)**

53. The "Eisenhower Doctrine," which pledged U.S. support to Middle Eastern countries resisting communism, was announced under which Secretary of State?

A) John Foster Dulles
B) Dean Acheson
C) Christian Herter
D) Henry Kissinger

Answer: **A)**

54. Which Secretary of State was in office during the Iran-Contra affair?

A) George Shultz
B) Alexander Haig
C) James Baker
D) Lawrence Eagleburger

Answer: **A)**

55. Who was the U.S. Secretary of State during the signing of the START I treaty?

A) James Baker
B) George Shultz
C) Lawrence Eagleburger
D) Colin Powell

Answer: **A)**

56. Which Secretary of State was a key proponent of the "New World Order" concept after the Cold War?

A) James Baker
B) Warren Christopher
C) Madeleine Albright
D) Colin Powell

Answer: **A)**

57. Who was the Secretary of State who laid the groundwork for the "Vietnamization" strategy in the Vietnam War?

A) Dean Rusk
B) Henry Kissinger
C) William P. Rogers
D) Cyrus Vance

Answer: **B)**

58. The "Carter Doctrine," which declared U.S. intentions to defend its interests in the Persian Gulf, was under which Secretary of State?

A) Cyrus Vance
B) Edmund Muskie
C) Alexander Haig
D) George Shultz

Answer: **B)**

59. Which Secretary of State was involved in the negotiations that led to the Treaty of San Francisco, formally ending the Pacific War?

A) Dean Acheson
B) John Foster Dulles
C) Christian Herter
D) Henry Kissinger

Answer: **A)**

60. The "Reagan Doctrine," which supported anti-communist resistance movements worldwide, was promoted under which Secretary of State?

A) Alexander Haig
B) George Shultz
C) James Baker
D) Lawrence Eagleburger

Answer: **B)**

61. Which U.S. Secretary of State was known for emphasizing human rights in foreign policy during the 1970s?

A) Cyrus Vance
B) Henry Kissinger
C) Edmund Muskie
D) Jimmy Carter (as President, not Secretary of State)

Answer: **A)**

62. Who was Secretary of State when the United States entered World War I?

A) William Jennings Bryan
B) Robert Lansing
C) Cordell Hull
D) Charles Evans Hughes

Answer: **B)**

63. The "Powell Doctrine," advocating for overwhelming force in military conflicts, was named after which Secretary of State?

A) Colin Powell
B) Madeleine Albright
C) Condoleezza Rice
D) Hillary Clinton

Answer: **A)**

64. Who served as Secretary of State during the negotiation of the Paris Agreement on climate change?

A) Hillary Clinton
B) John Kerry
C) Rex Tillerson
D) Mike Pompeo

Answer: **B)**

65. The "Logan Act," which prohibits unauthorized citizens from negotiating with foreign governments, was enacted during the presidency of which U.S. President?

A) George Washington
B) John Adams
C) Thomas Jefferson
D) James Madison

Answer: **B)**

66. Which Secretary of State was in office during the controversial Keystone XL Pipeline debates?

A) Condoleezza Rice
B) Hillary Clinton
C) John Kerry
D) Rex Tillerson

Answer: **C)**

67. The "Rogers Plan," aimed at resolving the Arab-Israeli conflict, was associated with which Secretary of State?

A) Dean Rusk
B) William P. Rogers
C) Henry Kissinger
D) Cyrus Vance

Answer: **B)**

68. Who was the U.S. Secretary of State during the acquisition of the Louisiana Territory?

A) Thomas Jefferson (as President, not Secretary of State)
B) James Madison
C) James Monroe
D) John Quincy Adams

Answer: **C)**

69. The "Fullbright Program," aimed at increasing mutual understanding through educational exchanges, was named after which U.S. Senator?

A) William Fullbright
B) James Fullbright
C) Henry Cabot Lodge
D) Charles Sumner

Answer: **A)**

70. Which Secretary of State was instrumental in the founding of the Asia-Pacific Economic Cooperation (APEC)?

A) George Shultz
B) James Baker
C) Warren Christopher
D) Madeleine Albright

Answer: **B)**

Part 2

1. What was the primary goal of the Monroe Doctrine, established in 1823?

A) To promote trade with Latin America
B) To prevent European colonization in the Americas
C) To establish English as a primary language in the Americas
D) To promote democracy in Eastern Europe

Answer: **B)**

2. Which President initiated the Open Door Policy with China at the turn of the 20th century?

A) Theodore Roosevelt
B) William McKinley
C) Woodrow Wilson
D) Franklin D. Roosevelt

Answer: **B)**

3. What was the main purpose of the Marshall Plan after World War II?

A) To rebuild European economies
B) To establish the United Nations
C) To start the Cold War
D) To end U.S. isolationism

Answer: **A)**

4. During which conflict was the Truman Doctrine first applied?

    A) World War II
    B) Korean War
    C) Greek Civil War
    D) Vietnam War

Answer: **C)**

5. Who was the U.S. President during the Louisiana Purchase?

    A) George Washington
    B) Thomas Jefferson
    C) James Madison
    D) John Adams

Answer: **B)**

6. The Cuban Missile Crisis occurred during the presidency of:

    A) John F. Kennedy
    B) Dwight D. Eisenhower
    C) Richard Nixon
    D) Lyndon B. Johnson

Answer: **A)**

7. Which President is associated with the policy of Detente?

    A) John F. Kennedy
    B) Jimmy Carter
    C) Ronald Reagan
    D) Richard Nixon

Answer: **D)**

8. The North American Free Trade Agreement (NAFTA) was signed under which President?

A) George H.W. Bush
B) Bill Clinton
C) George W. Bush
D) Barack Obama

Answer: **B)**

9. What was the primary objective of the Carter Doctrine?

A) To promote human rights worldwide
B) To prevent Soviet expansion in the Middle East
C) To increase trade with China
D) To support anti-communist regimes in Latin America

Answer: **B)**

10. Who was President during the signing of the Treaty of Paris, which ended the Spanish-American War?

A) William McKinley
B) Theodore Roosevelt
C) Woodrow Wilson
D) Franklin D. Roosevelt

Answer: **A)**

11. The "Pivot to Asia" policy is most closely associated with which U.S. President?

A) George W. Bush
B) Barack Obama
C) Donald Trump
D) Bill Clinton

Answer: **B)**

12. Which Secretary of State was primarily responsible for the purchase of Alaska from Russia?

A) William H. Seward
B) John Hay
C) Cordell Hull
D) Henry Kissinger

Answer: **A)**

13. The Good Neighbor Policy was implemented by which President?

A) Herbert Hoover
B) Franklin D. Roosevelt
C) Harry S. Truman
D) Dwight D. Eisenhower

Answer: **B)**

14. What international organization was established as a result of a proposal by U.S. President Franklin D. Roosevelt?

A) League of Nations
B) United Nations
C) NATO
D) WTO

Answer: **B)**

15. The Treaty of Versailles was signed under which U.S. President?

A) Woodrow Wilson
B) Calvin Coolidge
C) Herbert Hoover
D) Franklin D. Roosevelt

Answer: **A)**

16. Which U.S. President formulated the Fourteen Points as a basis for peace after World War I?

A) Theodore Roosevelt
B) Woodrow Wilson
C) Warren G. Harding
D) Franklin D. Roosevelt

Answer: **B)**

17. The Strategic Arms Limitation Talks (SALT) were conducted during the presidency of:

A) Lyndon B. Johnson
B) Richard Nixon
C) Gerald Ford
D) Jimmy Carter

Answer: **B)**

18. Which President was in office during the invasion of Grenada?

A) Ronald Reagan
B) Jimmy Carter
C) George H.W. Bush
D) Bill Clinton

Answer: **A)**

19. The Peace Corps was established by which President?

A) John F. Kennedy
B) Lyndon B. Johnson
C) Richard Nixon
D) Jimmy Carter

Answer: **A)**

20. Which international agreement aimed at reducing greenhouse gas emissions was signed during the presidency of Bill Clinton but never ratified by the Senate?

A) Kyoto Protocol
B) Paris Agreement
C) Montreal Protocol
D) Copenhagen Accord

Answer: **A)**

and continuing through question 70. Let me know if you'd like to continue with more questions or focus on a specific aspect of American foreign policy!

Continuing with more quiz questions on American foreign policy:

21. Which U.S. President led the country during the first Gulf War?

A) Ronald Reagan
B) George H.W. Bush
C) Bill Clinton
D) George W. Bush

Answer: **B)**

22. What is the primary purpose of the Rio Treaty, also known as the Inter-American Treaty of Reciprocal Assistance?

A) To create a free trade area in the Americas
B) To provide mutual defence against external aggression in the Western Hemisphere
C) To address environmental issues in Latin America
D) To promote democratic governance in the Americas

Answer: **B)**

23. Which U.S. President famously declared, "Speak softly and carry a big stick"?

A) Theodore Roosevelt
B) William Howard Taft
C) Woodrow Wilson
D) Franklin D. Roosevelt

Answer: **A)**

24. The Platt Amendment, which stipulated the conditions for the withdrawal of U.S. troops from Cuba, was enacted under which President?

A) William McKinley
B) Theodore Roosevelt
C) Herbert Hoover
D) Franklin D. Roosevelt

Answer: **B)**

25. Which U.S. President is credited with the creation of the United States Information Agency (USIA)?

A) Harry S. Truman
B) Dwight D. Eisenhower
C) John F. Kennedy
D) Lyndon B. Johnson

Answer: **B)**

26. The doctrine of pre-emptive war, often referred to as the "Bush Doctrine," was prominently featured during the presidency of:

A) George H.W. Bush
B) Bill Clinton
C) George W. Bush
D) Barack Obama

Answer: **C)**

27. Which U.S. President was responsible for initiating the Alliance for Progress, aimed at strengthening economic ties with Latin America?

A) John F. Kennedy
B) Lyndon B. Johnson
C) Richard Nixon
D) Jimmy Carter

Answer: **A)**

28. The U.S.-led NATO intervention in Kosovo occurred during the presidency of:

A) George H.W. Bush
B) Bill Clinton
C) George W. Bush
D) Barack Obama

Answer: **B)**

29. Who was the U.S. President during the signing of the START I Treaty, which aimed to reduce nuclear arms?

A) Ronald Reagan
B) George H.W. Bush
C) Bill Clinton
D) George W. Bush

Answer: **B)**

30. The "New Look" defense policy, which emphasized the role of nuclear weapons in deterrence, was associated with which President?

A) Harry S. Truman
B) Dwight D. Eisenhower
C) John F. Kennedy
D) Lyndon B. Johnson

Answer: **B)**

31. The decision to normalize diplomatic relations with Vietnam in 1995 was made under which President?

A) George H.W. Bush
B) Bill Clinton
C) George W. Bush
D) Barack Obama

Answer: **B)**

32. Which U.S. President initiated the embargo against Cuba that remains in effect today?

A) Dwight D. Eisenhower
B) John F. Kennedy
C) Lyndon B. Johnson
D) Richard Nixon

Answer: **A)**

33. The "Corollary to the Monroe Doctrine," which justified American intervention in Latin America, was introduced by which President?

A) William McKinley
B) Theodore Roosevelt
C) Woodrow Wilson
D) Franklin D. Roosevelt

Answer: **B)**

34. The Camp David Accords, which were brokered between Egypt and Israel, were facilitated by which U.S. President?

A) Jimmy Carter
B) Ronald Reagan
C) George H.W. Bush
D) Bill Clinton

Answer: **A)**

35. Which President was in office during the Iranian Hostage Crisis?

A) Gerald Ford
B) Jimmy Carter
C) Ronald Reagan
D) George H.W. Bush

Answer: **B)**

36. The "Lend-Lease Act," which provided military aid to allies during World War II, was signed by which President?

A) Franklin D. Roosevelt
B) Harry S. Truman
C) Dwight D. Eisenhower
D) John F. Kennedy

Answer: **A)**

37. The "Fair Deal," which included proposals for universal health care and education, was advocated by which President?

A) Harry S. Truman
B) Dwight D. Eisenhower
C) John F. Kennedy
D) Lyndon B. Johnson

Answer: **A)**

38. Who was the U.S. President during the acquisition of the Panama Canal Zone?

A) Theodore Roosevelt
B) William Howard Taft
C) Woodrow Wilson
D) Franklin D. Roosevelt

Answer: **A)**

39. The U.S. intervention in the Libyan civil war in 2011 occurred under which President?

A) George W. Bush
B) Barack Obama
C) Donald Trump
D) Bill Clinton

Answer: **B)**

40. Who was the U.S. President during the negotiations of the "Treaty of Wanghia," which opened Chinese ports to American trade?

A) Andrew Jackson
B) John Tyler
C) James K. Polk
D) Millard Fillmore

Answer: **C)**

41. Which President is associated with the doctrine that justified the U.S. intervention in the Dominican Republic in 1965?

A) John F. Kennedy
B) Lyndon B. Johnson
C) Richard Nixon
D) Jimmy Carter

Answer: **B)**

42. The Helms-Burton Act, which strengthened the U.S. embargo against Cuba, was signed by which President?

A) George H.W. Bush
B) Bill Clinton
C) George W. Bush
D) Barack Obama

Answer: **B)**

43. Which U.S. President oversaw the signing of the SALT II treaty, though it was never ratified by the Senate?

A) Gerald Ford
B) Jimmy Carter
C) Ronald Reagan
D) George H.W. Bush

Answer: **B)**

44. The "Point Four Program," which focused on technical assistance to developing countries, was initiated by which President?

A) Harry S. Truman
B) Dwight D. Eisenhower
C) John F. Kennedy
D) Lyndon B. Johnson

Answer: **A)**

45. Which President declared the War on Drugs, significantly affecting U.S. foreign policy in Latin America?

A) Richard Nixon
B) Jimmy Carter
C) Ronald Reagan
D) George H.W. Bush

Answer: **A)**

46. The INF Treaty, which aimed at eliminating intermediate-range nuclear missiles, was signed during the presidency of:

A) Jimmy Carter
B) Ronald Reagan
C) George H.W. Bush
D) Bill Clinton

Answer: **B)**

47. Which U.S. President initiated the "Thousand Days" reform agenda that included an emphasis on Latin American policy?

A) Dwight D. Eisenhower
B) John F. Kennedy
C) Lyndon B. Johnson
D) Richard Nixon

Answer: **B)**

48. Who was President during the establishment of the Peace Corps, which aimed at promoting international development and goodwill?

A) Dwight D. Eisenhower
B) John F. Kennedy
C) Lyndon B. Johnson
D) Richard Nixon

Answer: **B)**

49. Which President was responsible for the "Reagan Doctrine," which supported anti-communist insurgencies?

A) Jimmy Carter
B) Ronald Reagan
C) George H.W. Bush
D) Bill Clinton

Answer: **B)**

50. The "Agreed Framework" between the U.S. and North Korea, aimed at freezing North Korea's nuclear program, was signed under which President?

A) George H.W. Bush
B) Bill Clinton
C) George W. Bush
D) Barack Obama

Answer: **B)**

51. Which President's administration is most closely associated with the promotion of the "New World Order" after the Cold War?

A) Ronald Reagan
B) George H.W. Bush
C) Bill Clinton
D) George W. Bush

Answer: **B)**

52. The "Pax Americana" is a term often associated with the global influence of the United States under which President?

A) Franklin D. Roosevelt
B) Harry S. Truman
C) Dwight D. Eisenhower
D) John F. Kennedy

Answer: **C)**

53. Which President authorized the use of military force in the Libyan civil war in 2011?

A) George W. Bush
B) Barack Obama
C) Donald Trump
D) Bill Clinton

Answer: **B)**

54. The "Asia Reassurance Initiative Act," aimed at promoting U.S. interests in the Indo-Pacific region, was signed by which President?

A) Barack Obama
B) Donald Trump
C) George W. Bush
D) Bill Clinton

Answer: **B)**

55. Who was the U.S. President during the signing of the Intermediate-Range Nuclear Forces Treaty (INF) in 1987?

A) Ronald Reagan
B) George H.W. Bush
C) Bill Clinton
D) Jimmy Carter

Answer: **A)**

56. Which President oversaw the United States' entry into the League of Nations debate, although the U.S. ultimately did not join?

A) Woodrow Wilson
B) Franklin D. Roosevelt
C) Harry S. Truman
D) Dwight D. Eisenhower

Answer: **A)**

57. Which President led the initiative for the North American Leaders' Summit, a trilateral meeting between the U.S., Canada, and Mexico?

A) George W. Bush
B) Bill Clinton
C) Barack Obama
D) Donald Trump

Answer: **C)**

58. The "Johnson Doctrine" which asserted U.S. rights to intervene in the affairs of its neighbours if it felt necessary, was enacted under which President?

A) John F. Kennedy
B) Lyndon B. Johnson
C) Richard Nixon
D) Jimmy Carter

Answer: **B)**

59. Which President was in office during the "Ping-Pong Diplomacy" that helped open China to the West?

A) Richard Nixon
B) Jimmy Carter
C) Gerald Ford
D) Ronald Reagan

Answer: **A)**

60. Who was the U.S. President during the negotiation of the Anti-Ballistic Missile Treaty with the Soviet Union?

A) Lyndon B. Johnson
B) Richard Nixon
C) Jimmy Carter
D) Ronald Reagan

Answer: **B)**

61. Which President's administration was marked by the establishment of the "Wet foot, dry foot" policy concerning Cuban immigration?

A) Ronald Reagan
B) George H.W. Bush
C) Bill Clinton
D) George W. Bush

Answer: **C)**

62. Who was the U.S. President during the annexation of Hawaii?

A) Ulysses S. Grant
B) William McKinley
C) Theodore Roosevelt
D) Woodrow Wilson

Answer: **B)**

63. The "Nixon Doctrine" was announced during which international conflict?

A) Korean War
B) Vietnam War
C) Persian Gulf War
D) Bosnian War

Answer: **B)**

64. Which President is most closely associated with the initiation of the "War on Terror"?

A) Bill Clinton
B) George W. Bush
C) Barack Obama
D) Donald Trump

Answer: **B)**

65. Who was President when the United States first opened diplomatic relations with the People's Republic of China?

A) Lyndon B. Johnson
B) Richard Nixon
C) Gerald Ford
D) Jimmy Carter

Answer: **B)**

66. Which U.S. President initiated the Panama Canal treaties, leading to eventual control of the canal passing to Panama?

A) Lyndon B. Johnson
B) Richard Nixon
C) Gerald Ford
D) Jimmy Carter

Answer: **D)**

67. The "Bush Doctrine" emphasizing pre-emptive military action was a response to what event?

A) Fall of the Soviet Union
B) 9/11 terrorist attacks
C) Invasion of Kuwait
D) Rise of ISIS

Answer: **B)**

68. Which President led the United States during the Spanish-American War?

A) Grover Cleveland
B) William McKinley
C) Theodore Roosevelt
D) Woodrow Wilson

Answer: **B)**

69. Who was in office when the United States negotiated the Intermediate-Range Nuclear Forces (INF) Treaty?

A) Ronald Reagan
B) George H.W. Bush
C) Bill Clinton
D) Barack Obama

Answer: **A)**

70. Which President's foreign policy is known for the term "Big Stick Diplomacy"?

A) Abraham Lincoln
B) Theodore Roosevelt
C) Franklin D. Roosevelt
D) Harry S. Truman

Answer: **B)**

Domestic Policy

American domestic policy has evolved to address changing societal needs and conflicts, beginning with foundational issues like the establishment of a federal government and economic system. During the 19th century, policies focused on territorial expansion, slavery, and industrialization, culminating in the Civil War and Reconstruction efforts. The 20th century saw significant transformations with the New Deal responding to the Great Depression, civil rights movements advancing social justice, and the introduction of major social programs like Medicare. In recent decades, domestic policy has wrestled with healthcare reform, immigration policies, and responses to economic inequality and climate change, reflecting the nation's ongoing challenges and priorities.

Part 1

1. What major reform did President Franklin D. Roosevelt introduce as part of his New Deal programs?

   A) The Marshall Plan
   B) The Great Society
   C) Social Security Act
   D) Obamacare

Answer: **C)**

2. Which President signed the Affordable Care Act into law?

    A) Bill Clinton
    B) George W. Bush
    C) Barack Obama
    D) Donald Trump

Answer: **C)**

3. The Civil Rights Act of 1964, prohibiting discrimination based on race, color, religion, sex, or national origin, was signed by which President?

    A) John F. Kennedy
    B) Lyndon B. Johnson
    C) Richard Nixon
    D) Jimmy Carter

Answer: **B)**

4. Which U.S. President is most closely associated with the New Deal?

    A) Herbert Hoover
    B) Franklin D. Roosevelt
    C) Harry S. Truman
    D) Dwight D. Eisenhower

Answer: **B)**

5. The Emancipation Proclamation, which declared that all slaves in Confederate territory were to be set free, was issued by which President?

    A) Abraham Lincoln
    B) Andrew Johnson
    C) Ulysses S. Grant
    D) James Buchanan

Answer: **A)**

6. Which U.S. President was responsible for the establishment of the Environmental Protection Agency (EPA)?

A) Richard Nixon
B) Ronald Reagan
C) George H. W. Bush
D) Bill Clinton

Answer: **A)**

7. The 'War on Poverty' was a set of programs introduced by which President?

A) John F. Kennedy
B) Lyndon B. Johnson
C) Richard Nixon
D) Jimmy Carter

Answer: **B)**

8. Who was the U.S. President during the Louisiana Purchase?

A) George Washington
B) John Adams
C) Thomas Jefferson
D) James Madison

Answer: **C)**

9. Which U.S. President signed the legislation that established the Federal Reserve System?

A) William Howard Taft
B) Woodrow Wilson
C) Theodore Roosevelt
D) Warren G. Harding

Answer: **B)**

10. Who was the first African American to serve as the U.S. Secretary of State, appointed during George W. Bush's presidency?

A) Condoleezza Rice
B) Colin Powell
C) Eric Holder
D) Loretta Lynch

Answer: **B)**

11. The No Child Left Behind Act, which reauthorized the Elementary and Secondary Education Act, was signed by which President?

A) Bill Clinton
B) George W. Bush
C) Barack Obama
D) Donald Trump

Answer: **B)**

12. Which act, signed into law by Lyndon B. Johnson, aimed at overcoming legal barriers at the state and local levels that prevented African Americans from exercising their right to vote under the 15th Amendment?

A) Civil Rights Act of 1964
B) Voting Rights Act of 1965
C) Fair Housing Act
D) Equal Pay Act of 1963

Answer: **B)**

13. Which U.S. President launched the initiative known as 'Star Wars' to develop missile defense systems?

A) Richard Nixon
B) Gerald Ford
C) Jimmy Carter
D) Ronald Reagan

Answer: **D)**

14. Who was President when the Americans with Disabilities Act was signed into law?

A) Ronald Reagan
B) George H. W. Bush
C) Bill Clinton
D) George W. Bush

Answer: **B)**

15. Which President was in office during the passing of the Homestead Act, which allowed poor people to obtain land?

A) Andrew Johnson
B) Abraham Lincoln
C) Ulysses S. Grant
D) Rutherford B. Hayes

Answer: **B)**

16. The Interstate Highway System was authorized under which U.S. President?

A) Harry S. Truman
B) Dwight D. Eisenhower
C) John F. Kennedy
D) Lyndon B. Johnson

Answer: **B)**

17. Which President is credited with signing the Medicare and Medicaid programs into law?

A) John F. Kennedy
B) Lyndon B. Johnson
C) Richard Nixon
D) Jimmy Carter

Answer: **B)**

18. Which U.S. President first proposed what would eventually become known as the Food and Drug Administration (FDA)?

A) Theodore Roosevelt
B) Woodrow Wilson
C) Franklin D. Roosevelt
D) Harry S. Truman

Answer: **A)**

19. Which U.S. President was in office when the Department of Homeland Security was created?

A) Bill Clinton
B) George W. Bush
C) Barack Obama
D) Donald Trump

Answer: **B)**

20. The Wagner Act, which guaranteed the rights of most workers to organize labor unions and to bargain collectively, was signed under which President?

A) Franklin D. Roosevelt
B) Harry S. Truman
C) Dwight D. Eisenhower
D) John F. Kennedy

Answer: **A)**

21. Which President was responsible for the creation of the National Aeronautics and Space Administration (NASA)?

A) Dwight D. Eisenhower
B) John F. Kennedy
C) Lyndon B. Johnson
D) Richard Nixon

Answer: **A)**

22. Who signed the legislation that introduced the Supplemental Nutrition Assistance Program (SNAP), originally known as Food Stamps?

A) Lyndon B. Johnson
B) John F. Kennedy
C) Richard Nixon
D) Jimmy Carter

Answer: **B)**

23. The Sarbanes-Oxley Act, aimed at improving corporate governance and accountability, was signed by which President?

A) Bill Clinton
B) George W. Bush
C) Barack Obama
D) Donald Trump

Answer: **B)**

24. Which President was responsible for establishing the Peace Corps?

A) Dwight D. Eisenhower
B) John F. Kennedy
C) Lyndon B. Johnson
D) Richard Nixon

Answer: **B)**

25. The Brady Handgun Violence Prevention Act, which mandated federal background checks on firearm purchasers in the United States, was signed into law under which President?

A) George H. W. Bush
B) Bill Clinton
C) George W. Bush
D) Barack Obama

Answer: **B)**

26. Which U.S. President oversaw the passage of the Fair Labor Standards Act, which established minimum wage, overtime pay eligibility, recordkeeping, and child labor standards?

A) Franklin D. Roosevelt
B) Harry S. Truman
C) Dwight D. Eisenhower
D) John F. Kennedy

Answer: **A)**

27. Under which President was the Patriot Act, which expanded the government's surveillance capabilities following September 11, 2001, passed?

A) Bill Clinton
B) George W. Bush
C) Barack Obama
D) Donald Trump

Answer: **B)**

28. Which President initiated the project that would eventually be known as the Internet by funding ARPANET?

A) John F. Kennedy
B) Lyndon B. Johnson
C) Richard Nixon
D) Gerald Ford

Answer: **C)**

29. The legislation known as the Clean Air Act, which set the U.S. national air quality standards, was signed under which President?

A) Lyndon B. Johnson
B) Richard Nixon
C) Gerald Ford
D) Jimmy Carter

Answer: **B)**

30. Who was the President during the energy crisis of the 1970s and delivered a famous speech known as the "Crisis of Confidence" speech?

A) Richard Nixon
B) Gerald Ford
C) Jimmy Carter
D) Ronald Reagan

Answer: C)

31. Which President is associated with the establishment of the Earned Income Tax Credit (EITC)?

A) Richard Nixon
B) Gerald Ford
C) Jimmy Carter
D) Ronald Reagan

Answer: B)

32. The Family and Medical Leave Act, which provides eligible employees with unpaid, job-protected leave for certain family and medical reasons, was signed by which President?

A) George H. W. Bush
B) Bill Clinton
C) George W. Bush
D) Barack Obama

Answer: B)

33. Which U.S. President was in office during the signing of the Immigration and Nationality Act of 1965, which significantly changed the immigration policy of the United States?

A) John F. Kennedy
B) Lyndon B. Johnson
C) Richard Nixon
D) Jimmy Carter

Answer: B)

34. Who was President when the National Labor Relations Act, also known as the Wagner Act, was passed?

A) Herbert Hoover
B) Franklin D. Roosevelt
C) Harry S. Truman
D) Dwight D. Eisenhower

Answer: **B)**

35. The Dodd-Frank Wall Street Reform and Consumer Protection Act, aimed at reducing risks in the U.S. financial system, was signed by which President?

A) George W. Bush
B) Barack Obama
C) Donald Trump
D) Joe Biden

Answer: **B)**

36. Which President signed the Americans with Disabilities Act, which prohibits discrimination based on disability?

A) Ronald Reagan
B) George H. W. Bush
C) Bill Clinton
D) George W. Bush

Answer: **B)**

37. Who was President during the establishment of the Department of Energy in 1977?

A) Gerald Ford
B) Jimmy Carter
C) Ronald Reagan
D) George H. W. Bush

Answer: **B)**

38. The Children's Health Insurance Program (CHIP), providing health coverage to children in families with incomes too high to qualify for Medicaid, was signed into law by which President?

A) George H. W. Bush
B) Bill Clinton
C) George W. Bush
D) Barack Obama

Answer: **B)**

39. Which U.S. President oversaw the implementation of the Glass-Steagall Act, which separated commercial and investment banking?

A) Herbert Hoover
B) Franklin D. Roosevelt
C) Harry S. Truman
D) Dwight D. Eisenhower

Answer: **B)**

40. Who was President when the Fair Housing Act, intended to prevent discrimination in housing, was signed into law?

A) Lyndon B. Johnson
B) Richard Nixon
C) Gerald Ford
D) Jimmy Carter

Answer: **A)**

41. Which President introduced the concept of 'Reagonomics,' policies that included tax cuts, decreased social spending, increased military spending, and deregulation of domestic markets?

A) Richard Nixon
B) Jimmy Carter
C) Ronald Reagan
D) George H. W. Bush

Answer: **C)**

42. Under which President was the Department of Veterans Affairs elevated to a Cabinet-level executive department?

A) Ronald Reagan
B) George H. W. Bush
C) Bill Clinton
D) George W. Bush

Answer: **B)**

43. The legislation known as the Personal Responsibility and Work Opportunity Reconciliation Act, which significantly changed welfare policy, was signed by which President?

A) George H. W. Bush
B) Bill Clinton
C) George W. Bush
D) Barack Obama

Answer: **B)**

44. Who was President when the Pure Food and Drug Act, establishing the Food and Drug Administration, was enacted?

A) Theodore Roosevelt
B) William Howard Taft
C) Woodrow Wilson
D) Warren G. Harding

Answer: **A)**

Part 2

1. Which policy was established to address economic instability during the Great Depression?

A) New Deal
B) Fair Deal
C) Square Deal
D) New Frontier

Answer: **A)**

2. What was the primary goal of the Affordable Care Act?

A) To reduce military spending
B) To expand healthcare coverage
C) To deregulate the banking sector
D) To increase federal taxes

Answer: **B)**

3. The Civil Rights Act of 1964 aimed to end discrimination based on what?

A) Age and disability
B) Race, color, religion, sex, or national origin
C) Political affiliation
D) Income level

Answer: **B)**

4. What was the main purpose of the Social Security Act of 1935?

A) To regulate interstate commerce
B) To provide aid to farmers
C) To provide support for the elderly and unemployed
D) To establish national parks

Answer: **C)**

5. What does the Environmental Protection Agency (EPA) primarily regulate?

A) Educational standards
B) Environmental protection
C) Financial markets
D) Transportation safety

Answer: **B)**

6. The 'War on Poverty' introduced programs primarily to address what?

A) Foreign policy issues
B) Economic inequality
C) Corporate tax rates
D) Military spending

Answer: **B)**

7. Which act was designed to provide affordable housing and close the wealth gap in urban areas?

A) The Homestead Act
B) The National Housing Act
C) The Fair Housing Act
D) The Affordable Housing Act

Answer: **C)**

8. What does the Patriot Act focus on?

A) Environmental regulations
B) Educational reform
C) Surveillance and security
D) Healthcare reform

Answer: **C)**

9. The No Child Left Behind Act focuses on which area of policy?

A) Healthcare
B) Education
C) Economic development
D) Military preparedness

Answer: **B)**

10. What is the primary focus of the Dodd-Frank Act?

A) Climate change
B) Financial regulation
C) Healthcare affordability
D) Educational funding

Answer: **B)**

11. The Clean Air Act, first enacted in the 1960s, aims to regulate the emissions of which of the following?

A) Radioactive materials
B) Air pollutants
C) Water pollutants
D) Noise pollution

Answer: **B)**

12. Medicare and Medicaid were established to do what?

A) Regulate the pharmaceutical industry
B) Provide health insurance to specific groups
C) Encourage private healthcare
D) Fund medical research

Answer: **B)**

13. Which act is aimed at protecting consumer data and preventing identity theft?

A) Consumer Protection Act
B) Fair Credit Reporting Act
C) Internet Security Act
D) Data Privacy Act

Answer: **B)**

14. What was the main goal of the American Recovery and Reinvestment Act of 2009?

A) To reduce federal debt
B) To stimulate economic recovery
C) To overhaul the healthcare system
D) To reform education

Answer: **B)**

15. Which policy initiative focuses on increasing renewable energy production and energy efficiency?

A) Clean Power Plan
B) Green New Deal
C) Sustainable Energy Act
D) Energy Independence Act

Answer: **A)**

16. The Voting Rights Act of 1965 was enacted to ensure protection against discrimination in what area?

A) Employment
B) Voting
C) Education
D) Housing

Answer: **B)**

17. What does the Federal Reserve Act regulate?

A) Agricultural policies
B) Monetary policy
C) Environmental policies
D) Educational policies

Answer: **B)**

18. Which act was signed into law to improve accountability and prevent fraud in corporate environments?

A) Sarbanes-Oxley Act
B) Dodd-Frank Act
C) Federal Transparency Act
D) Corporate Accountability Act

Answer: **A)**

19. The Americans with Disabilities Act focuses on rights for which group?

A) Elderly
B) Veterans
C) Disabled
D) Children

Answer: **C)**

20. What is the primary aim of the Temporary Assistance for Needy Families (TANF) program?

A) Provide job training
B) Offer student loans
C) Support low-income families
D) Fund medical research

Answer: **C)**

21. The Federal Trade Commission (FTC) is primarily concerned with what aspect of government regulation?

A) Education policy
B) Consumer protection
C) Energy sustainability
D) National security

Answer: **B)**

22. What was the primary purpose of the Emergency Economic Stabilization Act of 2008?

A) To reform education
B) To address the housing market crisis
C) To improve healthcare access
D) To stabilize the financial system

Answer: **D)**

23. The Supplemental Nutrition Assistance Program (SNAP) aims to assist in what area?

A) Providing educational resources
B) Supporting renewable energy
C) Offering nutritional assistance
D) Enhancing national security

Answer: **C)**

24. Which policy is primarily associated with providing federal aid for primary and secondary education?

A) Health Education Act
B) Elementary and Secondary Education Act
C) Higher Education Act
D) Education Reform Act

Answer: **B)**

25. The Glass-Steagall Act, enacted during the Great Depression, was intended to address issues in which sector?

A) Agriculture
B) Education
C) Banking
D) Healthcare

Answer: **C)**

26. What is the main focus of the Fair Labor Standards Act?

A) Preventing unfair labor practices
B) Setting minimum wage, overtime pay standards, and child labor laws
C) Regulating the tech industry
D) Protecting consumer data

Answer: **B)**

27. The Clean Water Act focuses on regulating pollutants in what area?

A) Air
B) Soil
C) Water
D) Noise

Answer: **C)**

28. Which act was designed to protect endangered species and their habitats?

A) National Park Protection Act
B) Environmental Safety Act
C) Endangered Species Act
D) Wildlife Conservation Act

Answer: **C)**

29. The Sherman Antitrust Act was implemented to address issues in which of the following areas?

A) Education reform
B) Market competition
C) Environmental protection
D) Healthcare management

Answer: **B)**

30. The Family Educational Rights and Privacy Act (FERPA) deals with what type of information?

A) Employee data in corporations
B) Consumer credit information
C) Student educational records
D) Healthcare records

Answer: **C)**

31. Which act requires employers to provide reasonable accommodation for disabled employees?

A) Americans with Disabilities Act
B) Equal Employment Opportunity Act
C) Workforce Innovation and Opportunity Act
D) Family and Medical Leave Act

Answer: **A)**

32. The Brady Handgun Violence Prevention Act focuses on what specific aspect of law enforcement?

A) Expanding police powers
B) Establishing national parks
C) Background checks for firearms purchases
D) Enhancing border security

Answer: **C)**

33. What was the main purpose of the Wagner Act?

A) To provide healthcare benefits
B) To protect workers' rights to unionize and bargain collectively
C) To regulate interstate commerce
D) To promote educational reforms

Answer: **B)**

34. Which policy was designed to increase transparency in government spending?

A) The Freedom of Information Act
B) The Federal Reserve Transparency Act
C) The Government Accountability Act
D) The Transparency in Regulatory Analysis of Impacts on the Nation Act

Answer: **A)**

35. The establishment of the Consumer Financial Protection Bureau (CFPB) was a result of which act?

A) Dodd-Frank Wall Street Reform and Consumer Protection Act
B) Sarbanes-Oxley Act
C) Credit CARD Act
D) Federal Trade Commission Act

Answer: **A)**

36. Which program is designed to assist veterans in acquiring housing?

A) Veterans Health Administration
B) Veterans Educational Assistance Program
C) Veterans Housing Benefit Program
D) Veterans Employment and Training Service

Answer: **C)**

37. The National Environmental Policy Act (NEPA) mandates federal agencies to evaluate what before taking major actions?

A) Economic impact
B) Educational benefits
C) Environmental impact
D) Healthcare effects

Answer: **C)**

38. Which act regulates the collection and distribution of personal credit information?

A) Fair Credit Reporting Act
B) Consumer Credit Protection Act
C) Credit CARD Act
D) Electronic Fund Transfer Act

Answer: **A)**

39. What is the primary aim of the Public Service Loan Forgiveness (PSLF) program?

A) To forgive student loans for those working in private sector high-income jobs
B) To forgive student loans for those working in public service jobs after making 120 qualifying payments
C) To provide immediate debt relief for all federal student loan borrowers
D) To reduce interest rates on all student loans

Answer: **B)**

40. The Health Insurance Portability and Accountability Act (HIPAA) primarily protects what type of information?

A) Educational data
B) Patient health information
C) Consumer financial information
D) Employee work history

Answer: **B)**

41. The G.I. Bill, originally passed in 1944, was designed to assist veterans in what way?

A) Providing healthcare
B) Offering unemployment benefits
C) Funding education and housing
D) Ensuring job placement

Answer: **C)**

42. Which policy initiative focuses on providing nutrition assistance to low-income pregnant women, infants, and children?

A) Medicaid
B) TANF
C) SNAP
D) WIC

Answer: **D)**

43. The Fair Housing Act aims to prevent discrimination in housing based on what criteria?

A) Age
B) Employment status
C) Race, color, religion, sex, familial status, or national origin
D) Education level

Answer: **C)**

44. Which legislation was enacted to control and regulate air quality?

A) Clean Water Act
B) Clean Air Act
C) Endangered Species Act
D) Safe Drinking Water Act

Answer: **B)**

45. The National School Lunch Program provides what type of assistance?

A) Healthcare services
B) Educational grants
C) Free or reduced-cost meals to students
D) Housing subsidies

Answer: **C)**

46. The Occupational Safety and Health Act (OSHA) aims to ensure what?

A) Fair labor wages
B) Workplace safety and health standards
C) Environmental protection
D) Educational opportunities

Answer: **B)**

47. Which act established the modern system of social welfare in the United States?

A) Social Security Act
B) Medicare Act
C) Medicaid Act
D) Welfare Reform Act

Answer: **A)**

48. What does the Family and Medical Leave Act (FMLA) provide to eligible employees?

A) Paid vacation time
B) Unpaid, job-protected leave for family and medical reasons
C) Health insurance subsidies
D) Retirement benefits

Answer: **B)**

49. Which legislation was designed to improve the quality of air and reduce air pollution?

A) Environmental Protection Act
B) Clean Air Act
C) Air Quality Control Act
D) Pollution Prevention Act

Answer: **B)**

50. The Federal-Aid Highway Act of 1956 led to the creation of what?

A) Federal Reserve System
B) Interstate Highway System
C) Social Security System
D) National Park System

Answer: **B)**

51. What was the purpose of the Homestead Act of 1862?

A) To establish national parks
B) To provide land to settlers for farming
C) To regulate interstate commerce
D) To fund public education

Answer: **B)**

52. Which act focuses on the regulation of campaign financing?

A) Federal Campaign Act
B) Bipartisan Campaign Reform Act
C) Election Finance Act
D) Political Funding Act

Answer: **B)**

53. The National Defense Education Act (NDEA) was enacted in response to which event?

A) World War II
B) Korean War
C) Launch of Sputnik by the Soviet Union
D) Cuban Missile Crisis

Answer: **C)**

54. Which act is designed to control water pollution by regulating the discharge of pollutants into U.S. waters?

A) Safe Drinking Water Act
B) Clean Water Act
C) Water Quality Improvement Act
D) Federal Water Pollution Control Act

Answer: **B)**

55. The Personal Responsibility and Work Opportunity Reconciliation Act of 1996 reformed what area of policy?

A) Healthcare
B) Welfare
C) Education
D) Immigration

Answer: **B)**

56. The Housing and Community Development Act of 1974 introduced which program to provide affordable housing?

A) Section 8 Housing
B) Public Housing Initiative
C) Low-Income Housing Tax Credit
D) Urban Development Grant

Answer: **A)**

57. What was the main purpose of the Federal-Aid Highway Act?

A) To provide federal funding for public schools
B) To construct a national interstate highway system
C) To support agricultural subsidies
D) To establish national parks

Answer: **B)**

58. Which act is designed to ensure safe and healthful working conditions for employees?

A) Fair Labor Standards Act
B) Occupational Safety and Health Act
C) Employment Rights Act
D) Workforce Protection Act

Answer: **B)**

59. The National Labor Relations Act (Wagner Act) was enacted to protect the rights of which group?

A) Students
B) Workers
C) Veterans
D) Elderly

Answer: **B)**

60. Which legislation was created to provide a comprehensive framework for regulating the safety of food, drugs, and cosmetics?

A) Federal Food, Drug, and Cosmetic Act
B) Pure Food and Drug Act
C) Food Safety Modernization Act
D) Consumer Product Safety Act

Answer: **A)**

61. The Economic Opportunity Act of 1964 was a centerpiece of which major initiative?

A) New Deal
B) Fair Deal
C) Great Society
D) War on Poverty

Answer: **D)**

62. The Safe Drinking Water Act focuses on what aspect of public health?

A) Air quality
B) Food safety
C) Water quality
D) Workplace safety

Answer: C)

63. The Federal Aviation Administration (FAA) was established to regulate and oversee what?

A) Maritime navigation
B) Automobile safety
C) Air travel and aviation safety
D) Railroad operations

Answer: C)

64. Which act was enacted to address the economic fallout from the COVID-19 pandemic?

A) CARES Act
B) Affordable Care Act
C) Economic Stimulus Act
D) American Recovery Act

Answer: A)

65. The National Labor Relations Act established which organization to oversee labor practices?

A) Occupational Safety and Health Administration
B) National Labor Relations Board
C) Federal Labor Commission
D) Workers' Rights Bureau

Answer: B)

66. Which act aims to prevent workplace discrimination based on age for individuals 40 and older?

A) Age Discrimination in Employment Act
B) Equal Employment Opportunity Act
C) Employment Non-Discrimination Act
D) Workers' Rights Act

Answer: **A)**

67. The Freedom of Information Act (FOIA) allows public access to what type of information?

A) Military secrets
B) Government records
C) Personal financial data
D) Healthcare records

Answer: **B)**

68. The Comprehensive Environmental Response, Compensation, and Liability Act (CERCLA) is commonly known as what?

A) Clean Air Act
B) Safe Drinking Water Act
C) Superfund
D) Environmental Protection Act

Answer: **C)**

69. The Children's Health Insurance Program (CHIP) was designed to cover which group?

A) Elderly individuals
B) Unemployed adults
C) Low-income children
D) Veterans

Answer: **C)**

70. Which policy requires federal agencies to produce an environmental impact statement for major projects?

A) National Environmental Policy Act
B) Clean Water Act
C) Clean Air Act
D) Endangered Species Act

Answer: **A)**

71. The Federal Insecticide, Fungicide, and Rodenticide Act (FIFRA) regulates what?

A) Prescription drugs
B) Pesticide distribution, sale, and use
C) Water pollution
D) Automobile emissions

Answer: **B)**

72. The Magnuson-Stevens Fishery Conservation and Management Act focuses on which aspect of environmental policy?

A) Air quality
B) Water quality
C) Marine fisheries management
D) Wildlife conservation

Answer: **C)**

73. The Head Start program provides what type of assistance?

A) Healthcare services for the elderly
B) Early childhood education, health, nutrition, and parent involvement services to low-income children and families
C) Job training for unemployed adults
D) Housing subsidies for veterans

Answer: **B)**

74. The Community Reinvestment Act (CRA) requires banks to meet the needs of borrowers in what areas?

A) Urban areas only
B) Suburban areas only
C) The communities in which they operate, including low- and moderate-income neighborhoods
D) Rural areas only

Answer: **C)**

75. Which act aimed to improve the accuracy of financial reporting and restore investor confidence in the wake of corporate scandals?

A) Sarbanes-Oxley Act
B) Glass-Steagall Act
C) Securities Act of 1933
D) Dodd-Frank Act

Answer: **A)**

76. The Violence Against Women Act (VAWA) provides support for victims of what?

A) Child abuse
B) Domestic violence, sexual assault, and stalking
C) Human trafficking
D) Financial fraud

Answer: **B)**

77. The National Flood Insurance Program (NFIP) provides insurance to property owners in what type of areas?

A) High-crime areas
B) Flood-prone areas
C) Earthquake-prone areas
D) Tornado-prone areas

Answer: **B)**

78. The Federal Housing Administration (FHA) primarily assists with what?

A) Medical insurance
B) Home mortgage insurance
C) Educational grants
D) Small business loans

Answer: **B)**

79. Which act was designed to address the exploitation of children and child labor?

A) Children's Rights Act
B) Fair Labor Standards Act
C) Child Protection Act
D) Youth Employment Act

Answer: **B)**

80. The National School Lunch Act was established to ensure that children receive what?

A) School supplies
B) Healthcare
C) Nutritious meals
D) Educational scholarships

Answer: **C)**

81. The Occupational Safety and Health Administration (OSHA) was created under which act?

A) Fair Labor Standards Act
B) Social Security Act
C) Occupational Safety and Health Act
D) Labor Relations Act

Answer: **C)**

82. The Federal-Aid Highway Act led to the development of which system?

A) Public transit systems
B) Interstate Highway System
C) Railroads
D) National parks

Answer: **B)**

83. The Affordable Care Act introduced marketplaces for what purpose?

A) Buying and selling agricultural products
B) Purchasing health insurance
C) Trading financial securities
D) Regulating utilities

Answer: **B)**

84. The Public Health Service Act authorizes programs for what area of public policy?

A) National defense
B) Public health and research
C) Education funding
D) Environmental protection

Answer: **B)**

85. The Federal Emergency Management Agency (FEMA) is responsible for what?

A) Regulating air travel
B) Providing disaster response and recovery
C) Managing national parks
D) Enforcing labor laws

Answer: **B)**

86. The Hatch Act restricts the political activities of which group?

A) Military personnel
B) Federal employees
C) Corporate executives
D) Public school teachers

Answer: **B)**

87. The Elementary and Secondary Education Act (ESEA) was enacted to improve what?

A) Higher education
B) Primary and secondary education
C) Technical and vocational training
D) Adult education programs

Answer: **B)**

88. The Federal Deposit Insurance Corporation (FDIC) provides insurance for what type of financial institution?

A) Credit unions
B) Savings and loan associations
C) Commercial banks
D) Investment banks

Answer: **C)**

89. The Clean Power Plan aims to reduce emissions of what substance?

A) Methane
B) Carbon dioxide
C) Sulfur dioxide
D) Nitrogen oxide

Answer: **B)**

90. The Patient Protection and Affordable Care Act includes provisions for what key component?

A) Reducing environmental pollution
B) Increasing healthcare coverage and affordability
C) Enhancing national security
D) Expanding educational opportunities

Answer: **B)**

91. The Fair Credit Billing Act provides protections for consumers in what area?

A) Medical billing
B) Utility billing
C) Credit card billing
D) Property tax billing

Answer: **C)**

92. The Homestead Act of 1862 provided land to settlers under what condition?

A) They must be veterans
B) They must improve the land
C) They must build a school
D) They must operate a business

Answer: **B)**

93. The Freedom of Information Act (FOIA) allows citizens to request access to what?

A) Private business records
B) Government records
C) Medical records
D) Financial records

Answer: **B)**

94. The Gramm-Leach-Bliley Act repealed parts of which earlier legislation?

A) Securities Act of 1933
B) Glass-Steagall Act
C) Federal Reserve Act
D) Banking Act of 1935

Answer: **B)**

95. The Community Development Block Grant (CDBG) program provides funds for what purpose?

A) Military equipment
B) Community development and infrastructure
C) Agricultural subsidies
D) Space exploration

Answer: **B)**

96. Which act establishes standards for safe drinking water?

A) Clean Water Act
B) Water Pollution Control Act
C) Safe Drinking Water Act
D) Water Quality Act

Answer: **C)**

97. The Consumer Product Safety Commission (CPSC) is responsible for regulating what?

A) Financial products
B) Food and drugs
C) Consumer products to ensure safety
D) Telecommunications

Answer: **C)**

98. The Elementary and Secondary Education Act (ESEA) is the primary law governing what?

A) College funding
B) Public K-12 education
C) Early childhood education
D) Technical schools

Answer: **B)**

99. The Electronic Fund Transfer Act (EFTA) provides protection for consumers using what?

A) Checks
B) Credit cards
C) Electronic fund transfers
D) Mortgage loans

Answer: **C)**

100. The Federal Fair Housing Act prohibits discrimination in housing based on which criteria?

A) Employment status
B) Family size
C) Race, color, religion, sex, national origin, disability, and familial status
D) Credit score

Answer: **C)**

101. The Children's Health Insurance Program (CHIP) provides health coverage for which group?

A) Elderly individuals
B) Low-income children
C) Unemployed adults
D) Veterans

Answer: **B)**

102. The Equal Pay Act requires equal pay for equal work regardless of what?

A) Age
B) Gender
C) Education level
D) Employment history

Answer: **B)**

103. Which policy focuses on preventing youth tobacco use and regulating tobacco advertising?

A) Clean Air Act
B) Tobacco Control Act
C) Food and Drug Act
D) Public Health Service Act

Answer: **B)**

104. The Public Health Service Act includes provisions for funding what type of facilities?

A) Community health centers
B) Private hospitals
C) Military clinics
D) Veterinary offices

Answer: **A)**

105. The Personal Responsibility and Work Opportunity Reconciliation Act was primarily focused on reforming what?

A) Healthcare
B) Welfare
C) Education
D) Immigration

Answer: **B)**

106. The Agricultural Adjustment Act (AAA) was aimed at stabilizing what?

A) Commodity prices and farm income
B) Urban housing
C) Industrial output
D) Military spending

Answer: **A)**

107. The Patient Protection and Affordable Care Act includes a mandate for what?

A) All employers to provide paid sick leave
B) Individuals to have health insurance or pay a penalty
C) All citizens to invest in the stock market
D) Companies to reduce carbon emissions

Answer: **B)**

108. The Safe Drinking Water Act (SDWA) requires the EPA to set standards for what?

A) Air quality
B) Pesticide use
C) Drinking water quality
D) Soil conservation

Answer: **C)**

109. The Freedom of Information Act (FOIA) is intended to increase transparency in what?

A) Private corporations
B) Government agencies
C) Non-profit organizations
D) Educational institutions

Answer: **B)**

110. The Emergency Economic Stabilization Act of 2008 created a program to purchase what?

A) Foreign currencies
B) Troubled assets from financial institutions
C) Real estate properties
D) Military equipment

Answer: **B)**

111. The Energy Policy Act of 2005 includes provisions to encourage what?

A) Offshore drilling
B) Renewable energy development
C) Automobile manufacturing
D) Logging in national forests

Answer: **B)**

112. The Occupational Safety and Health Administration (OSHA) is part of which government department?

A) Department of Health and Human Services
B) Department of Labor
C) Department of Commerce
D) Department of the Interior

Answer: **B)**

113. The Federal-Aid Highway Act resulted in the construction of what major infrastructure?

A) National railroads
B) Interstate highways
C) Public transit systems
D) Airports

Answer: **B)**

114. The Americans with Disabilities Act (ADA) prohibits discrimination based on what?

A) Race
B) Gender
C) Disability
D) Age

Answer: C)

115. The Health Insurance Portability and Accountability Act (HIPAA) primarily protects what type of information?

A) Educational data
B) Financial data
C) Personal health information
D) Employment history

Answer: C)

116. The Endangered Species Act provides for the conservation of what?

A) Water resources
B) Air quality
C) Threatened and endangered plants and animals
D) Soil health

Answer: C)

117. The Clean Water Act regulates the discharge of pollutants into what?

A) Air
B) Soil
C) Water
D) Food

Answer: C)

118. The Federal Fair Housing Act aims to prevent discrimination in housing based on which factors?

A) Employment status and income level
B) Race, color, religion, sex, national origin, disability, and familial status
C) Age and education level
D) Political affiliation and voting history

Answer: **B)**

119. The Freedom of Information Act (FOIA) allows public access to records from which type of entities?

A) Private corporations
B) Government agencies
C) Non-profit organizations
D) International bodies

Answer: **B)**

120. The Elementary and Secondary Education Act (ESEA) focuses on funding and standards for what level of education?

A) Higher education
B) Primary and secondary education
C) Vocational training
D) Adult education

Answer: **B)**

Constitution of the United States

The Constitution of the United States, adopted in 1787, serves as the supreme law of the land, outlining the framework for federal government and embodying principles of federalism and separation of powers. It begins with the Preamble, which sets the stage for its seven original articles that establish the roles of the three branches of government: legislative (Congress), executive (President), and judicial (Supreme Court). The document also details the methods of amending the Constitution and the federal relationship with the states. Significantly, it has been amended 27 times to address issues ranging from individual rights to changes in governmental structure, with the first ten amendments known as the Bill of Rights ensuring specific personal freedoms.

1. Which article of the U.S. Constitution outlines the powers of the President?

    A) Article I
    B) Article II
    C) Article III
    D) Article IV

Answer: **B)**

2. How many amendments are there in the Bill of Rights?

    A) 10
    B) 12
    C) 15
    D) 20

Answer: **A)**

3. The principle of "judicial review" is established in which Supreme Court case?

    A) Marbury v. Madison
    B) Brown v. Board of Education
    C) Roe v. Wade
    D) Miranda v. Arizona

Answer: **A)**

4. Which amendment to the Constitution guarantees freedom of speech?

    A) 1st Amendment
    B) 2nd Amendment
    C) 4th Amendment
    D) 5th Amendment

Answer: **A)**

5. How many articles are there in the U.S. Constitution?

    A) 7
    B) 9
    C) 10
    D) 13

Answer: **A)**

6. The principle of "separation of powers" is established in which part of the Constitution?

    A) Preamble
    B) Article I
    C) Article II
    D) Article III

Answer: **B)**

7. Who has the power to declare war according to the Constitution?

    A) President
    B) Congress
    C) Supreme Court
    D) State Governors

Answer: **B)**

8. The "Supremacy Clause" of the Constitution establishes:

    A) The authority of the President over state governments
    B) The authority of state governments over the federal government
    C) The authority of federal law over state law
    D) The authority of state law over federal law

Answer: **C)**

9. Which amendment abolished slavery in the United States?

    A) 13th Amendment
    B) 14th Amendment
    C) 15th Amendment
    D) 16th Amendment

Answer: **A)**

10. The Constitution grants the power to regulate commerce to which branch of government?

A) Executive
B) Legislative
C) Judicial
D) States

Answer: **B)**

11. How many senators are there in the United States Senate?

A) 50
B) 100
C) 435
D) 538

Answer: **B)**

12. The "Due Process" clause of the 5th Amendment protects against:

A) Double jeopardy
B) Self-incrimination
C) Unreasonable searches and seizures
D) Deprivation of life, liberty, or property without due process of law

Answer: **D)**

13. How many total amendments have been added to the U.S. Constitution?

A) 27
B) 30
C) 32
D) 35

Answer: **A)**

14. The U.S. Constitution was adopted in which year?

    A) 1776
    B) 1787
    C) 1791
    D) 1800

Answer: **B)**

15. Which amendment grants the right to a trial by jury in civil cases?

    A) 6th Amendment
    B) 7th Amendment
    C) 8th Amendment
    D) 9th Amendment

Answer: **B)**

16. The "Elastic Clause" of the Constitution is found in which article?

    A) Article I
    B) Article II
    C) Article III
    D) Article IV

Answer: **A)**

17. Which amendment guarantees the right to bear arms?

    A) 1st Amendment
    B) 2nd Amendment
    C) 3rd Amendment
    D) 4th Amendment

Answer: **B)**

18. The Constitution requires that a census be taken every:

A) 4 years
B) 6 years
C) 8 years
D) 10 years

Answer: **D)**

19. The process of amending the Constitution is outlined in:

A) Article I
B) Article II
C) Article III
D) Article V

Answer: **D)**

20. The "Full Faith and Credit Clause" requires states to:

A) Recognize the laws and judicial decisions of other states
B) Treat all citizens equally under the law
C) Abide by the rulings of the Supreme Court
D) Respect the separation of powers

Answer: **A)**

21. How many branches of government are established by the Constitution?

A) 1
B) 2
C) 3
D) 4

Answer: **C)**

22. The "Great Compromise" resolved the debate over:

A) Representation in Congress
B) Slavery
C) Taxation
D) The Bill of Rights

Answer: **A)**

23. The Constitution grants the power to impeach federal officials to which body?

A) Senate
B) House of Representatives
C) Supreme Court
D) President

Answer: **B)**

24. Which amendment protects citizens from unreasonable searches and seizures?

A) 4th Amendment
B) 5th Amendment
C) 6th Amendment
D) 8th Amendment

Answer: **A)**

25. The number of representatives each state has in the House of Representatives is based on:

A) Population
B) Geographic size
C) Economic status
D) State government structure

Answer: **A)**

26. The "Electoral College" is established by which article of the Constitution?

A) Article I
B) Article II
C) Article III
D) Article IV

Answer: **B)**

27. Which amendment protects individuals from self-incrimination?

A) 4th Amendment
B) 5th Amendment
C) 6th Amendment
D) 8th Amendment

Answer: **B)**

28. The Constitution establishes the process for presidential succession in which amendment?

A) 20th Amendment
B) 22nd Amendment
C) 25th Amendment
D) 27th Amendment

Answer: **C)**

29. The "Necessary and Proper Clause" is also known as the:

A) Commerce Clause
B) Supremacy Clause
C) Elastic Clause
D) Full Faith and Credit Clause

Answer: **C)**

30. Which amendment protects against cruel and unusual punishment?

    A) 4th Amendment
    B) 5th Amendment
    C) 6th Amendment
    D) 8th Amendment

Answer: **D)**

31. The "Commerce Clause" of the Constitution grants Congress the power to:

    A) Regulate commerce between states
    B) Levy taxes
    C) Declare war
    D) Appoint Supreme Court justices

Answer: **A)**

32. Which amendment guarantees the right to a speedy and public trial?

    A) 5th Amendment
    B) 6th Amendment
    C) 7th Amendment
    D) 8th Amendment

Answer: **B)**

33. The Constitution establishes the procedure for electing the President through:

    A) Popular vote
    B) Electoral College
    C) Congressional appointment
    D) Supreme Court nomination

Answer: **B)**

34. The principle of "federalism" in the Constitution refers to:

    A) The division of powers between national and state governments
    B) The separation of powers between branches of government
    C) The process of amending the Constitution
    D) The right to a fair and speedy trial

Answer: **A)**

35. Which amendment guarantees the right to a trial by jury in criminal cases?

    A) 5th Amendment
    B) 6th Amendment
    C) 7th Amendment
    D) 8th Amendment

Answer: **B)**

36. The Constitution grants the power to levy taxes to which branch of government?

    A) Executive
    B) Legislative
    C) Judicial
    D) State governments

Answer: **B)**

37. The "First Amendment" to the Constitution protects:

    A) Freedom of speech, religion, and the press
    B) The right to bear arms
    C) The right to a fair trial
    D) Protection against unreasonable searches and seizures

Answer: **A)**

38. The Constitution grants the power to interpret laws to which branch of government?

A) Executive
B) Legislative
C) Judicial
D) State governments

Answer: **C)**

39. Which amendment guarantees the right to a fair trial and legal representation?

A) 5th Amendment
B) 6th Amendment
C) 7th Amendment
D) 8th Amendment

Answer: **B)**

40. The Constitution establishes the process for ratifying treaties in:

A) Article I
B) Article II
C) Article III
D) Article VI

Answer: **B)**

41. Which amendment guarantees the right to petition the government for grievances?

A) 1st Amendment
B) 2nd Amendment
C) 4th Amendment
D) 10th Amendment

Answer: **A)**

42. The "Equal Protection Clause" of the Constitution is found in which amendment?

A) 5th Amendment
B) 14th Amendment
C) 19th Amendment
D) 26th Amendment

Answer: **B)**

43. Which amendment guarantees the right to vote regardless of race, color, or previous condition of servitude?

A) 13th Amendment
B) 14th Amendment
C) 15th Amendment
D) 19th Amendment

Answer: **C)**

44. The Constitution establishes the principle of "limited government" by:

A) Granting certain powers to the federal government and reserving the rest to the states or the people
B) Granting all powers to the federal government
C) Granting all powers to the states
D) Granting all powers to the President

Answer: **A)**

45. Which amendment guarantees the right to equal protection under the law?

A) 4th Amendment
B) 5th Amendment
C) 14th Amendment
D) 15th Amendment

Answer: **C)**

46. The Constitution establishes the principle of "popular sovereignty," meaning that:

A) All political power rests with the people
B) All political power rests with the President
C) All political power rests with Congress
D) All political power rests with the Supreme Court

Answer: **A)**

47. Which amendment guarantees the right to a fair and reasonable bail?

A) 5th Amendment
B) 6th Amendment
C) 7th Amendment
D) 8th Amendment

Answer: **D)**

48. The Constitution establishes the process for amending the Constitution in which article?

A) Article I
B) Article II
C) Article III
D) Article V

Answer: **D)**

49. Which amendment guarantees the right to freedom of religion?

A) 1st Amendment
B) 2nd Amendment
C) 3rd Amendment
D) 4th Amendment

Answer: **A)**

50. The Constitution establishes the principle of "federal supremacy" through the:

A) Supremacy Clause
B) Necessary and Proper Clause
C) Commerce Clause
D) Establishment Clause

Answer: A)

51. Which amendment guarantees the right to a speedy and public trial in criminal cases?

A) 5th Amendment
B) 6th Amendment
C) 7th Amendment
D) 8th Amendment

Answer: B)

52. The principle of "federalism" in the Constitution refers to:

A) The division of powers between national and state governments
B) The separation of powers between branches of government
C) The process of amending the Constitution
D) The right to a fair and speedy trial

Answer: A)

53. Which amendment protects against unreasonable searches and seizures?

A) 4th Amendment
B) 5th Amendment
C) 6th Amendment
D) 8th Amendment

Answer: A)

54. The Constitution grants the power to levy taxes to which branch of government?

A) Executive
B) Legislative
C) Judicial
D) State governments

Answer: **B)**

55. The "First Amendment" to the Constitution protects:

A) Freedom of speech, religion, and the press
B) The right to bear arms
C) The right to a fair trial
D) Protection against unreasonable searches and seizures

Answer: **A)**

56. The Constitution establishes the process for electing the President through:

A) Popular vote
B) Electoral College
C) Congressional appointment
D) Supreme Court nomination

Answer: **B)**

57. The principle of "federal supremacy" through the Constitution is established by the:

A) Supremacy Clause
B) Necessary and Proper Clause
C) Commerce Clause
D) Establishment Clause

Answer: **A)**

58. Which amendment guarantees the right to petition the government for grievances?

A) 1st Amendment
B) 2nd Amendment
C) 4th Amendment
D) 10th Amendment

Answer: **A)**

59. The Constitution establishes the process for ratifying treaties in:

A) Article I
B) Article II
C) Article III
D) Article VI

Answer: **B)**

60. Which amendment guarantees the right to freedom of religion?

A) 1st Amendment
B) 2nd Amendment
C) 3rd Amendment
D) 4th Amendment

Answer: **A)**

61. The Constitution establishes the principle of "popular sovereignty," meaning that:

A) All political power rests with the people
B) All political power rests with the President
C) All political power rests with Congress
D) All political power rests with the Supreme Court

Answer: **A)**

62. Which amendment guarantees the right to equal protection under the law?

A) 4th Amendment
B) 5th Amendment
C) 14th Amendment
D) 15th Amendment

Answer: **C)**

63. The Constitution establishes the principle of "limited government" by:

A) Granting certain powers to the federal government and reserving the rest to the states or the people
B) Granting all powers to the federal government
C) Granting all powers to the states
D) Granting all powers to the President

Answer: **A)**

64. Which amendment guarantees the right to vote regardless of race, color, or previous condition of servitude?

A) 13th Amendment
B) 14th Amendment
C) 15th Amendment
D) 19th Amendment

Answer: **C)**

65. The Constitution establishes the process for amending the Constitution in which article?

A) Article I
B) Article II
C) Article III
D) Article V

Answer: **D)**

66. Which amendment protects against cruel and unusual punishment?

A) 4th Amendment
B) 5th Amendment
C) 6th Amendment
D) 8th Amendment

Answer: **D)**

67. The Constitution grants the power to interpret laws to which branch of government?

A) Executive
B) Legislative
C) Judicial
D) State governments

Answer: **C)**

68. Which amendment guarantees the right to a trial by jury in criminal cases?

A) 5th Amendment
B) 6th Amendment
C) 7th Amendment
D) 8th Amendment

Answer: **B)**

69. The "Equal Protection Clause" of the Constitution is found in which amendment?

A) 5th Amendment
B) 14th Amendment
C) 19th Amendment
D) 26th Amendment

Answer: **B)**

70. The Constitution establishes the process for presidential succession in which amendment?

A) 20th Amendment
B) 22nd Amendment
C) 25th Amendment
D) 27th Amendment

Answer: **C)**

71. Which amendment guarantees the right to a fair trial and legal representation?

A) 5th Amendment
B) 6th Amendment
C) 7th Amendment
D) 8th Amendment

Answer: **B)**

72. The Constitution grants the power to regulate commerce to which branch of government?

A) Executive
B) Legislative
C) Judicial
D) States

Answer: **B)**

73. Which amendment guarantees the right to bear arms?

A) 1st Amendment
B) 2nd Amendment
C) 3rd Amendment
D) 4th Amendment

Answer: **B)**

74. The Constitution grants the power to declare war according to the Constitution to which body?

A) President
B) Congress
C) Supreme Court
D) State Governors

Answer: **B)**

75. Which amendment protects individuals from self-incrimination?

A) 4th Amendment
B) 5th Amendment
C) 6th Amendment
D) 8th Amendment

Answer: **B)**

76. The "Due Process" clause of the 5th Amendment protects against:

A) Double jeopardy
B) Self-incrimination
C) Unreasonable searches and seizures
D) Deprivation of life, liberty, or property without due process of law

Answer: **D)**

77. The Constitution grants the power to impeach federal officials to which body?

A) Senate
B) House of Representatives
C) Supreme Court
D) President

Answer: **B)**

78. Which amendment guarantees the right to a trial by jury in civil cases?

A) 6th Amendment
B) 7th Amendment
C) 8th Amendment
D) 9th Amendment

Answer: **B)**

79. The Constitution requires that a census be taken every:

A) 4 years
B) 6 years
C) 8 years
D) 10 years

Answer: **D)**

80. The "Electoral College" is established by which article of the Constitution?

A) Article I
B) Article II
C) Article III
D) Article IV

Answer: **B)**

81. Which amendment protects against unreasonable searches and seizures?

A) 4th Amendment
B) 5th Amendment
C) 6th Amendment
D) 8th Amendment

Answer: **A)**

82. The Constitution grants the power to levy taxes to which branch of government?

A) Executive
B) Legislative
C) Judicial
D) State governments

Answer: **B)**

83. The "First Amendment" to the Constitution protects:

A) Freedom of speech, religion, and the press
B) The right to bear arms
C) The right to a fair trial
D) Protection against unreasonable searches and seizures

Answer: **A)**

84. The Constitution establishes the process for electing the President through:

A) Popular vote
B) Electoral College
C) Congressional appointment
D) Supreme Court nomination

Answer: **B)**

85. The principle of "federal supremacy" through the Constitution is established by the:

A) Supremacy Clause
B) Necessary and Proper Clause
C) Commerce Clause
D) Establishment Clause

Answer: **A)**

86. Which amendment guarantees the right to petition the government for grievances?

A) 1st Amendment
B) 2nd Amendment
C) 4th Amendment
D) 10th Amendment

Answer: **A)**

87. The Constitution establishes the process for ratifying treaties in:

A) Article I
B) Article II
C) Article III
D) Article VI

Answer: **B)**

88. Which amendment guarantees the right to freedom of religion?

A) 1st Amendment
B) 2nd Amendment
C) 3rd Amendment
D) 4th Amendment

Answer: **A)**

89. The Constitution establishes the principle of "popular sovereignty," meaning that:

A) All political power rests with the people
B) All political power rests with the President
C) All political power rests with Congress
D) All political power rests with the Supreme Court

Answer: **A)**

90. Which amendment guarantees the right to equal protection under the law?

A) 4th Amendment
B) 5th Amendment
C) 14th Amendment
D) 15th Amendment

Answer: **C)**

State Politics

State politics in the United States exhibit a rich diversity of governance styles and policies, reflective of the country's federal structure which allows individual states significant autonomy. Each state operates under its own constitution, electing a governor and legislators to create and implement state laws and policies. Key issues often vary by state due to regional priorities and economic conditions, encompassing topics such as taxation, education, healthcare, and environmental regulation. Additionally, state politics can serve as testing grounds for policies that may later influence national politics, showcasing the dynamic interplay between state and federal systems.

1. What is the primary role of a state governor?

A) To make federal laws
B) To serve in the state's judiciary
C) To execute state laws
D) To represent the state in international affairs

Answer: **C)**

2. Which state has a unicameral legislature?

A) Nebraska
B) Texas
C) California
D) Florida

Answer: **A)**

3. How many states allow for some form of direct democracy?

A) 12
B) 24
C) 34
D) 50

Answer: **B)**

4. In which state do judges of the State Supreme Court serve for life terms?

A) None
B) Rhode Island
C) New Jersey
D) Massachusetts

Answer: **A)**

5. What is required to override a gubernatorial veto in most states?

A) A simple majority in the state legislature
B) A two-thirds majority in the legislature
C) Three-fourths majority in the state legislature
D) Unanimous consent in the state legislature

Answer: **B)**

6. Which state has a governor who can only serve one term?

A) Virginia
B) New York
C) California
D) Texas

Answer: **A)**

7. In which state is the Attorney General not elected by the public?

A) Maine
B) Arizona
C) Michigan
D) Ohio

Answer: **A)**

8. Which state's constitution is known for being the longest in the United States?

A) Alabama
B) California
C) Texas
D) New York

Answer: **A)**

9. What is the minimum age requirement for someone to serve as a state governor in most states?

A) 18 years
B) 21 years
C) 25 years
D) 30 years

Answer: **D)**

10. Which state allows the recall of elected officials, including the governor?

A) Florida
B) New York
C) California
D) Massachusetts

Answer: **C)**

11. Which state has a non-partisan legislature?

A) Nebraska
B) Oregon
C) Kentucky
D) Louisiana

Answer: **A)**

12. As of 2024, which state does NOT have a balanced budget requirement?

A) Vermont
B) Ohio
C) Texas
D) California

Answer: **A)**

13. Which state first introduced the initiative process to allow citizens to propose legislation directly?

A) Oregon
B) California
C) Wisconsin
D) Massachusetts

Answer: **A)**

14. How often do state legislative elections occur in the majority of the United States?

    A) Every year
    B) Every two years
    C) Every four years
    D) Every six years

Answer: **B)**

15. What power do state governors typically have that the U.S. President does not?

    A) The power to declare war
    B) The power to pardon
    C) The line-item veto
    D) The power to enact laws without legislative approval

Answer: **C)**

16. Which state's governor has the shortest term in office at two years?

    A) New Hampshire
    B) Vermont
    C) Kentucky
    D) Mississippi

Answer: **A)**

17. In which state is the Secretary of State not an elected position?

    A) Utah
    B) Pennsylvania
    C) Texas
    D) Wisconsin

Answer: **B)**

18. Which state passed a law in 2019 that requires presidential candidates to release their tax returns to appear on the ballot?

A) New York
B) California
C) Illinois
D) Washington

Answer: **B)**

19. What type of legislature does the state of Minnesota have?

A) Unicameral
B) Bicameral
C) Tricameral
D) Nonpartisan

Answer: **B)**

20. Which state was the first to legalize same-sex marriage through legislative action?

A) Massachusetts
B) California
C) Vermont
D) New York

Answer: **C)**

21. Which state's governor is part of a plural executive, meaning they do not control the election of other executive officials?

A) Texas
B) Georgia
C) Florida
D) New York

Answer: **A)**

22. What function does a state's Lieutenant Governor typically serve?

A) Head of the state police
B) Presiding officer of the state Senate
C) Chief financial officer of the state
D) Attorney General

Answer: **B)**

23. Which state constitution explicitly allows for the formation of a state militia, separate from the National Guard?

A) California
B) Texas
C) Virginia
D) Alaska

Answer: **B)**

24. In which state do all judicial appointments have to be confirmed by a Legislative Council?

A) Maine
B) Arizona
C) Alaska
D) Delaware

Answer: **C)**

25. Which state implemented the first modern state sales tax?

A) Mississippi
B) New York
C) Illinois
D) California

Answer: **A)**

26. What is unique about the New Jersey State Legislature in terms of its structure?

A) It has three chambers
B) It is unicameral
C) It has a Senate and a General Assembly
D) Senators serve two-year terms

Answer: **C)**

27. In which state does the Secretary of State act as the lieutenant governor?

A) Arizona
B) Tennessee
C) Wisconsin
D) New Jersey

Answer: **B)**

28. Which state has the power of gubernatorial impeachment solely vested in the Senate, with no role for the House?

A) Virginia
B) Illinois
C) Texas
D) Oregon

Answer: **A)**

29. What is the role of a state Comptroller?

A) Oversees state elections
B) Manages state financial operations
C) Handles transportation issues
D) Oversees public health

Answer: **B)**

30. Which state allows its residents to participate in "Taxpayer Bill of Rights" refunds when state revenues exceed a certain amount?

A) Colorado
B) Florida
C) Texas
D) New York

Answer: **A)**

31. What unique power does the Nevada legislature have concerning gambling legislation?

A) It can ban gambling statewide without a referendum
B) It meets every year to discuss only this issue
C) It must approve all new casino licenses
D) It does not regulate gambling; local governments do

Answer: **C)**

32. Which state has had the most women serve as governor?

A) Arizona
B) Kansas
C) Michigan
D) Oregon

Answer: **A)**

33. What is a common requirement for someone to be elected state treasurer?

A) Must be a certified public accountant
B) No criminal record
C) Must have prior governmental experience
D) Must be at least 30 years old

Answer: **B)**

34. Which state was the first to have an African American woman serve as governor?

A) Georgia
B) New York
C) Illinois
D) None of the above

Answer: **D)**

35. What legislative body is responsible for impeaching the governor in most states?

A) The state senate
B) The state house of representatives
C) Both chambers together
D) The state supreme court

Answer: **B)**

36. Which state allows the public to elect the head of the Department of Natural Resources?

A) California
B) Montana
C) Minnesota
D) None of the above

Answer: **D)**

37. What is the primary responsibility of a state Secretary of Agriculture?

A) Regulating state utilities
B) Promoting agricultural products and practices
C) Overseeing public education systems
D) Managing state parks and recreation

Answer: **B)**

38. Which state gives its governor the least veto power?

A) Rhode Island
B) North Carolina
C) Vermont
D) Wisconsin

Answer: **B)**

39. In what state does the Insurance Commissioner also act as the Fire Marshal?

A) Florida
B) Georgia
C) California
D) Oregon

Answer: **C)**

40. What unique method does Louisiana use for its state elections?

A) Closed primary system
B) Jungle primary system
C) Nonpartisan blanket primary
D) Top-two primary

Answer: **B)**

41. Which state was the first to enact a law that permits family members to initiate gun seizures if they believe the individual poses a risk?

A) Connecticut
B) California
C) Indiana
D) Washington

Answer: **C)**

42. Which state holds the distinction of having the most extensive constitution, often noted for its detailed policy prescriptions?

A) Alabama
B) California
C) Texas
D) Ohio

Answer: **A)**

43. In which state do voters have the ability to recall elected officials from any level of government, including local?

A) Oregon
B) California
C) Wisconsin
D) All of the above

Answer: **D)**

44. What is a primary function of the State Auditor?

A) Enforcing the state's criminal code
B) Managing state investments
C) Overseeing public accounts and conducting audits
D) Regulating banking institutions

Answer: **C)**

45. Which state has a governor who appoints all county sheriffs?

A) No state
B) Alaska
C) Delaware
D) Hawaii

Answer: **A)**

46. In which state does the governor have no veto power?

A) Alabama
B) Vermont
C) North Carolina
D) None

Answer: **D)**

47. Which state was the first to allow women the right to vote?

A) New York
B) Wyoming
C) Massachusetts
D) California

Answer: **B)**

48. Which state has the highest number of amendments to its constitution?

A) Alabama
B) California
C) Florida
D) Texas

Answer: **A)**

49. Which state uses a commission-based approach for redistricting, removing the legislature from the process?

A) Arizona
B) Iowa
C) California
D) All of the above

Answer: **D)**

50. What is the primary role of a state's Secretary of State?

A) Overseeing public education
B) Managing state defense forces
C) Supervising elections and maintaining public records
D) Budget management and fiscal policy

Answer: **C)**

51. Which state has a nonpartisan "blanket" primary for state elections?

A) Washington
B) Louisiana
C) Nebraska
D) Maine

Answer: **A)**

52. In which state are judges of the highest court selected by a non-partisan commission and appointed by the governor?

A) Missouri
B) Florida
C) New Jersey
D) New York

Answer: **A)**

53. Which state's legislature meets only every other year?

A) California
B) Texas
C) New York
D) Illinois

Answer: **B)**

54. What unique legislative body does Maryland have for evaluating the performance of public officials?

A) Executive Review Committee
B) Public Service Commission
C) Legislative Policy Committee
D) Judicial Disabilities Commission

Answer: **C)**

55. Which state has implemented term limits for its state legislators?

A) New York
B) Florida
C) Oregon
D) Michigan

Answer: **D)**

56. What unique voting method does Maine use for state elections?

A) Ranked-choice voting
B) Cumulative voting
C) Approval voting
D) Proportional representation

Answer: **A)**

57. Which state has the smallest legislature in terms of the number of members?

A) Alaska
B) Delaware
C) Rhode Island
D) Nevada

Answer: **B)**

58. Which state constitution includes a right to privacy?

A) Florida
B) California
C) Montana
D) All of the above

Answer: **D)**

59. In what state does the governor serve a two-year term instead of four?

A) New Hampshire
B) Vermont
C) Both A and B
D) None of the above

Answer: **C)**

60. What state first passed an environmental bill of rights?

A) Pennsylvania
B) California
C) Montana
D) Alaska

Answer: **C)**

61. Which state's governor can veto individual spending items in budget bills?

A) Only California
B) Only Texas
C) Both California and Texas
D) All states

Answer: **C)**

62. Which state was the first to establish a state-funded public school system?

A) Massachusetts
B) New York
C) Virginia
D) Pennsylvania

Answer: **A)**

63. What is a significant power held by the Governor of Texas compared to other states?

A) The ability to veto state constitutional amendments
B) The power to appoint all judges without election
C) Extensive use of the line-item veto on legislation
D) None of the above

Answer: **C)**

64. Which state's constitution explicitly allows for the independent review of legislative salaries by a citizen's commission?

A) Michigan
B) Washington
C) Alaska
D) Oregon

Answer: **B)**

65. In which state do citizens have the power to repeal legislation via referendum without any legislative involvement?

A) California
B) Ohio
C) Florida
D) All of the above

Answer: **D)**

66. Which state has the oldest continuously operating legislative body in the Western Hemisphere?

A) Virginia
B) Massachusetts
C) New York
D) Pennsylvania

Answer: **A)**

67. In which state is the Secretary of State also the Lieutenant Governor?

A) Texas
B) Tennessee
C) Georgia
D) New Jersey

Answer: **B)**

68. What state does NOT allow the impeachment of its governor?

A) Oregon
B) California
C) New Jersey
D) None of the above

Answer: **D)**

69. Which state implemented the first state income tax?

A) Wisconsin
B) Massachusetts
C) New York
D) Ohio

Answer: **A)**

70. Which state gives the most power to its lieutenant governor compared to other states?

A) California
B) Texas
C) Maryland
D) Florida

Answer: **C)**

71. Which state has a governor without the power to issue executive orders?

A) North Carolina
B) Rhode Island
C) Vermont
D) None of the above

Answer: **D)**

72. In which state do voters elect the state's education commissioner?

A) Florida
B) California
C) Texas
D) None of the above

Answer: **D)**

73. Which state allows its legislature to convene special sessions without the governor's consent?

A) Alaska
B) Nevada
C) Idaho
D) All of the above

Answer: **D)**

74. What unique feature does the New Hampshire legislature have regarding its size?

A) It is the largest state legislature
B) It is the smallest state legislature
C) It has the most committees of any state legislature
D) It has the fewest number of sessions per year

Answer: **A)**

75. Which state first allowed no-excuse absentee voting?

A) California
B) Oregon
C) Michigan
D) Pennsylvania

Answer: **A)**

76. Which state has the longest term for a state senator at six years?

A) Alabama
B) Louisiana
C) New Jersey
D) None of the above

Answer: **D)**

77. What role does the Attorney General play in state government?

A) Chief education officer
B) Chief legal officer
C) Chief financial officer
D) None of the above

Answer: **B)**

78. Which state was the first to pass legislation requiring health insurance coverage for pre-existing conditions?

A) Massachusetts
B) California
C) Vermont
D) New York

Answer: **A)**

79. Which state has the power to dismiss local governments?

A) Florida
B) Michigan
C) California
D) New York

Answer: **B)**

80. In which state does the state legislature not have the power to pass a budget without the governor's approval?

A) Nevada
B) Rhode Island
C) Arizona
D) None of the above

Answer: **D)**

81. Which state grants its governor the power to appoint all county and city public defenders?

A) New Jersey
B) Florida
C) California
D) None of the above

Answer: **D)**

82. What state has a Board of Pardons that includes its governor as a voting member?

A) Pennsylvania
B) Texas
C) Nebraska
D) All of the above

Answer: **A)**

83. Which state's constitution provides for the election of a state poet laureate?

A) Minnesota
B) Louisiana
C) Illinois
D) None of the above

Answer: **D)**

84. What unique voting requirement does Colorado have for amending its state constitution?

A) Simple majority vote
B) Two-thirds majority vote in two consecutive elections
C) Majority vote in the legislature, then a simple majority public vote
D) Majority vote that exceeds 55% of voters

Answer: **D)**

85. Which state has the only officially bilingual constitution in the United States?

A) New Mexico
B) Hawaii
C) Louisiana
D) Alaska

Answer: **B)**

86. In which state does the Chief Justice of the Supreme Court also oversee the state bar association?

A) Oregon
B) Texas
C) New York
D) None of the above

Answer: **D)**

87. Which state was the first to legalize recreational marijuana through legislative action rather than a ballot initiative?

A) Colorado
B) Vermont
C) California
D) Washington

Answer: **B)**

88. What role does the state comptroller play in Texas?

A) Manages the state's public schools
B) Oversees the state's finances, including tax collection and budget planning
C) Regulates the state's natural resources
D) None of the above

Answer: **B)**

89. Which state allows for the impeachment of judges by the public through a voting process?

A) Alabama
B) California
C) Ohio
D) None of the above

Answer: **D)**

90. In which state is there a mandatory retirement age of 70 for all judges?

A) New York
B) Florida
C) Pennsylvania
D) All of the above

Answer: **D)**

91. Which state has a legislative body that meets every other year, making it one of the least frequently convening legislatures in the country?

A) Montana
B) Nevada
C) Texas
D) Oregon

Answer: **B)**

92. What unique power does the Governor of Alaska have regarding natural resources?

A) Direct control over all oil and gas leasing on state lands
B) The power to set annual fishing quotas
C) The ability to veto mining permits
D) None of the above

Answer: **D)**

93. Which state was the first to allow women to hold any political office, including governor?

A) Wyoming
B) Utah
C) Kansas
D) New York

Answer: **A)**

94. In which state do state Supreme Court justices serve for life, similar to federal judges?

A) None
B) Massachusetts
C) Rhode Island
D) Louisiana

Answer: **A)**

95. Which state allows its residents to use a 'None of the Above' option on ballots for state elections?

A) Nevada
B) Oregon
C) Maine
D) None of the above

Answer: **A)**

96. What is unique about the election process for the North Dakota Education Board?

A) It is appointed by the state legislature
B) Board members are elected by a statewide vote
C) The governor appoints all members with no confirmation needed
D) Members are selected by local school boards

Answer: **B)**

97. Which state has the largest number of amendments to its constitution, largely due to its comprehensive detail on local governance?

A) Alabama
B) California
C) Texas
D) Ohio

Answer: **A)**

98. What state first introduced the 'jungle primary' system, where candidates of all parties appear on the same primary ballot?

A) Louisiana
B) California
C) Washington
D) None of the above

Answer: **A)**

99. Which state requires the highest percentage of voter signatures to qualify an initiative for the ballot, based on the number of voters in the last gubernatorial election?

A) California
B) Illinois
C) Florida
D) Oregon

Answer: **C)**

100. In what state does the Constitution provide for the establishment of a 'Council of State' that advises the governor?

A) North Carolina
B) Texas
C) Ohio
D) Florida

Answer: **A)**

Printed in Great Britain
by Amazon